Ned Rorem

Ned Rorem. Photo by Jack Mitchell.

Ned Rorem

A Bio-Bibliography

Arlys L. McDonald

Bio-Bibliographies in Music, Number 23

Donald L. Hixon, Series Adviser

GREENWOOD PRESS
New York • Westport, Connecticut • London

Library of Congress Cataloging-in-Publication Data

McDonald, Arlys L.
    Ned Rorem, a bio-bibliography / Arlys L. McDonald.
        p.   cm.—(Bio-bibliographies in music, ISSN 0742-6968 ; no.
    23)
    Discography: p.
    Bibliography: p.
    "Rorem bibliography" : p.
    Includes index.
    ISBN 0-313-25565-2 (lib. bdg. : alk. paper)
    1. Rorem, Ned, 1923-   —Bibliography. 2. Rorem, Ned, 1923-   —
    Discography. I. Title. II. Series.
    ML134.R67M3   1989
    780'.92—dc20
    [B]   89-2139

British Library Cataloguing in Publication Data is available.

Library of Congress Catalog Card Number: 89-2139
ISBN: 0-313-25565-2
ISSN: 0742-6968

First published in 1989

Greenwood Press, Inc.
88 Post Road West, Westport, Connecticut 06881

Printed in the United States of America

The paper used in this book complies with the
Permanent Paper Standard issued by the National
Information Standards Organization (Z39.48-1984).

10 9 8 7 6 5 4 3 2 1

Contents

Preface

Ned Rorem occupies a position of influence and importance in American music both as a composer and as an author. His numerous works are frequently performed, and his writings provide insights into contemporary music that have rarely been equaled. It is hoped that the information organized and annotated in this volume will serve as a resource for those seeking information by and about this distinguished American composer and his works.

The book is divided into four sections:

1) A brief biography;

2) A complete list of works and performances which includes Rorem's plays and books (W282-W297), works in preparation (W298-W300), as well as his musical compositions (W1-W281). The latter have been classified by genre and arranged alphabetically within each category. Each entry is preceded by a "W" (W1, W2, etc.) and provides such information as the date of composition and publication, publisher, duration, medium of performance, literary source, commission, dedication, and dates of premiere and performances. "See" references refer to citations which are found in the bibliography. A directory of publishers and their addresses concludes this section;

3) A discography of commercially produced sound recordings arranged by label and number. Each item is preceded by a "D" (D1, D2, etc.) and provides such information as contents, performers, date of issue, and album title. "See" references refer to citations which are found in other sections;

4) A bibliography of writings by and about Ned Rorem. These have been organized alphabetically by author with anonymous works interspersed by title. Each entry is preceded by a "B" (B1, B2, etc.) and includes a short

annotation and/or quote from the article. Articles by
Rorem appear as items B520-B644. His books and plays are
found in the "Works and Performances" section as items
W282-W297. "See" references refer to citations which are
found in other sections.

Three appendices are included. Appendix I provides an
alphabetical list of Rorem's compositions, including individual songs in cycles, distinctive sub-titles, working titles
and titles of unpublished works mentioned in the "Works and
Performances." Appendix II is a chronological list of compositions. Appendix III provides a list of the literary sources
for Rorem's works. Each entry is followed by a "W" number
(W1, W2, etc.) which references a title in the "Works and Performances" section. An index, which includes subjects, and
personal, corporate and geographical names, concludes the
volume.

Acknowledgments

During the preparation of this volume, many persons and institutions contributed time, support and encouragement. In particular, I should like to extend my thanks to the following individuals.

For providing specialized bibliographical assistance:

J. Richard Abell, Head of the History Department, Public Library of Cincinnati and Hamilton County, Cincinnati, OH; Richard Barrios, Boosey & Hawkes Publishing Co., New York City; Robert Biddlecome, Associate General Manager, Aspen Music Festival; Cindy Birt, Head of Reference, Whittier Public Library, Whittier, CA; William J. Dane, Art & Music Collection, Newark Public Library, Newark, NJ; Joan L. Dobson, Local Historian, Dallas Public Library, Dallas, TX; Dorothy Donio, Miami-Dade Public Library, Miami, FL; Richard M. Duris, Temple University Library, Philadelphia, PA; Marc T. Faw, Music Librarian, University of Oklahoma, Norman, OK; Sylvia Goldstein, Boosey & Hawkes Publishing Co., New York City; David Gollon, Music Librarian, Pitkin County Library, Aspen, CO; Patti Graham, Reference Librarian, Wake County Public Libraries, Raleigh, NC; Gretchen Grogan, Santa Fe Chamber Music Festival, Santa Fe, NM; John Gruen, New York City; Susan H. Hitchens, Music Librarian, University of Kansas, Lawrence, KS; Tye Hogan, Graduate Student, University of Nebraska, Lincoln, NE; Katharine Holum, Music Librarian, University of Minnesota, Minneapolis, MN; Nancy R. Horlacher, Dayton Collection, Dayton and Montgomery County Public Library, Dayton, OH; Martin W. Jasicki, Entertainment Editor, Tribune-Star, Terre Haute, IN; James J. Jatkevicius, New Haven Free Public Library, New Haven, CT; Rick Johnson, KNME-TV, Albuquerque, NM; Judy Klinger, Reference Librarian, Public Library, Santa Fe, NM; Joe Levy, Assistant to Doug Simmons, Village Voice, New York City; Katheryn P. Logan, Music and Art Department, The Carnegie Library of Pittsburgh, Pittsburgh, PA; Susan H. McClure, Reference Librarian, Chapel Hill Public Library, Chapel Hill, NC; Susan Messerli, Music Librarian, University of Nebraska, Lincoln, NE; Bill Morrison, Entertainment Editor, The News and

x   Acknowledgments

Observer-The Raleigh Times, Raleigh, NC; Cheryl Morton, Fine
Arts Division, Akron-Summit County Public Library, Akron, OH;
Holly Oberle, Music Librarian, University of Miami, Miami, FL;
Genevieve Oswald, Dance Collection, New York Public Library;
Diane O. Ota, Curator of Music, Boston Public Library, Boston,
MA; Myron B. Patterson, Music Librarian, University of Utah,
Salt Lake City, UT; Deborah L. Pierce, Librarian, Music Lis-
tening Center, University of Washington Libraries, Seattle,
WA; Sally Raye, Reference Librarian, Public Library of Nash-
ville and Davidson County, Nashville, TN; Don L. Roberts, Head
Music Librarian, Northwestern University, Evanston, IL; John
H. Roberts, Music Librarian, University of Pennsylvania, Phil-
adelphia, PA; Lois I. Rowell, Reference Librarian, Music/Dance
Library, Ohio State University, Columbus, OH; Nancy Shear,
Nancy Shear Arts Services and WNYC Radio, New York City;
Stanley Shiebert, Librarian, Art/Music Department, Seattle
Public Library, Seattle, WA; Lisa A. Sisley, Manhattan Public
Library, Manhattan, KS; Wendy Sistrunk, Boston, MA; Joan L.
Sorger, Head of Main Library, Cleveland Public Library, Cleve-
land, OH; Bob Stanford, Editor-in-Chief, In Touch, North Hol-
lywood, CA; Walter Verdehr, Professor of Music, Michigan State
University, East Lansing, MI; John von Rhein, Music Critic,
Chicago Tribune; Rod Walker, Choral Director, Kansas State
University, Manhattan, KS; James B. Wright, Music Librarian,
University of New Mexico; and "CJ" of the San Jose Public Li-
brary and "Kathy" of the Albuquerque Publishing Co., who did
not further identify themselves.

For specialized editorial assistance:

    Donald L. Hixon, University of California, Irvine, and
Series Adviser, Bio-Bibliographies in Music, Greenwood Press;
Eleanor Ferrall, Reference Librarian, Arizona State Univer-
sity.

For providing institutional support:

    Donald Riggs, Dean of the University Libraries, Arizona
State University; Maxine Reneker, Associate Librarian for Pub-
lic Services, Arizona State University Libraries; the staff of
Inter-Library Loan, Arizona State University; Margaret A.
Heath and Vivian G. Kohler, Computing Services, Arizona State
University.

For providing information assistance:

    A special thanks is given to Mr. Ned Rorem for answering
numerous question-filled letters, providing information which
otherwise would have been unavailable, and clearing up con-
flicts of information which are inevitable in a research
project such as this.

For providing personal encouragement:

    To those who encouraged and supported me, my special
thanks, not only for their interest, but for their patience
and understanding as well.

Ned Rorem

Biography

I'm a composer who happens to write, not an author who
happens to compose...my prose and music fill opposing
needs. (1)

Ned Rorem, noted American composer, performing musician,
and distinguished author, was born in Richmond, Indiana, October 23, 1923. He was the second of two children born to
Clarence Rufus Rorem, a medical economist and a founder of
Blue Cross, and Gladys Miller Rorem, an activist in various
peace movements and Society of Friends projects.
     When Rorem was eight months old, his father left his
position on the faculty of Earlham College in Richmond and
moved the family to Chicago. While his parents were not especially musical, they were cultivated and well-bred people who
were interested in providing a cultural and artistic environment for their children. Thus, Rorem and his older sister,
Rosemary, were taken at an early age to concerts of such legendary pianists as Ignace Paderewski, Serge Rachmaninoff, and
Josef Hofmann, and to the dance programs of Mary Wigman, Ruth
Page and the Ballets Russes.
     Ned Rorem gave evidence of his unusual musical gifts
while he was still very young, quickly surpassing his sister
during their initial piano lessons. After a series of piano
teachers from whom he says he learned piano but not music, he
began to study with the first of three women teachers who were
to make a lasting impression on his work. Nuta Rothschild
introduced him to the music of Debussy and Ravel, and opened
the door to his love of French music and all things French.

Our first meeting opened the gates of heaven. This was
no lesson but a recital. She played Debussy's "L'Isle
joyeuse" and "Golliwogg's Cake Walk," and during those
minutes I realized for the first time that there was what
music was supposed to be. I didn't realize this "modern
stuff" repelled your average Music Lover, for it was an
awakening sound that immediately, as we Quakers say,
spoke to my condition, a condition nurtured by Mrs. Rothschild, who began to immerse me in "impressionism." (2)

At the age of 12, he had a similar experience with his next teacher, Margaret Bonds, a young black woman, who was only ten years his senior. Through her he learned the American contemporary music of Charles Griffes and John Alden Carpenter as well as American jazz. He had been composing little tunes for some time, but it was Margaret Bonds who taught him to notate them.

> So unswervingly convinced was I of music, from the age of seven on, it never occurred to me that all other boys and girls didn't go home after school and write pieces too. (3)

In 1938, Rorem began to study piano with Belle Tannenbaum, who gave him his initial introduction to classical piano repertoire. Under her tutelage, he learned the first movement of Grieg's Piano Concerto which he performed in June 1940 with the American Concert Orchestra under the direction of William Fantozzi. During that same month, he graduated, at age 16, from high school at the University of Chicago Lab School.

Rorem's first formal study of theory and harmony was with Leo Sowerby, an eminent teacher, composer and organist at the American Conservatory in Chicago. It was also about this time, at age 15, that Rorem first met Paul Goodman, beginning a friendship and association with the poet which would continue until Goodman's death in 1972.

> My first songs date from then, all of them settings of Paul Goodman's verse. I may have written other kinds of songs since, but none better. That I have never in the following decades wearied of putting his words to music is the highest praise I can show him; since I put faith in my own work, I had first to put faith in Paul's...He was my Goethe, my Blake, and my Apollinaire. (4)

Despite rather lackluster academic credentials, Rorem was accepted at Northwestern University's School of Music on the basis of his "creative potential." (5) His entrance audition was so impressive that he was encouraged to study piano as well as composition. So, in addition to his studies in composition with Dr. Alfred Nolte, Rorem studied piano with Harold Van Horne. During this time at Northwestern, he displayed an insatiable appetite for expanding his knowledge of piano literature, and concentrated on learning all the standard works of Beethoven, Bach and Chopin.

In 1943, he accepted a scholarship from the Curtis Institute in Philadelphia. There he studied counterpoint and composition with Rosario Scalero and dramatic forms with Gian-Carlo Menotti. Scalero's emphasis on counterpoint exercises did not endear himself to the young composer.

> What I retained from Curtis was not the wisdom of a dusty maestro but the still vital friendship of young pianists, notably Eugene Istomin and Shirley Gabis Rhoads; also the rich flock of wartime jeunesse: Gary Graffman, Seymour Lipkin, Jacob Latiener, Theodore Lettvin. (6)

Indeed, Rorem has maintained many of these early friendships from both the Curtis years and the Juilliard ones which were to follow.   Many of these friends are the same artists who first performed his music and continue to do so at present.

Despite Scalero's lack of encouragement, Rorem continued to compose.   During the summer of 1943, he had the satisfaction of hearing the first performance of his Seventieth Psalm sung by the Army Music School Chorus under the direction of William Strickland at the National Gallery of the Library of Congress.   His Four-Hand Piano Sonata, which was composed while he was a student at Curtis, was first performed the following year at the Statler Hotel in New York during a Blue Cross meeting.

He left Curtis in 1944, and despite the objections of his parents, went to New York to live.   As his parents had stopped his allowance, he supported himself by becoming Virgil Thomson's copyist in exchange for orchestration lessons and $20 a week.   While Rorem considers himself self-taught in composition, he credits Virgil Thomson for teaching him the skills of orchestration which he has employed so successfully.   "What Virgil taught me was craft, not creation, but craft is the only thing that can be taught." (7)

Virgil Thomson introduced him to his next piano teacher, Betty Crawford.   Through her efforts, he obtained a job as Martha Graham's accompanist for $2 per hour.   This job was of short duration.   Miss Graham fired him, as Rorem explained, for "...my lack of the pianistic thrust needed to impel collective contractions and releases." (8)   Ironically, twenty-three years later, she used his composition, Eleven Studies for Eleven Players, for her ballet, Dancing Ground, which was successfully premiered in New York in 1967.   Martha Graham was not the only artist for whom he served as accompanist.   In 1947, he also supported himself as the accompanist for Eva Gauthier's vocal coaching sessions.

Finally, at the urging of his father, Rorem returned to school, this time enrolling at Juilliard, where he completed his Bachelor's degree in 1946 and his Master's degree in 1948. Here he studied composition with Bernard Wagenaar, but during the summers of 1946 and 1947, he was fortunate in receiving fellowships for study with Aaron Copland at the Berkshire Music Center at Tanglewood.

Since literature is one of Rorem's major interests, most of his efforts during the Juilliard years were expended on songs.   However, he occasionally wrote incidental music to plays, some ballets and even music for a puppet show.   While the chronological list of his works shows a healthy number of titles for one so young, it does not show his total output for this period.   About these several hundred unpublished songs he has said:

Incidentally, much of the unpublished stuff is not so much juvenalia as simply well-written music that never quite came to life.   But I must re-examine it: maybe today it could live.   Then again, probably not. (9)

Two events during 1948 gave a substantial boost to the young composer's career.   The Lordly Hudson, a setting of one

of Paul Goodman's poems, was declared the "best published song
of the year" by the Music Library Association, and his Overture in C was awarded the Gershwin Memorial Award, the first
of many awards during the years which followed. About Overture in C Rorem says, "The piece didn't deserve the prize, but
I did." (10)

The 1940s were formative years for Rorem.

The forties, therefore, were my years of deciding who I
was and it was a question of almost flipping a coin as to
what I was going to be when I grew up--a composer or a
writer or a poet or a dancer, or what have you. By 1950,
I guess I knew. (11)

The Gershwin Award provided the opportunity to fulfill a
desire he had long entertained. "I took the thousand dol-
lars and went to France for three months, but stayed nine
years." (12) Rorem has said he did not become French by living in France; he was already French when he lived in Chicago
and New York. He was drawn to the French aesthetic tradition
from his early childhood when he first became acquainted with
the music of Debussy and Ravel, and as a result, French impressionism became deeply rooted in his sensibilities and love
of music. It was only natural that he should be drawn to
France. During the first two years of his sojourn, however,
he spent extended periods of time in Morocco where he lived in
the home of a friend, Dr. Guy Ferrand. This proved to be of
great benefit to Rorem. He learned the French language, and
without the distractions and social life of the large city,
wrote an extraordinary number of works, including some twenty
large-scale compositions.
    The Gershwin Award was followed by the Lili Boulanger
Award in 1950, the Prix de Biarritz for his ballet Mélos in
1951, and a Fulbright Fellowship in 1951. With the receipt of
the latter, Rorem left Morocco and returned to Paris to study
with Arthur Honegger.
    It is interesting to note that Rorem was probably one of
the few American composers who studied in France who did not
study with the famed teacher Nadia Boulanger.

She weighed the pros and cons but concluded that at
twenty-four I was now formed--her nudging could only
falsify what she termed my nature bête. (13)

One of the first individuals he met upon his return to
Paris from Morocco in 1951 was the Vicomtesse Marie Laure de
Noailles, an extremely wealthy, talented, and influential
patroness of the Arts. In the cultured milieu of her homes,
Rorem was introduced to all the leading French artists, mu-
sicians, poets, writers and theatrical figures of the day.
Rorem attributed much of his success to this woman.

Back in 1951 my obstreperousness in the company of Marie
Laure was both feigned and short-lived: an expression of
dazzlement at so easily meeting half of legendary Europe
at her table. Once the novelty wore off, my Quaker sense
informed me that, above all she's offered the leisure to
work. She has not only provided three pianos, sponsored

concerts, clothed and fed and housed me, but has been the main cause of my staying on to compose in France for so long. (14)

This stimulating environment opened up all kinds of opportunities for the young composer but surprisingly it did not deter him from composition. The years Rorem spent under her patronage resulted in a large body of work, almost unheard of for one so young.

> I think one of the things Marie Laure liked about me was the fact that I would get up after lunch and say "Excuse me" and go to work in my room. This, no matter where I was or with whom. That's how I got the catalogue of music I now have. (15)

In addition to building his catalogue of music, Rorem, whose talent for prose equals his talent for composition, began to keep a diary of his experiences in France. He had kept a diary intermittently since he was a child, and with Marie Laure's encouragement, became a keen observer of the musical, literary, cultural and social life of France and America from the 1950s through to the present. His chatty and sometimes self-indulgent diaries are a candid mixture of his observations and insights about music and the other arts. They contain aphorisms, gossipy character portraits of major artists, composers, conductors, performers and literary personages, as well as revealingly frank personal accounts of his own homosexual affairs and problems with alcohol, drugs and depression. With the publication of the first of the series of his diaries in 1966, Rorem made all this a matter of public record, causing a furor in the artistic and performing world, offending and shocking many, but also leaving a valuable first-hand record of the composer and the world in which he lives.
Rorem began contributing articles for publication as early as 1949 when he wrote an article about the ethnic music of Morocco for Musical America. Through the years he has had essays, book reviews, articles and music criticism published in journals and major newspapers in this country and abroad. Many of the articles have now been cumulated and published in his books. Several times he has commented that his music and literary talents complement one another, with music showing his need for order, his writing the need for chaos.
His prose as well as his music is essential in knowing and understanding the complexity of Ned Rorem.

> May I assume you are aware of my ten [sic] published books? No biography, however cursory, could afford to ignore my prose. I am the sum of my parts, of course, and almost everything I have to say about music (as well as about every aspect of my life) is in the diaries and collections of essays. (16)

Rorem is a stimulating author who writes with style and precision. He has used this talent to good advantage in his essays, encouraging the performance of contemporary music, and as an advocate in urging economic support for composers. His essays are also a principal source of information about many

of the major 20th-century composers.   Through personal acquaintance, he provides insights which would not otherwise be
available about these individuals and their works.   His thor-
ough knowledge of music, art and literature, linked to his
apparent outspokenness and willingness to discuss controversial topics, have also resulted in frequent invitations to
appear as a guest panelist on radio, and television, and on
the lecture circuit.

While Rorem himself is highly regarded as an incisive and
witty music critic, who is frequently compared to Virgil Thomson, he has little personal regard for the music critic in
general.   His feud with Richard Goldstein in the New York
Times is legendary, and he withheld no punches when he addressed the National Symposium of Critics in Santa Fe in 1982.
His expressed viewpoint is that "Reviews of my music have
never taught me a thing.   They are basically useless, and form
opinions (after the fact) for those who have none." (17)

Rorem has long been an advocate for the performance of
contemporary music, but he recognizes the fact that he has not
had some of the difficulties other composers or authors have
had in having their works performed and published.

> I really feel fortunate that I have what a lot of people
> never have.   I've won major prizes.   I make a living as a
> composer--which is unusual in America--and I'm appreci-
> ated pretty much for what I like best to do.   I write
> exactly what I want to write with no compromises and it
> gets played.   And my books get published.   Like everybody
> else I don't think I get played enough or that my books
> get advertised enough--but still, there they are. (18)

Not only has Rorem used his writing and influence to en-
courage the performance of contemporary music, he also has
taken an active stance in encouraging it.   Rorem is unusual
among composers in that he is also a performer of both his own
music, and that of others.   He, in tandem with composer
William Flanagan, initiated a series of concerts called "Music
for the Voice by Americans."   These extended from 1959 through
1962 and were followed by similar concerts throughout the
years, such as "Composers Showcase Concerts" in 1969; "Hear
America First Concerts" in 1973; and "Meet the Moderns" in
1978.

Rorem made three trips from France to the United States
during the mid 1950s.   These were mainly for premieres and
performances of his music or for publication purposes.   It was
not until 1958 that he decided to return permanently.   By then
his works were beginning to attract attention.   Conductors
such as Reiner and Ormandy were programming his music and his
songs were being premiered by such prestigious sopranos as
Phyllis Curtin and Eleanor Steber.

As documented in his diaries, his return to New York did
not change his flamboyant lifestyle, yet he retained his disciplined schedule of composition.

> In the old days I would get ferociously drunk, but I
> would also be ferociously sober and work prodigiously
> hard.   After all, I am a prolific composer.   Nobody can

be drunk all the time, anymore than one can be unhappy all the time. (19)

His problems with alcohol did not diminish overnight. He describes years in the 1950s and the 1960s as "my drinking decade." (20) He tried to gain control of his alcoholism by going to AA meetings and taking antabuse, but this was not really effective until 1967 when he met James Holmes, a friend who became a stabilizing influence in his life. Since then, Rorem has settled into a less hectic alcohol-free lifestyle.

Upon his return to the United States, Rorem began to concentrate more on instrumental music or combinations of vocal and instrumental music, although as he has explained, he views all music as vocal.

I always think vocally. Even when writing for violin or timpani, it's the vocalist in me trying to get out. Music is, after all, a song [sung?] expression, and any composer worthy of the name is intrinsically a singer whether he allows it or not. (21)

An example of this is found on the occasion when Rorem used some of his early unpublished songs in his later instrumental compositions.

It's of interest to note that the third movement of my six-movement Violin Concerto (1984) is literally the same music as Boy with a Baseball Glove, minus the words, with the vocal line ascribed to the solo violin and the piano accompaniment orchestrated. (22)

Rorem's "borrowing" has not been restricted to songs, however. Carried further, Eclogues (1953) was used in Sinfonia (1956-1957); Burlesque (1955) was used in A Quaker Reader (1976); and five of the twelve movements of A Birthday Suite (1967) have been orchestrated and incorporated into Winter Pages (1981), Remembering Tommy (1970), Sunday Morning (1977), The Santa Fe Songs (1979-1980) and Septet (1984-1985).

Prior to the mid 1950s, Rorem chose texts from poets from all literary periods. Since then, however, most of his choices have been 20th-century Americans such as Paul Goodman, Theodore Roethke, Kenneth Koch, Howard Moss, Witter Bynner, and especially Walt Whitman. Problems of copyright releases plagued him on some of his early songs. Two Poems of Edith Sitwell which were composed in 1948 were not published until 1982 when he finally obtained copyright clearance. Julien Green's L'Autre Someil which Rorem set as Another Sleep in 1951, was premiered by Donald Gramm in Town Hall in 1956, but never published.

They are not published because Green would not give his permission. Too bad, they're among my best songs-- certainly my most original of that period. (23)

He has composed few single songs since 1960. Songs composed since then are mostly in cycles or combined with instrumental accompaniment. Because of his unflagging interest in literature, Rorem's music is a union of literature, music and visual imagery.   His instrumental works frequently use pro-grammatic ideas such as those found in <u>Eagles</u> or <u>Lions</u>.

> Music has no intrinsic literary meaning beyond what its composer lends to it through titles and program notes, but since I'm amused by words as well as musical sounds, I like to use poetic concepts (as opposed to so-called abstract music concepts) as skeletons on which to add the flesh of sound. (24)

Much of his work since 1960 has been on commission.   He has received commissions from such prestigious organizations as the Ford Foundation, Koussevitsky Foundation, Elizabeth Sprague Coolidge Foundation, and New York City Opera, as well as lesser ones including schools, churches, performing groups and private individuals.   In addition to those mentioned pre-viously, he has continued to receive major grants and awards: Guggenheim Fellowships were received in 1957 and 1977; and an award in 1968 from the National Institute of Arts and Letters, of which he was made a member in 1979.   For his book <u>Critical Affairs: a Composer's Journal</u> he won the ASCAP--Deems Taylor Award in 1971 and repeated it in 1975 for <u>The Final Diary</u>; and finally, the jewel of them all, the Pulitzer Prize in 1976 for <u>Air Music</u>.

> I feel very, very, very lucky that I'm able to support myself as a composer of serious music...My income is not so much from royalties as from commissions, prizes, fellowships and official handouts, such as the National Endowment of the Arts and the Guggenheim Fellowship which I am now living on. (25)

Sometimes Rorem is working on several commissions at one time.   During 1974-75, he received seven commissions, all of which were major works completed for the American Bicentennial celebration: <u>Assembly and Fall</u>; <u>Air Music</u>; <u>Book of Hours</u>; <u>Eight Piano Etudes</u>; <u>Serenade</u>; <u>Sky Music</u>; and <u>Women's Voices</u>. A clue to his tremendous effort and vitality lies in the an-swer he gave when asked for whom he wrote:

> I definitely write for an audience.   Also since my music is mostly commissioned, I know who the audience will be. But I write for approval too; I want to be approved of by my parents, by the boys who beat me up in grammar school, by my peers, and by the young.   A small order.   The pur-pose of my work is not to make money, but if I didn't make money at it, I might stop.   I need, first of all, to live, but I also need daily reassurance that I'm appreci-ated or I get paranoid.   The reassurance comes from hav-ing a piece asked for, paid for, played, reviewed and published. (26)

In 1959, shortly after Rorem returned from France, he was offered the Slee Professorship at the University of Buffalo. This was the first of three major teaching positions he would accept over the next 20 years.   In 1965, he went to the Uni-versity of Utah at Salt Lake City as composer-in-residence and Professor of Composition.   Both positions were of short dura-tion, for as Rorem said about the Utah appointment:

> This is the kind of assignment that should not last more
> than two years as a teacher begins to believe what he
> says after that long a time and becomes sterile. (27)

His third position has been of much longer duration. In 1980,
he was appointed co-director with David Loeb to the Under-
graduate Department of Composition at Curtis Institute, a
position he retains at present. He obviously has some mixed
feelings about teaching.

> I don't happen to like to teach. On those occasions when
> I have taught, at universities, it's interested me only
> because I'm pretty good at seeing what bogs down a young
> composer, then at helping him see more clearly who he
> thinks he is. But I don't have a Socratic bone in my
> body. I do like to show off and in showing off, I'm
> instructive. (28)

Throughout the years, Rorem has been involved with drama,
composing a number of operas, and writing incidental music to
plays such as Tennessee Williams' Suddenly Last Summer (1957)
and The Milk Train Doesn't Stop Here Anymore (1964). He also
wrote a score for the film, Panic in Needle Park (1971) which
unfortunately was not used when the film was finally issued.
Ironically, some of the material was later used in the Pulitzer Prize winning Air Music (1976).
    Miss Julie was written for the New York City Opera on a
grant from the Ford Foundation, but was poorly received at its
premiere in 1965. This was a major disappointment for Rorem.
After extensive revision, it was again performed in 1979, this
time to more appreciative critics. His interest in drama has
not been restricted to opera or incidental music. Two of his
one-act plays were performed off-Broadway in 1970 and he was
the librettist for his own one-act opera, The Robbers.
    A major change in lifestyle was made in 1974 when Rorem
bought a house on Nantucket where he now spends his summers
and holidays enjoying a more peaceful life. As he described
the summer of 1974, "I wrote Air Music, made pies, felt no
competition, was content." (29)
    Rorem has spent three summers in Santa Fe as composer-
in-residence and performer during the Santa Fe Chamber Music
Festival where The Santa Fe Songs were premiered in 1980,
Winter Pages performed in 1982, and Scenes from Childhood
premiered in 1985. He and his work have been prominently
featured at other festivals such as Aspen, the Spoleto Festival in Charleston, South Carolina, and the New World Festival
of the Arts in Miami.
    After receiving the Pulitzer Prize, Rorem was further
honored by Northwestern University on June 18, 1977, when he
was awarded an honorary doctorate acknowledging his achieve-
ments.   Recognition also came from his hometown of Chicago
when Mayor Harold Washington declared March 22-23, 1984 to be
"Ned Rorem Days." On May 13, 1984, he was presented with a
plaque from the Fund for Human Dignity for educating the public about the lives of lesbians and gay men.
    There is in Rorem a man of contrast and complexity. He
is one of the most accomplished composers of art song, yet he
won the Pulitzer Prize for an instrumental composition. He is
an author as well as a composer, entertaining a literary

following quite apart from music circles. He is a respected
music critic who mistrusts music criticism. He is an atheist
who composes sacred music because he believes not in the text
per se, but the quality of the text. Rorem professes to dis-
like the organ and the guitar, yet he has written two long
suites and a concerto for organ and a suite for guitar which
have become major additions to the literature for those instruments.

1988, the year of Rorem's 65th birthday, finds him completing still more commissions: a choral work for the Gay
Men's Chorus of New York; Goodbye My Fancy, an oratorio based
on texts by Walt Whitman; and Society of Friends, for large
orchestra and chorus. Some twenty concerts of his works are
being performed on the occasion of his birthday, including
premieres of Bright Music, a quintet for flute, two violins,
cello and piano; an orchestral version of A Quaker Reader; and
a work for organ and four brass which was premiered under the
title of Fanfare and Flourish but originally had been called
Praising Charles.

Rorem has not let up the pace of his work, continuing in
the same manner as he has done since he was quite young, for
as he has said:

> Anyone can be drunk, anyone can be in love, anyone can
> waste time and weep, but only I can pen my songs in the
> remaining years or minutes. (30)

1. "TNB Interviews Ned Rorem." NATS Bulletin, 39 no. 2 (1982), 5.
2. Ned Rorem, Setting the Tone: Essays and a Diary (New York: Coward-McCann, 1983), 19.
3. _____ , "Vocabulary." Christopher Street, 1 no. 11 (May 1977), 11.
4. _____ , Setting the Tone, 358-359.
5. Ibid., 122.
6. Ibid., 23.
7. Richard Dyer, "Ned Rorem Tells All." Boston Globe, (September 30, 1984), 15.
8. Ned Rorem, Music and People (New York: George Braziller, 1968), 205.
9. _____ , letter to the author, April 1, 1988.
10. Richard Dyer, "Ned Rorem Tells All," 15.
11. John Gruen, The Party's Over Now: Reminiscences of the Fifties (New York: The Viking Press, 1972), 74.
12. Ned Rorem, letter to the author, May 24, 1988.
13. _____ , Setting the Tone, 138.
14. _____ , The Paris and New York Diaries of Ned Rorem 1951-1961 (San Francisco: North Point Press, 1983), 202.
15. John Gruen, The Party's Over Now, 79.
16. Ned Rorem, letter to the author, December 7, 1986.
17. _____ , The Paris and New York Diaries, 122.
18. Gordon Emerson, "On Razor's Edge with Ned Rorem." New Haven Register, (October 23, 1983), sec. 3, 1.
19. Richard Dyer, "Ned Rorem Tells All," 15.
20. John Gruen, The Party's Over Now, 81.
21. Philip Ramey, "Ned Rorem: Not Just a Song Composer." Keynote, 4 no. 3 (1980), 14.
22. Ned Rorem, letter to the author, April 1, 1988.
23. Ibid.
24. Maurice Hinson, "Great Composers of Our Time: Ned Rorem." Piano Quarterly, 28 (1980), 10.
25. Max Millard, "Westsider Ned Rorem." Westsider, (June 17, 1978), 28.
26. Nancy Plum, "A Conversation with Ned Rorem." Voice, (November/December 1985), 8.
27. "35 mm Music Man." Utah Alumnus, 43 (Winter 1967), 20.
28. Steven Greco, "Ned Rorem: in Prose, in Music—a Master of Composition." The Advocate, (October 4, 1979), 35.
29. Ned Rorem. "A Nantucket Diary." Geo, 6 (October 1984), 30.
30. _____ , "A Composer Offers Some Candid Thoughts on His Art." New York Times, (May 1, 1983), sec. 2, 21.

Works and Performances

The "See" references, e.g., See: B52, W49, refer to citations found in the "Bibliography" and "Works" sections.

I. SONGS AND SONG CYCLES WITH PIANO

W1. ABSALOM. (1972; Boosey & Hawkes; 2-1/2 min.)
     See: W77

     Voice and piano.
     Text by Paul Goodman.
     Composed: New York City, December 1946; orchestral
       version, 1947.

W2. ALLELUIA. (1949, 1977; Hargail Music, Inc.; Boosey &
     Hawkes; 3 min.)
     See: B31, B374, B664, B777

     Voice and piano.
     Dedicated to Jennie Tourel.
     Composed: New York City, June 1946.

     Premiere:

         1946 (Autumn): New York City, Carnegie Recital
         Hall; Janet Fairbank, soprano; Henry Jackson,
         piano.

     Selected performances:

         1959 (Feb 24): New York City; Carnegie Recital
         Hall; Patricia Neway, soprano; Ned Rorem, piano.
         1973 (Mar 27): New York City; Eleanor Steber.
         1973 (Aug 1): Marlboro, VT; Ellen Phillips,
         mezzo-soprano; Ned Rorem, piano.

W3. ANACREONTICHE. (unpublished)

     Song cycle.

Text by Jacopo Vitorelli; in Italian.
Composed: 1954.

W4.   AN ANGEL SPEAKS TO THE SHEPHERDS.   (1956; Southern
Music; 5 min.)

Voice and piano.
Text from St. Luke 2:9-15.
Dedicated to Jean Stein.
Composed: Hyères, Aug. 27-31, 1952.

W5.   ANOTHER SLEEP. (unpublished)
See: B127, B306, B503

Song cycle.
Text by Julien Green.
Dedicated to Gérard Souzay.
Composed: Morocco, 1951.

Premiere:

1956 (Jan 27): New York City; Town Hall; Donald
Gramm, bass-baritone; Harold Eisberg, piano.

W6.   AS ADAM EARLY IN THE MORNING.   (1961; Henmar Press;
C. F. Peters; 2 min.)
See: W30

Voice and piano.
Text by Walt Whitman.
Commissioned by and dedicated to Wilder Luke Burnap.
Composed: Hyères, July 24, 1957.

W7.   BAWLING BLUES.   (1984; Red Ozier Press)
See: W294

Voice and piano.
Text by Paul Goodman.
Composed: September 8, 1947.
In Paul's Blues.

Premiere:

1947: New York City; Mary's Bar; John and Frank
Etherton.

W8.   BOY WITH A BASEBALL GLOVE.   (unpublished)
See: W246

Voice and piano.
Text by Paul Goodman.
Used as the third movement of Violin Concerto.
Composed: 1953.

W9.   THE CALL. (1953; Elkan-Vogel)
See: W31, W130

Voice and piano.
Text is anonymous 15th c.

Also published as "My Blood So Red" in From an Unknown Past.
Composed: Fez, Morocco, 1951.

W10. CATULLUS: ON THE BURIAL OF HIS BROTHER. (1969; Boosey
& Hawkes; 2 min.)
See: W78

Voice and piano.
Text by Catullus; translated by Aubrey Beardsley.
Dedicated to David Lloyd.
Composed: Philadelphia, May 6-7, 1947.

W11. A CHRISTMAS CAROL. (1953; Elkan-Vogel; 1-1/2 min.)
See: B20, B76, B256, B379

Voice and Piano.
Text anonymous from 1500 A.D.
Composed: Marrakech, 1952.

Selected Performance:

1960 (Feb 8): New York City; Carnegie Recital
Hall; Reri Grist, soprano; Ned Rorem, piano.

W12. CLOUDS. (1968; Boosey & Hawkes; 2 min.)
See: B435; W26, W100

Voice and piano.
Text by Paul Goodman.
Published with For Susan and What Sparks and Wiry
Cries under the title Three Poems of Paul Goodman.
Dedicated to David Diamond.
Composed: Paris, September 20, 1953.

W13. CONVERSATION. (1969; Boosey & Hawkes)

Voice and piano.
Text by Elizabeth Bishop.
Dedicated to James Roland Holmes.
Composed: Paris, May 20, 1957.

W14. CRADLE SONG. (1968; Henmar Press; C. F. Peters)
See: W114

High voice and piano.
Originally with orchestra in Six Songs for High
Voice.
Text is anonymous 16th c.
Composed: Paris, December 17, 1953.

W15. CYCLE OF HOLY SONGS. (1955; Southern Music; 10 min.)
See: B59, B182, B664, B732, B741; W167

Song cycle; voice and piano.
Texts from the Psalms.
Composed: Paris, October 1951.
Contents: Psalm 134 (dedicated to Jerome Robbins);
Psalm 142 (dedicated to Pino Fasani); Psalm 148

(dedicated to Heddy De Ré); Psalm 150 (dedicated
to Hughes Cuenod). Psalms 134 and 150 also arranged for SATB under the title Two Holy Songs.

Premiere:

1952 (Feb 24): Washington, DC; Nell Tangeman,
mezzo-soprano.

Selected performances:

1959 (Feb 24): New York City; Carnegie Recital
Hall; Patricia Neway, soprano; Ned Rorem, piano.
1967 (Feb 5): Salt Lake City, UT; University of
Utah; Suzanne Sanborn, soprano; Ned Rorem,
piano.

W16. DAWN ANGEL. (unpublished)

Voice and piano.
Text by Parker Tyler.
Composed: New York City, September 1945.

W17. DOLL'S BOY. (1944; privately printed)

Voice and piano.
Text by e.e. cummings.
Privately printed with cover by Alvin Ross.
Composed: 1944.

W18. EARLY IN THE MORNING. (1958; Henmar Press; C. F. Peters; 2 min).
See: B146, B219, B515, W30

Voice and piano.
Text by Robert Hillyer.
Dedicated to Pierre Quézel.
Composed: 1955.

Selected performances:

1984 (Mar 30): Glendale, CA; Brand Library; Anne
Marie Ketchum, soprano; Adam Stern, piano.
1986 (Jan 19): Omaha; Strauss Performing Arts Center; Margaret Hemmen, mezzo-soprano.

W19. ECHO'S SONG. (1953; Boosey & Hawkes; 2 min.)
See: B256, B286; W77

Voice and piano.
Text by Ben Jonson.
Dedicated to "Xenia Gabis" (Shirley Rhoads).
Composed: New York City, February 15-16, 1948.

W20. ECLOGUES. (unpublished)
See: W240

Song cycle; six songs for voice and piano.
Texts by John Fletcher.

Two movements are later used in <u>Sinfonia</u>.
Composed: 1953.

W21.   <u>EPITAPH</u> (on Eleanor Freeman who died 1650, aged 21).
        (1953; Elkan-Vogel)
        <u>See</u>: B256; W91

        Voice and piano.
        Published with <u>To You</u>.
        Text is anonymous 15th c.
        Composed: Paris, 1953.

W22.   <u>FEED MY SHEEP</u>. (unpublished)

        Voice and piano.
        Text by Mary Baker Eddy.
        Commissioned by the Christian Science Church.
        Composed: 1966.

W23.   <u>FIVE POEMS OF WALT WHITMAN</u>.   (1970; Boosey & Hawkes; 8
        min.)
        <u>See</u>: B307, B664

        Voice and piano.
        Commissioned by Wilder Luke Burnap.
        Composed: Hyères, July 15-27, 1957 with the excep-
            tion of <u>Reconciliation</u> which was composed in New
            York City, March 11, 1946.
        Contents: Sometimes with One I Love (dedicated to
            Beverly Wolff); Look Down, Fair Moon (dedicated to
            Donald Gramm); Gliding o'er All (dedicated to
            Phyllis Curtin); Reconciliation (dedicated to
            Adele Addison): Gods (dedicated to Patricia
            Neway).

        <u>Premiere</u>:

        1958: Wilder Luke Burnap, baritone.

        <u>Selected performances</u>:

        1959 (Feb 24): New York City; Carnegie Recital
            Hall; Patricia Neway, soprano; Ned Rorem, piano
            (Look Down Fair Moon).
        1986 (Apr 18): Detroit; Detroit Institute of Arts;
            William Parker, baritone; Ned Rorem, piano
            (selections).

W24.   <u>FLIGHT FOR HEAVEN</u>.   (1952; Mercury Music; Theodore
        Presser; 14 min.)
        <u>See</u>: B181, B274, B338, B415, B503, B511, B661, B771

        Song cycle; bass voice and piano.
        Text by Robert Herrick.
        Dedicated to Doda Conrad.
        Composed: Paris and Fez, Morocco, May 1950.
        Contents: To Music, to Becalm His Fever; Cherry-
            Ripe; Upon Julia's Clothes; To Daisies, Not to
            Shut So Soon; Epitaph; Another Epitaph; To the

Willow-Tree; Comfort to a Youth That Had Lost His Love; To Anthea, Who May Command Him Anything (dedicated to Marie Laure).

Premiere:

1950 (Nov 19): New York City; League of Composers Concert; The Museum of Modern Art; Doda Conrad, bass; David Garver, piano.

Selected performances:

1981 (Mar 28): Hartford, CT; Trinity Episcopal Church; Robert Briggs, bass; Ned Rorem, piano.
1986 (Apr 18): Detroit; Detroit Institute of Arts; William Parker, baritone; Ned Rorem, piano.

W25. FOR POULENC. (1968; E. C. Schirmer; 3-1/2 min.)
      See: B246, B715; W29

Medium voice and piano.
Text by Frank O'Hara.
Also arranged for unison male chorus with piano.
Commissioned by Alice Esty.
Composed: New York City, June 23, 1963.

Premiere:

1964 (Jan 13): New York City; Carnegie Recital Hall; Memorial concert for Francis Poulenc; Alice Esty, soprano.

Selected performance:

1972 (Apr 26): New York City; Whitney Museum; Phyllis Curtin, soprano.

W26. FOR SUSAN. (1968; Boosey & Hawkes; 2 min.)
      See: B435; W12, W77, W100

Voice and piano.
Text by Paul Goodman.
Published with Clouds and What Sparks and Wiry Cries under the title Three Poems of Paul Goodman.
Dedicated to Susan Goodman.
Composed: Hyères, September 12, 1953.

W27. FOUR DIALOGUES. (1969; Boosey & Hawkes; 20 min.)
      See: B71, B229, B230, B340, B396, B780

Two voices and two pianos.
Text by Frank O'Hara.
Composed: London, Paris, Munich, Winter-Spring 1953-1954.
Contents: The Subway; The Airport; The Apartment; In Spain and in New York.

Premiere

1955 (Mar 23): Rome; Contessa Mimi Pecci-Blunt's palazzo; N. de Courson, soprano; V. Delafosse, tenor; John Moriarty and Ned Rorem, pianos.

Selected performances:

1965: New York City; New York Concert Ensemble; Anita Darian, soprano; John Stewart, tenor.
1966 (Jan 30): Salt Lake City, UT; University of Utah; Annual Chamber Music Festival.
1981 (Nov 14): Lansing, MI; Michigan State University Music Auditorium; Opera Company of Greater Lansing; Jean Herzberg, soprano, Michael Ballam, tenor; Kathryn Brown and Grace Karl, pianos; Annie Chadwick, director.

W28. FOUR POEMS OF TENNYSON. (1969; Boosey & Hawkes; 11 min.)
See: B73; W77, W78

Voice and piano.
Commissioned by and dedicated to Ellen Faull.
Composed: New York City, May-June 1963 (nos. 1-3) and Fez, Morocco, August 27, 1949 (no. 4).
Contents: Ask Me No More; Now Sleeps the Crimson Petal; Far-Far-Away; The Sleeping Palace.

Premiere:

1964 (Feb 8): New York City; Town Hall; Ellen Faull, soprano.

W29. FOUR SONGS. (1986; E. C. SCHIRMER; 9 MIN.)
See: B120; W25, W48, W49, W92

Voice and piano.
Each title published separately in 1968.
Contents: For Poulenc; The Midnight Sun; The Mild Mother; The Tulip Tree.

W30. 14 SONGS ON AMERICAN POETRY. (1958; Henmar Press; C. F. Peters)
See: W6, W18, W34, W47, W51, W54, W57, W70, W71, W72, W75, W85, W97, W104

Voice and piano.
Contents: As Adam Early in the Morning; Early in the Morning; I Am Rose; Memory; My Papa's Waltz; Night Crow; O You Whom I Often and Silently Come; Root Cellar; Sally's Smile; See How They Love Me; Snake; Such Beauty As Hurts to Behold; The Waking; Youth, Day, Old Age, and Night.

W31. FROM AN UNKNOWN PAST. (1953, 1963; Southern Music; 8 min.)
See: B85, B503; W9, W130

Voice and piano.

Arranged by the composer from the original version for SATB a cappella.

W32.   GLORIA. (1972; Boosey & Hawkes; 21 min.)
        See: B218, B319, B320, B343, B475, B492, B515, B684, B699, B747, B780

Two solo voices and piano.
Text from the Ordinary of the Mass.
Dedicated to Stuart Pope.
Composed: New York City and Peterborough, NH, May-June 1970.

Premiere:

1972 (Nov 26): New York City; Chapel of the Intercession; Phyllis Curtin, soprano; Helen Vanni, mezzo-soprano; Ned Rorem, piano.

Selected performances:

1973 (Nov 25): New York City; Alice Tully Hall; Phyllis Curtin, soprano; Beverly Wolff, mezzo-soprano; Ned Rorem, piano.
1982 (Jan 30): New York City; Katherine and Kristine Ciesinski, sopranos; Ned Rorem, piano.
1983 (Mar 2): New York City; Sotheby's; Composers Showcase Concerts; Katherine and Kristine Ciesinski, sopranos; Ned Rorem, piano.
1984 (Mar 23): Chicago; St. James Cathedral; Katherine and Kristine Ciesinski, sopranos.

W33.   HEARING. (1969; Boosey & Hawkes; 26 min.)
        See: B116, B239, B249, B780; W77

Song cycle; medium-low voice and piano.
Text by Kenneth Koch.
Dedicated to Carolyn Reyer.
Composed: New York City and Salt Lake City, November 1965-February 1966.
Contents: In Love with You; Down at the Docks; Poem; Spring; Invitation; Hearing.

Premiere:

1967 (May 9); New York City; Carolyn Reyer, mezzo-soprano; J. Benner, piano.

Selected performance:

1973 (Oct 3): New York City; New York Cultural Center; Florence Quivar, mezzo-soprano; Bruce Eberle, piano.

W34.   I AM ROSE. (1963; Henmar Press; C. F. Peters; 1/2 min.)
        See: B116, B374, B657, B712, B762; W30

Medium voice and piano.
Text by Gertrude Stein.

Dedicated to Marya Freund on her 80th birthday.
Composed: Paris, September 29, 1955.

Selected performances:

> 1959 (Nov 16): New York City; Carnegie Recital
> Hall; Regina Sarfaty, soprano; Ned Rorem, piano.
> 1968 (Dec 12): New York City; Town Hall; Phyllis
> Curtin, soprano; Ned Rorem, piano.
> 1973 (Aug 1): Marlboro, VT; Ellen Phillips,
> mezzo-soprano; Ned Rorem, piano.
> 1973 (Oct 3): New York City; New York Cultural
> Center; Florence Quivar, mezzo-soprano; Bruce
> Eberle, piano.
> 1984 (Apr 19): Philadelphia; Curtis Institute.
> Chrisselene Petropoulos, soprano; Vladimir
> Sokoloff, piano.

W35. I WILL ALWAYS LOVE YOU. (unpublished)
      See: B246

Voice and piano.
Text by Frank O'Hara.
Composed: 1950's.

Premiere:

> 1972 (Apr 26): New York City; Whitney Museum;
> Phyllis Curtin, soprano.

W36. IN A GONDOLA. (1963; Henmar Press; C. F. Peters)
      See: W114

High voice and piano.
Originally with orchestra in Six Songs for High
     Voice.
Text by Robert Browning.
Composed: Paris, December 2, 1953.

W37. JACK L'EVENTREUR. (1972; Boosey & Hawkes)
      See: B657; W78

Voice and piano.
Text by Marie Laure de Noailles.
Dedicated to André Dubois.
Composed: Hyères, July 27, 1953.

Premiere:

> 1954 (Feb): Germany; Chloe Owen, soprano.

Selected performance:

> 1959 (Nov 16): New York City; Carnegie Recital
> Hall; Phyllis Curtin, soprano; Ned Rorem, piano.

W38. JAIL-BAIT BLUES. (1984; Red Ozier Press)
      See: W294

Voice and piano.
Text by Paul Goodman.
Composed: 1947.
In Paul's Blues.

Premiere:

1947: New York City; Mary's Bar; John and Frank
Etherton.

W39. A JOURNEY. (1977; Boosey & Hawkes)

Voice and piano.
Text by Andrew Glaze.
Dedicated to "Alice" (Alice Esty).
Composed: New York City, April 23, 1976.

W40. KING MIDAS. (1970; Boosey & Hawkes; 24 min.)
      See: B21, B312, B692, B780; W72

Cantata for voices and piano.
Text by Howard Moss.
Dedicated to Elizabeth Ames.
Composed: Yaddo, New York City, Paris, Hyères, 1960-
1961.
Contents: The King's Speech; The Queen's Song; The
Princess' Speech; The Queen's Speech; The Hunts-
man's Song, The Gardener's Refrain; Address by
Dionysus; The Princess' Song (composed October 6,
1956, originally published by Henmar Press as See
How They Love Me); The King's Song, Dionysus'
Song; The King to the Princess, at the River Bank.

Premieres:

1962 (Mar 11): New York City; Carnegie Recital
Hall; Veronica Taylor, soprano; David Lloyd,
tenor; Ned Rorem, piano.

Selected Performance:

1962 (Mar 18): Boston; Gardner Museum; Veronica
Taylor, soprano; David Lloyd, tenor; Ned Rorem,
piano.

W41. LITTLE ELEGY. (1952; Hargail Press)
      See: B702, B777; W78

Voice and piano.
Text by Elinor Wylie.
Dedicated to Nell Tangeman.
Composed: New York City, March 29, 1949.

Premiere:

1949 (April): New York City; Times Hall; Nell
Tangeman, mezzo-soprano; Ned Rorem, piano.

W42. THE LORDLY HUDSON.   (1947; Mercury Music; Theodore
      Presser; 2-1/2 min.)

      Voice and piano.
      The Music Library Association's "best published song
          of the year."
      Text by Paul Goodman.
      Dedicated to Janet Fairbank.
      Composed: 1947.

      Selected performance:

          1986 (Apr 18): Detroit; Detroit Institute of Arts;
              William Parker; baritone; Ned Rorem, piano.

W43. THE LORD'S PRAYER.   (1957; Henmar Press; C. F. Peters;
      2 min.)

      Voice and piano or organ.
      Composed: Paris, July 2, 1957.

W44. LOVE.   (1969; Boosey & Hawkes; 2 min.)
      See: B664; W78

      Voice and piano.
      Text by Thomas Lodge.
      Dedicated "to Shirley Xenia Gabis Rhoads."
      Composed: Hyères, July 22, 1953.

      Premiere:

          1959 (Feb 24): New York City; Carnegie Recital
              Hall; Patricia Neway, soprano; Ned Rorem, piano.

W45. LOVE IN A LIFE.   (1972; Boosey & Hawkes; 4 min.)
      See: W77

      Voice and piano.
      Text by Robert Browning.
      Dedicated to Jacques Dupont.
      Composed: Hyères, July 16, 1951.

W46. LULLABY OF THE WOMAN OF THE MOUNTAIN.   (1956; Boosey &
      Hawkes; 2-1/2 min.)
      See: B664, B772; W78

      Medium voice and piano.
      Text by Padhraic Pearse; translated by Thomas Mac-
          Donagh.
      Composed: Fez, Morocco, August 18, 1950.

      Premiere:

          1959 (Feb 24): New York City; Carnegie Recital
              Hall; Patricia Neway, soprano; Ned Rorem, piano.

W47. MEMORY.   (1961; Henmar Press; C. F. Peters; 1 min.)
      See: B18, B57; W30

Voice and piano.
Text by Theodore Roethke.
Dedicated to Alice Esty.
Composed: New York City, May 27, 1959.

Premiere:

1960 (Apr 3): New York City; Carnegie Recital
Hall; Alice Esty, soprano; David Stimer, piano.

W48. THE MIDNIGHT SUN.   (1968; E. C. Schirmer; 1-1/2 min.)
      See: B657; W29

Medium voice and piano.
Text by Paul Goodman.
Dedicated to Joseph Adamiak.
Composed: Hyères, September 11, 1953.

Selected performance:

1959 (Nov 16): New York City; Carnegie Recital
Hall; Regina Sarfaty, soprano; Ned Rorem, piano.

W49. THE MILD MOTHER.   (1968; E. C. Schirmer; 1 min.)
      See: W29, W145

Medium voice and piano.
Text anonymous 15th c.; adapted by the composer.
Also published for unison chorus with piano, 1970.
Dedicated to Rosemarie Beck.
Composed: Philadelphia, November 28, 1952.

W50. MONGOLIAN IDIOT.   (unpublished)

Voice and piano.
Text by Karl Shapiro.
Composed: 1947.

Premiere:

1947 (Jul 20): Tanglewood; Zelda Goodman, soprano;
Ned Rorem, piano.

W51. MY PAPA'S WALTZ.   (1963; Henmar Press; C. F. Peters;
      1-1/2 min.)
      See: B18, B57, B764; W30

Medium voice and piano.
Text by Theodore Roethke.
Commissioned by and dedicated to Alice Esty.
Composed: Summer 1959.

Premiere:

1960 (Apr 3): New York City; Carnegie Recital
Hall; Alice Esty, soprano; David Stimer, piano.

Selected performance:

>1979 (Jan 29): Philadelphia; Curtis Institute; Randi Marrazzo, mezzo-soprano; Thomas Jaber, piano.

W52.   THE NANTUCKET SONGS.   (1981; Boosey & Hawkes; 18 min.)
        See: B130, B257, B258, B259, B359, B360, B419, B456,
        B655, B752

Song cycle; ten songs for voice and piano.
Commissioned by the Elizabeth Sprague Coolidge Foundation.
Composed: Nantucket, November 1978-May 1979.
Contents: From Whence Cometh Song? (Theodore Roethke); The Dance (William Carlos Williams); Go, Lovely Rose (Edmund Waller); Up-Hill (Christina Rossetti); Mother I Cannot Mind My Wheel (Walter Savage Landor); Fear of Death (John Ashbery); Thoughts of a Young Girl (John Ashbery); Ferry Me across the Water (Christina Rossetti); The Dancer (Edmund Waller).

Premiere:

>1979 (Oct 30): Washington, DC; Library of Congress; Phyllis Bryn-Julson, soprano; Ned Rorem, piano.

Selected performances:

>1980 (Nov 21): Chicago; Thorne Hall; Elsa Charlston, soprano; Ned Rorem, piano.
>1981 (Mar 22): New York City; Carnegie Hall; Leontyne Price, soprano; David Garvey, piano (The Dance; Ferry Me across the Water).
>1981 (Oct 4): Bethesda, MD; Bradley Hills Presbyterian Church; Phyllis Bryn-Julson, soprano; Ned Rorem, piano.
>1984 (Apr 4): Boston; Boston University; Lynn Torgrove, soprano.

W53.   NEAR CLOSING TIME.   (1984; Red Ozier Press)
        See: W294

Voice and piano.
Text by Paul Goodman.
Composed: September 21, 1947.
In Paul's blues.

Premiere:

>1947: New York City; Mary's Bar; John and Frank Etherton.

W54.   NIGHT CROW.   (1963; Henmar Press; C. F. Peters; 2 min.)
        See: B18, B57; W30

Medium Voice and piano.
Text by Theodore Roethke.

Dedicated to Alice Esty and David Stimer.
Composed: Fish Creek, WI, August 22, 1959.

Premiere:

1960 (Apr 3): New York City; Carnegie Recital Hall; Alice Esty, soprano; David Stimer, piano.

W55.   THE NIGHTINGALE. (1956; Boosey & Hawkes; 1 min.)
See: B72; W77

Voice and piano.
Text anonymous 16th c.
Dedicated to Muriel Smith.
Composed: Marrakech, August 11, 1951.

W56.   O DO NOT LOVE TOO LONG. (unpublished)
See: W89, W214

Voice and piano.
Text by W. B. Yeats.
One of six Yeats songs in an unpublished baritone cycle called To a Young Girl (the title song of which is published by Boosey and Hawkes).
Adapted to the fifth movement of Septet: "Scenes from Childhood."
Composed: 1951.

W57.   O YOU WHOM I OFTEN AND SILENTLY COME. (1961; Henmar Press; C. F. Peters)
See: B146; W30

Voice and piano.
Text by Walt Whitman.
Commissioned by Wilder Luke Burnap.
Dedicated to Maggy Magerstadt.
Composed: Hyères, July 16, 1957.

Premiere:

1958: Wilder Luke Burnap.

Selected performances:

1986 (Jan 29): Omaha, NE; Strauss Performing Arts Center; Margaret Hemmen, mezzo-soprano, Harold Payne, piano.
1986 (Apr 18): Detroit; Detroit Institute of Arts; William Parker, baritone; Ned Rorem, piano.

W58.   ON A SINGING GIRL. (1952; Hargail Press)
See: B777; W78

Voice and piano.
Text by Elinor Wylie.
Dedicated to Daniel Pinkham.
Composed: April 29, 1946.

W59. PENNY ARCADE. (unpublished)
      See: B37, B205, B242

      Song cycle; voice and piano.
      Text by Harold Norse.
      Composed: 1949.

      Premiere:

          1949 (May 19): New York City; Nell Tangeman,
          soprano; Ned Rorem, piano.

W60. PHILOMEL.   (1952; Hargail Music Press; Boosey &
      Hawkes; 3 min.)
      See: B777

      Medium voice and piano.
      Text by Richard Barnfield.
      Dedicated to Guy Ferrand.
      Composed: Fez, Morocco, June 9, 1950.

W61. PIPPA'S SONG. (1963; Henmar Press; C. F. Peters)
      See: B20; W114

      High voice and piano.
      Originally with orchestra in Six Songs for High
      Voice.
      Text by Robert Browning.
      Commissioned by Virginia Fleming.
      Dedicated to Thomas Thompson.
      Composed: Paris, December 3, 1953.

      Selected performance:

          1960 (Feb 8): New York City; Carnegie Recital
          Hall; Reri Grist, soprano; Ned Rorem, piano.

W62. POEM FOR F. (unpublished)

      Voice and piano.
      Text by Edouard Roditi.
      Composed: 1955.

W63. POÈMES POUR LA PAIX. (1970; Boosey & Hawkes; 13 min.)
      See: B492, B780, B783; W78

      Song cycle; voice and piano; also arranged by the
      composer for voice and string orchestra.
      Text from Paul Eluard's Anthologie vivante de la
      poesie du passe."
      Composed: Paris, May 13-25, 1953.
      Contents: Lay (Jehan Regnier): Ode (Pierre de Ron-
      sard); Sonnet I and II (Olivier de Magny); Sonnet
      (Jean Daurát); L'hymne de la paix (Jean-Antoine de
      Baif).

      Premiere:

1954 (Oct 23): Paris; Ecole Normale; Bernard Lefort, baritone; Ned Rorem, piano.

Selected performances:

1972 (Nov 26): New York City; Chapel of the Intercession; Sandra Walker, soprano.
1974 (Apr 4): Avignon, France; Paul Sperry, baritone; Marius Constant, conductor.

W64. POEMS OF LOVE AND THE RAIN.   (1965, 1986; Boosey & Hawkes; 28 min.)
See: B91, B178, B266, B314, B444, B465, B712, B780

Song cycle; mezzo-soprano and piano.
Commissioned by the Ford Foundation.
Dedicated to Regina Sarfaty.
Composed: New York City, December 1962-January 1963.
Contents: Prologue: from "The Rain" (Donald Windham); Stop All the Clocks, Cut Off the Telephone (W. H. Auden); The Air Is the Only (Howard Moss); Love's Stricken "Why" (Emily Dickinson); The Apparition (Theodore Roethke); Do I Love You (Jack Larson); In the Rain (e.e. cummings); Song for Lying in Bed during a Night Rain (Kenneth Pitchford); Interlude (Theodore Roethke); Epilogue: from "The Rain" (Donald Windham).

Premiere:

1964 (Apr 12): Madison, WI; Wisconsin Union Theatre; Regina Sarfaty, mezzo-soprano; Ned Rorem, piano.

Selected performances:

1965 (Apr 9): New York City; Metropolitan Museum; Grace Rainey Rogers Auditorium; Regina Sarfaty, mezzo-soprano; Ned Rorem, piano.
1968 (Dec 12): New York City; Town Hall; Beverly Wolff, mezzo-soprano; Ned Rorem, piano.
1973 (Apr 14): Albuquerque; University of New Mexico; Jeanne Grealish, mezzo-soprano; Ned Rorem, piano.

W65. A PSALM OF PRAISE.   (1946; Associated Music Publishers; 3 min.)

Medium voice and piano.
Text from Psalm 100.
Dedicated to David Diamond.
Composed: 1945.

W66. RAIN IN SPRING. (1956; Boosey & Hawkes; 1 min.)
See: B764, B772; W77

Voice and piano.
Text by Paul Goodman.

Dedicated to Henri Hell.
Composed: Paris, June 7, 1949.

Selected performance:

> 1979 (Jan 29): Philadelphia; Curtis Institute: Randi Marrazzo, mezzo-soprano; Thomas Jaber, piano.

W67. REQUIEM. (1950; Peer International; 2 min.)
      See: B157, B658

Voice and piano.
Text by Robert Louis Stevenson.
Composed: New York City, November 9-10, 1948.

W68. THE RESURRECTION. (1965; Southern Music)
      See: B690

Voice and piano.
Text from St. Matthew 27:62-66; 28.
Dedicated to Virgil Thomson.
Composed: Paris, August 2-20, 1952.

Selected performance:

> 1973 (Jul 15): London; Shirley Verrett, soprano; Warren Wilson, piano.

W69. RONDELAY. (1968; C. F. Peters)
      See: W114

High voice and piano.
Originally with orchestra in Six Songs for High Voice.
Text by John Dryden.
Composed: Paris, November 25, 1953.

W70. ROOT CELLAR. (1963; Henmar Press; C. F. Peters; 1-1/2 min.)
      See: B18, B57; W30

Medium voice and piano.
Text by Theodore Roethke.
Dedicated to Alice Esty.
Composed: Yaddo, June 12, 1959.

Premiere:

> 1960 (Apr 3): New York City; Carnegie Recital Hall; Alice Esty, soprano; David Stimer, piano.

W71. SALLY'S SMILE. (1957; Henmar Press; C. F. Peters; 1 min.)
      See: W30

Voice and piano.
Text by Paul Goodman.

Dedicated to Claude Lebon.
Composed: Hyères, September 12, 1953.

W72.   SEE HOW THEY LOVE ME.   (1958; Henmar Press, C. F. Pe-
       ters; 1-1/2 min.)
       See: W30, W40

       Voice and piano.
       Text by Howard Moss.
       Dedicated to Oliver Daniel.
       Composed: Paris, October 6-7, 1956.
       Included as no. 7 in King Midas, "The Princess'
       Song."

W73.   THE SERPENT.   (1974; Boosey & Hawkes; 2 min.)
       See: W77

       Voice and piano.
       Text by Theodore Roethke.
       Dedicated to Phyllis Curtin.
       Composed: May 21, 1970-April 14, 1972.

W74.   THE SILVER SWAN.   (1950; Peer International; 3 min.)
       See: B413, B662, B677

       Voice and piano.
       Text by Orlando Gibbons.
       Composed: New York City, February 25, 1949.

       Selected performance:

          1978 (Oct 8): Washington, DC; The White House;
          Leontyne Price, soprano.

W75.   SNAKE.   (1963; Henmar Press; C. F. Peters; 1-1/2 min.)
       See: B18, B57, B116; W30

       Medium voice and piano.
       Text by Theodore Roethke.
       Dedicated to Alice Esty.
       Composed: Fish Creek, WI, August 18-21, 1959.

       Premiere:

          1960 (Apr 3): New York City; Carnegie Recital
          Hall; Alice Esty, soprano; David Stimer, piano.

       Selected performance:

          1973 (Oct 3): New York City; New York Cultural
          Center; Florence Quivar, mezzo-soprano; Bruce
          Eberle, piano.

W76.   SOME TREES: Three Poems for Three Voices.   (1970;
       Boosey & Hawkes; 11 min.)
       See: B178, B315, B409, B712, B716, B780, B783

       Soprano, mezzo-soprano, bass-baritone and piano.
       Texts by John Ashbery.

Composed: New York City; April 2-29, 1968.
Contents: Some Trees; The Grapevine; Our Youth.

Premiere:

    1968 (Dec 12): New York City; Town Hall; Phyllis
    Curtin, soprano; Beverly Wolff, mezzo-soprano;
    Donald Gramm, bass-baritone; Ned Rorem, piano.

W77. SONG ALBUM: Volume One. (1980; Boosey & Hawkes)
     See: W1, W19, W23, W26, W28, W33, W45, W55, W66,
     W73, W89, W95

     Voice and piano.
     Contents: Absalom; Rain in Spring; For Susan; Look
     Down, Fair Moon; Sometimes with One I Love; Echo's
     Song; Far-Far-Away; The Nightingale; To a Young
     Girl; Love in a Life; Orchids; Spring; The Serpent.

W78. SONG ALBUM: Volume Two. (1982; Boosey & Hawkes)
     See: W10, W12, W28, W37, W41, W44, W46, W58, W63,
     W83, W88, W95, W99, W108, W122

     Voice and piano.
     Contents: Catullus: On the Burial of His Brother;
     Ask Me No More; Love; Spring "Nothing is So Beau-
     tiful as Spring"; A Child Asleep in Its Own Life;
     Lullaby of the Woman of the Mountain; I Strolled
     Across an Open Field; Clouds; The Land of Fear;
     Jack L'Eventreur; Ode; Little Elegy; Confitebor
     tibi; What If Some Little Pain; On a Singing Girl.

W79. SONG FOR A GIRL. (1963; Henmar Press; C. F. Peters)
     See: B20; W114

     High voice and piano.
     Originally with orchestra in Six Songs for High
      Voice.
     Text by John Dryden.
     Dedicated to Virginia Fleming.
     Composed: Paris, November 20-21, 1953.

     Selected performance:

       1960 (Feb 8): New York City; Carnegie Recital
       Hall; Reri Grist, soprano; Ned Rorem, piano.

W80. SONG OF CHAUCER. (unpublished)

     Voice and piano.
     Text by Geoffrey Chaucer.
     Composed: 1944.

W81. A SONG OF DAVID: Psalm 120. (1946; Associated Music
     Publishers; 2 min.)
     See: B93

     Voice and piano.
     Dedicated to "H.K."

Composed: 1945.
Also published in <u>Contemporary American Sacred Songs</u>.

W82. <u>SONG TO A FAIR YOUNG LADY, GOING OUT OF TOWN IN THE SPRING</u>. (1963; Henmar Press; C. F. Peters)
<u>See</u>: W114

High voice and piano.
Originally with orchestra in <u>Six Songs for High Voice</u>.
Text by John Dryden.
Composed: Paris, November 16, 1953.

W83. <u>SPRING: 'Nothing Is So Beautiful as Spring.'</u> (1953, 1981; Boosey & Hawkes)
<u>See</u>: B256, B260, B286, B664; W78

Voice and piano.
Text by Gerard Manley Hopkins.
Dedicated to Marie Laure de Noailles.
Composed: New York City, January 1947.

<u>Selected performances</u>:

1959 (Feb 24): New York City; Carnegie Recital Hall; Patricia Neway, soprano; Ned Rorem, piano.
1981 (Sep 23): Washington, DC; Kennedy Center; Rosalind Rees, soprano; Ned Rorem, piano.

W84. <u>SPRING AND FALL</u>. (1947; Mercury Music, Theodore Presser; 2 min.)
<u>See</u>: B657

Voice and piano.
Text by Gerard Manley Hopkins.
Dedicated to Mme. Eva Gauthier.
Composed: 1946.

<u>Selected performance</u>:

1959 (Nov 16): New York City; Carnegie Recital Hall; Regina Sarfaty, soprano; Ned Rorem, piano.

W85. <u>SUCH BEAUTY AS HURTS TO BEHOLD</u>. (1961; Henmar Press; C. F. Peters; 2-1/2 min.)
<u>See</u>: B260, B374; W30

Voice and piano.
Text by Paul Goodman.
Dedicated to Marc Blitzstein.
Composed: Hyères, July 10, 1957.

<u>Selected performances</u>:

1973 (Aug 1): Marlboro, VT; Ellen Phillips, mezzo-soprano; Ned Rorem, piano.
1981 (Sep 23): Washington, DC; Kennedy Center; Rosalind Rees, soprano; Ned Rorem, piano.

W86.   THREE CALAMUS POEMS.   (1986; Boosey & Hawkes; 10 min.)
       See: B6, B236

       Medium voice and piano.
       Texts by Walt Whitman.
       Commissioned by Donald Collup on a Solo Recital Fel-
         lowship from the National Endowment for the Arts.
       Composed: New York City and Nantucket, March-April
         1982.
       Contents: Of Him I Love Day and Night; I Saw in Lou-
         isiana a Live Oak Growing; To a Common Prostitute.

       Premiere:

          1983 (Apr 27): New York City; Town Hall; Donald
            Collup, baritone; Walter Huff, piano.

       Selected performance:

          1986 (Apr 18): Detroit: Detroit Institute of Arts;
            William Parker, baritone; Ned Rorem, piano.

W87.   THREE INCANTATIONS FROM A MARIONETTE TALE.   (1967,
       1969; Boosey & Hawkes; 2 min.)
       See: B109, B391; W269

       Song cycle; solo voice or unison chorus and piano.
       Texts by Charles Boultenhouse.
       Some of this material was previously used as inci-
         dental music for the puppet show, Fire Boy.
       Dedicated to John Bernard Myers.
       Composed: New York City, July 6, 1948.
       Contents: Cloudless Blue Claw; Now I Make a Circle;
         Boy into Animal.

       Selected performance:

          1971 (Mar 21): New York City; Alice Tully Hall;
            New Jersey Schola Cantorum; Fairleigh Dickinson
            University Chamber Orchestra.

W88.   THREE POEMS OF DEMETRIOS CAPETANAKIS: (1968; Boosey &
       Hawkes)
       See: W78

       Voice and piano.
       Dedicated to Betty Allen, John Lehmann and Marie
         Laure de Noailles.
       Composed: Paris and Hyères, June-July 1954.
       Contents: Abel; Guilt; The Land of Fear.

       Premiere:

          ca. 1969; New York City; Whitney Museum; Betty
            Allen, mezzo-soprano.

W89.   TO A YOUNG GIRL.   (1972; Boosey & Hawkes; 1-1/2 min.)
       See: W77

Voice and piano.
Text by W. B. Yeats.
Originally the last in a cycle of six songs for bar-
itone by the same title (unpublished).
Dedicated to Sylvia Goldstein.
Composed: Hyères, April 13, 1951.

Premiere:

1952: New York City; Museum of Modern Art; League
of Composers; Doda Conrad, soprano.

W90. TO JANE. (1976; Boosey & Hawkes; 1-1/2 min.)

Voice and piano.
Text by Percy B. Shelley.
Dedicated to Jane Wilson (Jane Wilson Gruen).
Composed: New York City, April 25, 1974.

W91. TO YOU. (1965; Elkan-Vogel; 1 min.)
See: B657, B664; W21

Voice and piano.
Text by Walt Whitman.
Published with Epitaph.
Commissioned by Wilder Luke Burnap.
Dedicated to Thomas Prentiss.
Composed: Hyères, July 17, 1957.

Premiere:

1958: Wilder Luke Burnap, baritone.

Selected performances:

1959 (Feb 24): New York City; Carnegie Recital
Hall; Patricia Neway, soprano; Ned Rorem, piano.
1959 (Nov 16): New York City; Carnegie Recital
Hall; Regina Sarfaty, soprano; Ned Rorem, piano.
1986 (Apr 18): Detroit; Detroit Institute of Arts;
William Parker, baritone; Ned Rorem, piano.

W92. THE TULIP TREE. (1968; E. C. Schirmer; 2 min.)
See: W29

Medium voice and piano.
Text by Paul Goodman.
Dedicated to Robert Phelps.
Composed: Hyères, September 10-11, 1953.

W93. TWO POEMS OF EDITH SITWELL. (1982; Boosey & Hawkes)
See: B34

Medium-high voice and piano.
Contents: You, the Young Rainbow (dedicated to
Rosalind Rees; composed: New York City, August 7,
1948); The Youth with the Red-Gold Hair (dedicated
to Charles Turner; composed: Truro, August 16,
1948).

Premieres:

    1950: Amerikahaus tour of Germany; Nell Tangeman,
    mezzo-soprano; Noel Lee, piano (You, the Young
    Rainbow).

Selected performance:

    1950 (May): Paris; American Embassy; Janet Hayes
    Walker, mezzo-soprano; Ned Rorem, piano (The
    Youth with the Red-Gold Hair).

W94. TWO POEMS OF PLATO. (unpublished)

    Song cycle in Greek; voice and piano.
    Text by Plato.
    Private commission.
    Composed: 1964.

W95. TWO POEMS OF THEODORE ROETHKE. (1969; Boosey &
    Hawkes; 3 min.)
    See: B18, B57, B309; W77, W78

    Voice and piano.
    Commissioned by and dedicated to Alice Esty.
    Contents: Orchids (composed: New York City, May
    21-26, 1959); I Strolled across an Open Field
    (composed: Buffalo, NY, Autumn, 1959).

Premiere:

    1960 (Apr 3): New York City; Carnegie Recital
    Hall; Alice Esty, soprano; David Stimer, piano.

W96. VISITS TO ST. ELIZABETHS (Bedlam). (1964; Boosey &
    Hawkes)
    See: B116, B248, B260, B374, B657, B664, B764

    Medium voice and piano.
    Text by Elizabeth Bishop.
    Dedicated to Robert Holton.
    Composed: Hyères, July-August 1957.

Premiere:

    1959 (Feb 24): New York City; Carnegie Recital
    Hall; Patricia Neway, soprano; Ned Rorem, piano.

Selected performances:

    1959 (Nov 16): New York City; Carnegie Recital
    Hall; Regina Sarfaty, soprano; Ned Rorem, piano.
    1969 (Feb 5): New York City; Whitney Museum; Betty
    Allen, mezzo-soprano; Ned Rorem, piano.
    1973 (Aug 1): Marlboro, VT; Ellen Phillips, mezzo-
    soprano; Ned Rorem, piano.
    1973 (Oct 3): New York City; New York Cultural
    Center; Florence Quivar, mezzo-soprano; Bruce
    Eberle, piano.

    1979 (Jan 29): Philadelphia; Randi Marrazzo,
    mezzo-soprano; Thomas Jaber, conductor.
    1981 (Sep 23): Washington, DC; Kennedy Center;
    Rosalind Rees, soprano; Ned Rorem, piano.

W97. THE WAKING. (1961); Henmar Press; C. F. Peters; 2-1/2
      min.)
      See: B18, B57, B219; W30

      Voice and piano.
      Text by Theodore Roethke.
      Dedicated to Alice Esty.
      Composed: Yaddo, June 9-11, 1959.

      Premiere:

        1960 (Apr 3): New York City; Carnegie Recital
        Hall; Alice Esty, soprano; David Stimer, piano.

      Selected performance:

        1984 (Mar 30): Glendale, CA; Brand Library; Anne
        Marie Ketchum, soprano; Adam Stern, piano.

W98. WAR SCENES. (1971; Boosey & Hawkes; 13 min.)
      See: B33, B66, B130, B216, B217, B218, B257, B294,
      B300, B320, B458, B515, B684, B699, B757, B764, B780

      Song cycle; medium-low voice and piano.
      Text by Walt Whitman from Specimen Days.
      Dedicated "to those who died in Vietnam, both sides,
        during the composition: 20-30 June 1969."
      "Designed for Gérard Souzay."
      Contents: A Night Battle; Specimen Case; An Inci-
        dent; Inauguration Ball; The Real War Will Never
        Get in the Books.

      Premiere:

        1969 (Oct 19): Washington, DC; Constitution Hall;
        Gérard Souzay, baritone; Dalton Baldwin, piano.

      Selected performance:

        1969 (Nov 5): New York City; Philharmonic Hall;
        Gérard Souzay, baritone; Dalton Baldwin, piano.
        1973 (Nov 25): New York City; Alice Tully Hall;
        Donald Gramm, baritone; Ned Rorem, piano.
        1975 (May 11): Philadelphia; Donald Gramm, bari-
        tone; Ned Rorem, piano.
        1979 (Jan 29): Philadelphia; Curtis Institute;
        Jack Clay, bass; Ned Rorem, piano.
        1980 (Feb 10): New York City; Alice Tully Hall;
        William Parker, baritone; William Huckaby,
        piano.
        1980 (Jul 25): Santa Fe; Santa Fe Chamber Music
        Festival; Santuario de Guadalupe; William Park-
        er, baritone; Ned Rorem, piano.

1980 (Aug 18): Seattle; Meany Theater; William Parker, baritone; Ned Rorem, piano.
1981 (Oct 4): Bethesda, MD; Bradley Hills Presbyterian Church; David Young, baritone; Ned Rorem, piano.
1982 (Feb 12): London; Wigmore Hall; William Parker, baritone.
1983 (Mar 2): New York City; Sotheby's; Composers Showcase Concert; William Parker, baritone; Ned Rorem, piano.
1984 (Apr 4): Boston; Boston University; Richard Morrison, baritone; Phillip Oliver, piano.
1986 (Apr 18): Detroit; Detroit Institute of Arts; William Parker, baritone; Ned Rorem, piano.

W99. WHAT IF SOME LITTLE PAIN... (1952; Hargail Music Press)
See: B777; W78

Medium voice and piano.
Text by Edmund Spenser.
Dedicated to Julien Green.
Composed: Fez, Morocco, December 20, 1949.

W100. WHAT SPARKS AND WIRY CRIES. (1968; Boosey & Hawkes; 2 min.)
See: B435, B664, W12, W26

Voice and piano.
Text by Paul Goodman.
Published with For Susan and Clouds under the title Three Poems of Paul Goodman.
Dedicated to James Roland Holmes.
Composed: France, 1952-1956.

Premiere:

1959 (Feb 24): New York City; Carnegie Recital Hall; Patricia Neway, soprano; Ned Rorem, piano.

W101. WHERE WE CAME. (1976; Boosey & Hawkes; 2 min.)

Voice and piano.
Text by Jean Garrigue.
Dedicated to Ben Weber.
Composed: Yaddo, February 15-17, 1974.

W102. WHISKY, DRINK DIVINE. (unpublished)

Voice and piano.
Text from an Irish folk poem.
Composed: 1951.

W103. WOMEN'S VOICES. (1979; Boosey & Hawkes; 22 min.)
See: B258, B343, B473, B515, B686, B752, B780

Song cycle; eleven songs for soprano and piano.
Commissioned by and dedicated to Joyce Mathis.
Composed: Nantucket and New York City, 1975-1976.

Contents: Now Let No Charitable Hope (Elinor Wylie);
A Birthday (Christina Rossetti); To My Dear and
Loving Husband (Anne Bradstreet); To the Ladies
(Mary Leigh, Lady Chudleigh); If Ever Hapless
Woman Had a Cause (Mary Sidney Herbert, Countess
of Pembroke); We Never Said Farewell (Mary Eliza-
beth Coleridge); The Stranger (Adrienne Rich);
What Inn Is This (Emily Dickinson); Defiled Is My
Name (Queen Anne Boleyn); Electrocution (Lola
Ridge); Smile, Death (Charlotte Mew).

Premiere:

1976 (Nov 4): New York City; Alice Tully Hall;
Joyce Mathis, soprano; Warren Wilson, piano.

Selected performances:

1980 (Nov 21): Chicago; Thorne Hall; Dorothy
Keyser, soprano; Ned Rorem, piano.
1982 (Jan 3): New York City; Susan Davenny Wyner;
Ned Rorem, piano.
1983 (Mar 2): New York City; Sotheby's; Composers
Showcase Concert; Katherine Ciesinski, soprano;
Ned Rorem, piano.

W104. YOUTH, DAY, OLD AGE, AND NIGHT.   (1958; Henmar Press;
C. F. Peters; 1-1/2 min.)
See: W30

Voice and piano.
Text by Walt Whitman.
Dedicated to Walter Hinrichsen.
Composed: Hyères, July 6, 1954.

II.   SONGS WITH INSTRUMENTAL ENSEMBLE

W105. AFTER LONG SILENCE.   (1982 Boosey & Hawkes; 24 min.)
See: B5, B233, B423, B519

Soprano, oboe, and string orchestra.
Commissioned by the New World Festival of the Arts,
Miami, Florida.
Composed: 1981-82.
Contents: After Long Silence (W. B. Yeats); Bit-
tersweet (G. Herbert); Mediocrity in Love Rejected
(T. Carew); A Red, Red Rose (R. Burns); On Mon-
sieur's Departure (Elizabeth I); String Interlude;
The Darkling Thrush (T. Hardy); The Sick Rose (W.
Blake); Vita summa brevis (E. Dowson); After Great
Pain (E. Dickinson).

Premiere:

1982 (Jun 11): Miami; New World Festival of the
Arts; Katherine Ciesinski, mezzo-soprano; André
Spiller, oboe, Camerata Bariloche of Argentina.

Selected performances:

1984 (Nov 17): New York; Delia Wallis, soprano; Y Chamber Symphony; Gerard Schwarz, conductor.

1985 (Jun 4): London; Wigmore Hall; Felicity Palmer, mezzo-soprano; London Sinfonietta.

W106. ARIEL. (1974; Boosey & Hawkes; 17 min.)
See: B218, B318, B320, B350, B374, B468, B653, B684, B738, B780

Soprano, clarinet and piano.
Texts by Sylvia Plath.
Dedicated to Phyllis Curtin.
Composed: New York City, May 1971.
Contents: Words; Poppies in July; The Hanging Man; Poppies in October; Lady Lazarus.

Premiere:

1971 (Nov 26): Washington, DC; Library of Congress; Phyllis Curtin, soprano; David Glazer, clarinet; Ryan Edwards, piano.

Selected performances:

1973 (Aug 1): Marlboro, VT; Carol Page, soprano; Richard Stoltzman, clarinet; Luis Batlle, piano.
1973 (Nov 26): New York City; Alice Tully Hall; Phyllis Curtin, soprano; Joseph Rabbai, clarinet; Ryan Edwards, piano.
1982 (Nov 5): New York City; Merkin Hall; Kristine Ciesinski, soprano; Jean Kopperud, clarinet; Cameron Grant, piano.
1983 (Oct 28): Washington, DC; Washington Music Ensemble's Festival Americana; Elizabeth Kirkpatrick, soprano.

W107. BACK TO LIFE. (1980; Boosey & Hawkes)
See: B4, B401, B511

Counter-tenor and double bass.
Text by Thom Gunn.
Composed: 1980.

Premiere:

1981 (Mar 23): Hartford, CT; Trinity Episcopal Church; Rod Hardesty, counter-tenor; Gary Karr, double bass.

W108. LAST POEMS OF WALLACE STEVENS. (1974; Boosey & Hawkes; 24 min.)
See: B91, B112, B130, B218, B260, B319, B320, B374, B475, B476, B511, B684, B699, B761; W78

Voice, cello and piano.
Commissioned by the David Ensemble.
Composed: December 1971-February 1972.

Contents: Not Ideas about the Thing but the Thing Itself; The River of Rivers in Connecticut; A Child Asleep in Its Own Life; The Planet on the Table; The Dove in Spring; Interlude; Of Mere Being; A Clear Day and No Memories.

Premieres:

1972 (Nov 13): New York City; Town Hall; Sheila Schonbrun, soprano; Jonathan Abramowitz, cello; Warren Wilson, piano.

Selected Performances:

1973 (Apr 14): Albuquerque, NM; University of New Mexico; Donna McRae, soprano; Joanna de Keyser, cello; Lois McLeod, piano.
1973 (Aug 1): Marlboro, VT; Diana Hoagland, soprano; Terry Braverman, cello; Ruth Laredo, piano.
1973 (Nov 25): New York City; Alice Tully Hall; Betti McDonald, soprano; Jeffry Solow, violoncello; Jerome Lowenthal, piano.
1981 (Mar 28): Hartford, CT; Trinity Episcopal Church; Betti McDonald, soprano; Jeffrey Krieger, violoncello; Alexander Farkas, piano.
1981 (Sep 23): Washington, DC; Kennedy Center; Rosalind Rees, soprano; Sharon Robinson, cello; Jerome Lowenthal, piano.
1983 (Mar 22): New York City; YMHA; Lucy Shelton, soprano; Sharon Robinson, cello; Ned Rorem, piano.
1984 (Apr 4): Boston; Boston University; Joan Heller, soprano; William Rounds, cello; Warren George Wilson, piano.
1986 (Mar 19): Philadelphia; Philadelphia Camerata; Marian vander Loo, mezzo-soprano; Charles Forbes, cello; Peter Helm, piano.

W109. MOURNING SCENE FROM SAMUEL.   (1963; Henmar Press; C. F. Peters; 6 min.)
See: B59, B374, B396, B664

Medium voice and string quartet.
Text from II Samuel 1:19-27.
Dedicated to Lee Hoiby.
Composed: Tanglewood, July 20, 1947.

Selected performances:

1959 (Feb 24): New York City; Carnegie Recital Hall; Jerold Siena, baritone; Ned Rorem, piano.
1959 (Aug 12): Marlboro, VT; Barry Hanner, baritone; Bjoern Andreasson and Takaoki Sugitani, violins; Rhoda Rhea, viola; Ann Goodman, cello.
1966 (Jan 30): Salt Lake City; University of Utah; Annual Chamber Music Festival.

W110. THE SANTA FE SONGS: Twelve Poems of Witter Bynner. (1980; Boosey & Hawkes; 25 min.)

See: B3, B5, B36, B66, B118, B132, B273, B283, B291, B297, B366, B420, B457, B458, B469, B485, B489, B513, B767, B778; W183

Song cycle; medium voice, violin, viola, cello and piano.
"Commissioned by the Santa Fe Chamber Music Festival for the 1980 season."
Composed: Nantucket and New York City, December 1979-March 1980.
Some material from A Birthday Suite is incorporated into this work.
Contents: Santa Fe; Opus 101; Any Other Time; Sonnet; Coming Down the Stairs; He Never Knew; El Musico; The Wintry-Mind; Water-Hyacinths; Moving Leaves; Yes I Hear Them; The Sowers.

Premiere:

    1980 (July 27): Santa Fe; Santa Fe Chamber Music Festival; Greer Garson Theatre, College of Santa Fe; William Parker, baritone; Ani Kavafian, violin; Heiichiro Ohyama, viola; Timothy Eddy, cello; Ned Rorem, piano.

Selected performances:

    1980 (Aug 19): Seattle; Meany Theatre; same performers as the premiere.
    1980 (Aug 25): New York City; Alice Tully Hall; same performers as the premiere.
    1982 (Aug 3): Aspen, CO; Leslie Guinn, baritone; Ned Rorem, piano.
    1985 (Aug 18-19): Santa Fe; Santa Fe Chamber Music Festival; William Parker, baritone; Daniel Phillips, violin; Geraldine Walther, viola; Timothy Eddy, cello, Ned Rorem, piano.

W111. SCHUYLER SONGS. (1988; Boosey & Hawkes; 25 min.)
    See: B408

Song cycle; eight poems for voice and orchestra.
Texts by James Schuyler.
Commissioned by the Fargo-Moorhead Symphony for Phyllis Bryn-Julson.
Composed: 1987.

Premiere:
1988 (Apr 23): Fargo, ND; Fargo-Moorhead Symphony; Phyllis Bryn-Julson, soprano; J. Robert Hanson, conductor.

W112. SERENADE ON FIVE ENGLISH POEMS. (1978; Boosey & Hawkes) 18 min.)
    See: B229, B322, B455, B512, B745, B749, B751, B780

Voice, violin, viola, and piano.
Commissioned by Walter and Virginia Wojno for the Cuyahoga Valley Arts Ensemble.

Dedicated to Miriam Fried and Paul Biss.
Composed: Nantucket and New York City, November–December 1975.
Contents: Instrumental Interlude; Hold Back Thy House, Dark Night (John Fletcher); Th'Expense of Spirit (William Shakespeare); Flower in the Crannied Wall (Alfred Lord Tennyson); When Will You Ever, Peace (Gerard Manley Hopkins); Instrumental Interlude; Never Weatherbeaten Sail (Thomas Campion).

Premiere:

1976 (May 23): Akron, OH; Akron Art Institute; Grace Reginald, mezzo–soprano; Miriam Fried, violin; Paul Biss, viola; Margaret Baxtresser, piano.

Selected Performance:

1977 (Nov 20): New York City; Guggenheim Museum; Cantilena Players.

W113. SIX IRISH POEMS. (1971; Southern Music Publishing; 18 min.)
See: B760

Medium voice and orchestra; also published for voice and piano.
Texts by George Darley.
Dedicated to Nell Tangeman.
Composed: Torino, Paris and Fez, February–May 1950.
Contents: Lay of the Forlorn; Robin's Cross; Chorus of Spirits; The Call of the Morning; Runilda's Chant; The Sea Ritual.

Premiere:

1951 (Jul 4): Nell Tangeman, mezzo–soprano; L'Orchestre de la Radiodiffusion Francaise; Tony Aubin, conductor.

Selected performance:

1984 (Dec 9): Philadelphia; Curtis Institute; Beth McLeod, soprano; Curtis Institute Orchestra; Jose Serebrier, conductor.

W114. SIX SONGS FOR HIGH VOICE. (1963, 1968; Henmar Press; C. F. Peters; 12 min.)
See: B276, B306; W14, W36, W61, W69, W79, W82

Voice and orchestra.
Individual titles published separately and in collection with piano accompaniment.
Composed: 1953.
Contents: Cradle Song; In a Gondola; Pippa's Song; Rondelay; Song for a Girl; Song to a Fair Young Lady Going Out of Town in the Spring.

Premiere:

>1954 (Nov): Paris; Virginia Fleming, soprano; Orchestre de la Salle Gaveau; Jean Martinon, conductor.

Selected performances:

>1956 (Jan 27): New York City; Town Hall; Virginia Fleming, soprano, Ned Rorem, piano.
>1956: New York City; Town Hall; Mattiwilda Dobbs, soprano.
>1978 (Apr 28): Geanie Faulkner, soprano; Brooklyn Philharmonic Symphony Orchestra; Lukas Foss, conductor.

W115. SUN: Eight Poems in One Movement. (1969; Boosey & Hawkes; 26 min.)
See: B2, B5, B111, B203, B251, B316, B486, B626, B780

Voice and orchestra; also published for voice and piano.
Commissioned by the Lincoln Center Fund for the Lincoln Center Festival '67.
Composed: Yaddo, Saratoga, NY, October 1966.
Contents: To the Sun (King Ikhnaton); Sun of the Sleepless (Lord Byron); Dawn (Paul Goodman); Day (William Blake): Catafalque (Robin Morgan); Full Many a Glorious Morning (William Shakespeare); Sundown Lights (Walt Whitman); From "What Can I Tell My Bones?" (Theodore Roethke).

Premiere:

>1967 (Jul 1): New York City; Philharmonic Hall; Jane Marsh, soprano; New York Philharmonic; Karel Ancerl, conductor.

Selected performances:

>1969 (May 8): Rochester, NY; Joyce Castle, soprano; Eastman-Rochester Symphony Orchestra; Howard Hanson, conductor.
>1979 (Oct 18-19): Cleveland; Irene Gubrud, soprano; Cleveland Orchestra; Loren Maazel, conductor.
>1982 (Aug 1): Aspen, CO: Kristine Ciesinski, soprano; Richard Dufallo, conductor.

III.   CHORAL MUSIC

W116. ALL GLORIOUS GOD. (1962; Henmar Press; C. F. Peters; 2 min.)

SATB chorus a cappella.
Text from the Episcopal Hymnal, U.S.A. (1841).
Dedicated to the Rev. Albert C. Miller (1866-1955).
Composed: Hyères, August 15-17, 1955.

W117. <u>ALL HAIL THE POWER OF JESUS' NAME</u>. (unpublished)
    <u>See: W128</u>

    SATB chorus.
    This is the same as "In Christ There Is No East or
    West" from <u>Four Hymns</u>; different text superimposed.

    <u>Selected performance</u>:

        1988 (May 11): New York City; 65th anniversary
        year of the composer; The Church of St. Matthew
        and St. Timothy; James Holmes, music director.

W118. <u>AN AMERICAN ORATORIO</u>.   (1984; Boosey & Hawkes; 40
    min.)
    <u>See: B7, B15, B16, B17, B98, B153, B180, B237, B275,
    B289</u>, B425, B431, B466, B652, B748, B750, B756

    Tenor solo, mixed chorus, and orchestra.
    Texts by Emma Lazarus, Edgar Allan Poe, Henry Wads-
        worth Longfellow, Mark Twain, Sidney Lanier,
        Herman Melville, Stephen Crane, and Walt Whitman.
    Commissioned by the Mendelssohn Choir of Pittsburgh.
    Composed: Nantucket, July 1983.

    <u>Premiere</u>:

        1985 (Jan 4): Pittsburgh; Heinz Hall; Mendelssohn
        Choir; Pittsburgh Symphony Orchestra; Robert
        Page, conductor.

    <u>Selected performances</u>:

        1985 (Apr 11): New York City; Schola Cantorum of
        New York; Manhattan School of Music Orchestra;
        Hugh Ross, conductor.
        1986 (Mar 13-15): Cleveland; Cleveland Symphony
        Orchestra and Chorus; Robert Page, conductor.
        1986 (Mar 23): Washington, DC; Paul Hill Chorale.
        1986 (Apr 24-26): Chicago; Orchestra Hall; Chicago
        Symphony Orchestra and Chorus; Margaret Hillis,
        conductor.

W119. <u>ARISE, SHINE</u> (Surge, illuminare).   (1979; Boosey &
    <u>Hawkes</u>; 4 min.)
    See: B351

    SATB chorus and organ.
    Text from the Third Song of Isaiah.
    Commissioned by Christ Church Cathedral, Hartford,
        CT; Trinity Church, Hartford, CT; and St. James'
        Church, West Hartford, CT.
    Composed: New York City, January 1-17, 1977.

    <u>Premieres</u>:

        1979 (Jun 5): Hartford, CT; Trinity Church; Men
        and Boys Choirs of Christ Church Cathedral and
        St. James' Church.

1979 (Jun 27): Hartford, CT; Trinity College Chapel; Men and Boys Choirs of Christ Church Cathedral and St. James' Church; for the Regional Convention of the American Guild of Organists.

Selected performance:

1982 (Dec 12): New York City; Greek Church of the Annunciation; George Tsontakis, conductor.

W120. ARMENIAN LOVE SONGS. (unpublished)
See: B67, B102, B220

SATB chorus.
Text by Nahapet Kuchak (16th c.).
Commissioned by the Armenian Benevolent Union for the State Chorus of Armenia.
Composed: 1987.

Premiere:

1987 (Sep 17): Los Angeles; Scottish Rite Auditorium; State Chorus of Armenia; Ovannes Tchekidjian, director.

Selected performance:

1987 (Oct 3): New York City; Avery Fisher Hall; State Choir of Armenia; Ovannes Tchekidjian, director.

W121. CANTICLE OF THE LAMB. (1972; Boosey & Hawkes; 2 min.)
See: B492

SATB chorus a cappella.
Text by Ned Rorem.
Composed: Yaddo, February 16, 1971.

Premiere:

1972 (Nov 26): New York City; Chapel of the Intercession; Chapel Concert Choir; James Holmes, conductor.

W122. CANTICLES. (1972; Boosey & Hawkes; 15 min.)
See: B319, B475, B492; W78

English settings of liturgical songs; in 2 sets.
Composed: Fire Island Pines, Yaddo and New York City; January 1971-July 1972.
Contents: Set I: Confitebor tibi (Unison; dedicated to James Holmes): Magnificat anima mea (SA or TB); Nunc dimittis (SAT).--Set II: Benedictus es Domine (SATB); Phos Hilarion (SATB); Ecce Deus (SATBB).

Premiere:

1972 (Nov 26): New York City; Chapel of the Intercession; Chapel Concert Choir; James Holmes, conductor.

W123. <u>CHRIST THE LORD IS RIS'N TODAY</u>. (1962; Henmar Press; C. F. Peters; 2 min.)

SATB chorus a cappella.
Text by Charles Wesley.
Dedicated to John Brodbin Kennedy.
Composed: Hyères, August 15-17, 1955.

W124. <u>THE CORINTHIANS</u>: for Mixed Voices and Organ.   (1960; Henmar Press; C. F. Peters; 9 min.)
<u>See</u>: B351

Mixed chorus (SSAATTBB) and organ.
Text from I Corinthians, chapter 13.
Dedicated to William Flanagan.
Composed: Paris, July 19, 1953.

Premiere:

1953 (Fall): Washington, DC; Washington Cathedral; Paul Callaway, conductor.

W125. <u>DEATH OF MOSES</u>. (1987; Boosey & Hawkes; 5 min.)
<u>See</u>: B88, B234, B408, B768

SATB chorus and organ.
Text from Deuteronomy 34:1-8, 10-12.
Commissioned by and dedicated to Richard Westenburg and Musica Sacra.
Composed: October 14-25, 1987.

Premiere:

1988 (Jan 28): New York City; Alice Tully Hall; Musica Sacra; Richard Westenburg, conductor.

W126. <u>A FAR ISLAND</u>. (1961; Elkan-Vogel; 2 min.)

SSA chorus a cappella.
Text by Kenward Elmslie.
Dedicated to Joseph LeSueur.
Composed: Hyères, July 1953.

W127. <u>FIVE PRAYERS FOR THE YOUNG</u>. (1956; Theodore Presser; 8 min.)

SSA chorus a cappella.
Eurydice Choral Award, 1954.
Composed: 1953.
Contents: A Nursery Darling (L. Carroll; dedicated to Jane and Jay Harrison and Paige Julie); A Dirge (Shelley; dedicated to Philippe Erlanger); Now I Lay Me Down to Sleep (Shelley; dedicated to Morris Golde); Fragment: Wine of the Fairies (Shelley; dedicated to Paul and Rachel; Mary and Christo-

pher); The Virgin's Cradle-Hymn (Coleridge; dedicated to Aaron Copland).

W128. <u>FOUR HYMNS</u>. (1973; Boosey & Hawkes; 8 min.)
<u>See</u>: B35; W117

Two for unison with keyboard; two SATB chorus a cappella.
Composed: 1973.
Contents: Come, Pure Hearts (unison; text 12 c. Latin); I Heard a Sound (SATB a cappella; text by G. Thring); In Christ There Is No East or West (unison; Text by H. Oxenham); Jerusalem, My Happy Home (SATB a cappella; text 16th c.)

W129. <u>FOUR MADRIGALS</u>. (1948; Mercury Music; Theodore Presser; 9 min.)
<u>See</u>: B148, B285, B466, B770

SATB chorus a cappella.
Text by Sappho; translated by C. M. Bowra.
Composed: Autumn 1947.
Contents: Parting (dedicated Hugh Ross); Flowers for the Graces (dedicated to Rufus Rorem): Love (dedicated to Gladys Rorem); An Absent Friend (dedicated to Bernard Wagenaar).

<u>Premiere</u>:

1948: Tanglewood; Hugh Ross, conductor.

<u>Selected performance</u>:

1969 (Nov 9): Trenton, NJ; New Jersey State Museum; Modern Madrigal Singers.

W130. <u>FROM AN UNKNOWN PAST</u>. (1953; Southern Music; 8 min.)
<u>See</u>: B109, B717, B747; W31

SATB chorus a cappella.
Also arranged for voice and piano by the composer.
Texts from anonymous poem 16th c. Christ Church ms.; John Dowland, William Shakespeare (?), and anonymous sources.
Composed: 1951.
Contents: The Lover in Winter Plaineth for the Spring (Georg Redlich); Hey Nonny No! (Marie Laure); My Blood So Red (The Call) (Julien Green); Suspiria (Nadia Boulanger); The Miracle (Nora and Georges Auric); Tears (Don Dalton); Crabbed Age and Youth (Guy Ferrand).

<u>Selected performances</u>:

1969 (May 25): Upper Montclair, NJ: Montclair State College; Lois Winter, soprano; Helene Miles, contralto; Phillip Olson, tenor; Michael Stewart, bass.

1971 (Mar 22): New York City; Alice Tully Hall; New Jersey Schola Cantorum; Fairleigh Dickinson University Chamber Orchestra.
1984 (Mar 23): Chicago; St. James Cathedral; William Ferris Chorale.

W131. GENTLE VISITATIONS. (1961; Elkan Vogel; 2 min.)

SSA chorus a cappella.
Text by Percy B. Shelley.
Dedicated to Morris Golde.
Composed: Hyères, July 1953.

W132. GIVE ALL TO LOVE. (1981; Boosey & Hawkes; 6 min.)
See: B4

Two-part mixed chorus (SA or TB) and piano.
Text by Ralph Waldo Emerson.
Dedicated to Gregg Smith.
Composed: New York City, March 4-14, 1981.

Premiere:

1981 (July): Saranac Lake Festival; Gregg Smith Singers.

W133. HE SHALL RULE FROM SEA TO SEA. (1968; Boosey & Hawkes; 5 min.)
See: B240, B351

SATB chorus and organ.
Text from Feast of Christ the King: Psalm 71, Dn 7.
Commissioned by Peter J. Basch, James A. Burns, and Marie Lambert.
Dedicated to the Saint Nicholas Boy Choir Festival.
Composed: Yaddo, July 1967.

Premiere:

1968 (June): New York City.

W134. HOMER: Three Scenes from 'The Iliad'. (1986; Boosey & Hawkes; 22 min.)

SATB chorus, flute, oboe, bassoon, trumpet, piano, 3 strings.
Text from The Iliad by Homer.
Commissioned by Franklin and Marshall College.
Composed: 1986.
Contents: Sing Goddess; Priam and Helen on the Wall of Troy; Hector's Funeral.

Premiere:

1987 (Apr 12): Lancaster, PA; Franklin and Marshall College.

W135. I FEEL DEATH... (1967; Boosey & Hawkes; 1 min.)

TTB chorus a cappella.
Text by John Dryden
Composed: Hyères, September 8, 1953.

W136. IN TIME OF PESTILENCE: Six Short Madrigals on Verses
of Thomas Nashe. (1974; Boosey & Hawkes; 7 min.)
See: B10, B40, B56, B86, B472

SATB chorus a cappella.
Commissioned by the Kansas State University Concert
Choir Commissioning Project, Rod Walker, director.
Composed: New York City, August–December 1973.
Contents: Adieu, Farewell Earth's Bliss; Beauty Is
but a Flower; Haste Therefore Each degree; Rich
Men, Trust Not in Wealth; Strength Stoops unto the
Grave; With His Wantoness.

Premieres:

1974 (Mar 3): Manhattan, KS; All Faith's Chapel;
Kansas State University; Kansas State University
Choir; Rod Walker, director.

Selected performance:

1986 (May 20): Omaha, NE; Strauss Center for the
Performing Arts; Contemporary Music Festival;
University of Nebraska Chamber Choir; C. M.
Shearer, conductor.

W137. LAUDEMUS TEMPUS ACTUM.   (1966; Boosey & Hawkes; 3
min.)

SATB chorus and orchestra; also arranged by the com-
poser for keyboard accompaniment.
Text by the composer.
Composed: New York City, May–June 1964.

W138. LETTERS FROM PARIS.   (1969; Boosey & Hawkes; 25 min.)
See: B109, B255, B316, B370, B409, B747, B780

SATB chorus and small orchestra.
Texts from Janet Flanner's Paris Journal.
Commissioned by the Koussevitzky Foundation in the
Library of Congress.
Dedicated to Serge and Natalie Koussevitzky.
Composed: Salt Lake City, March 3–July 30, 1966.
Contents: Spring; The French Telephone; Summer;
Colette; Autumn; The Sex of the Automobile; Win-
ter; Mistinguett; Spring Again.

Premiere:

1969 (Apr 25): Ann Arbor; University of Michigan;
Thomas Hillbish, conductor.

Selected performances:

1971 (Mar 21): New York City; Alice Tully Hall;
New Jersey Schola Cantorum; Fairleigh Dickinson

University Chamber Orchestra; Louis Hooker, conductor.
1978 (Oct 29): Washington, DC; Coolidge Auditorium
of Library of Congress; Paul Callaway, conductor.
1984 (Mar 23): Chicago; St. James Cathedral;
William Ferris Chorale.

W139. LIFT UP YOUR HEADS. (The Ascension). (1964; Boosey &
Hawkes; 4 min.)
See: B351

SATB chorus, wind ensemble and organ; also arranged
for brass, timpani and organ.
Text by John Beaumont.
Dedicated to Francis Poulenc.
Composed: Yaddo, Saratoga Springs and New York City,
August 26-September 6, 1963.

Premiere:

1964 (May 4): Washington, DC; Washington Cathedral; Wayne Dirksen, conductor.

W140. LITTLE LAMB, WHO MADE THEE? (1982; Boosey & Hawkes; 4
min.)

SATB chorus and organ.
Text by William Blake.
Commissioned by Christ Church, New Brunswick.
Composed: Nantucket, May 1982.

W141. LITTLE PRAYERS. (1976; Boosey & Hawkes; 30 min.)
See: B83, B477, B780; W165

Soprano and baritone solos, mixed chorus and orches-
tra.
Unaccompanied interludes have been published sepa-
rately under the title Three Prayers.
Texts by Paul Goodman.
Commissioned by the Colleges of Mid-America, Inc.,
with assistance of the Iowa and South Dakota Arts
Councils, and the Sullivan Music Foundation.
Composed: Saratoga, NY, February-July 1973.

Premieres:

1974 (Apr 20): Sioux Falls; Irene Gubrud, soprano;
William Powers, baritone; Colleges of Mid-
America Chorus; Sioux Falls Symphony; George
Trautwein, conductor.
1974 (Apr 21): Sioux city, IA; Irene Gubrud, so-
prano; William Powers, baritone; Colleges of
Mid-America Chorus; Sioux City Symphony; Leo
Kucinski, conductor.

W142. THE LONG HOME. (unpublished)

SATB chorus with orchestra.
Composed: 1946.

Premiere:

　　1946: Washington, DC; Washington Cathedral; Paul
　　Callaway, conductor.

W143. LOVE DIVINE, ALL LOVES EXCELLING.   (1968; Boosey &
　　　　Hawkes; 2 min.)

SATB chorus a cappella.
Text by Charles Wesley.
Composed: September 8-12, 1966.

W144. MERCY AND TRUTH ARE MET.   (1983; Boosey & Hawkes; 3
　　　　min.)
　　　　See: B448

SATB chorus and organ.
Text from Psalm 85:10-13.
"Commissioned for the reconsecration of Immanuel
　　Episcopal Church, New Castle, Delaware."
Composed: New York City and Nantucket, March-Septem-
　　ber 1982.

Selected performance:

　　1984 (Jan 14): New York City; St. Peter's Church;
　　Gregg Smith Singers.

W145. THE MILD MOTHER.   (1970; E. C. Schirmer)
　　　　See: W49

Unison chorus with piano.
Arranged from original version for medium voice and
piano.

W146. MIRACLES OF CHRISTMAS.   (1971; Boosey & Hawkes; 17
　　　　min.)
　　　　See: B223, B309, B351

SATB chorus and organ (or piano).
Text by Ruth Apprich Jacob.
"Commissioned by and dedicated to The Garden City
　　Community church, Long Island, NY."
Composed: Yaddo, June 1-15, 1959.

Premiere:

　　1959 (Dec 20): Long Island, NY; Garden City Commu-
　　nity Church.

Selected performance:

　　1980 (Dec 13-14): Washington, DC; Washington
　　Cathedral; Paul Callaway, conductor.

W147. MISSA BREVIS.   (1974; Boosey & Hawkes; 16 min.)

See: B466

Four solo voices (SATB) and mixed chorus a cappella.
Text from the Ordinary of the Mass.
Commissioned by the Cleveland Chapter, American
    Guild of Organists, for the 1974 National Conven-
    tion.
Composed: New York City, August-December 1973.

Premiere:

1974 (June): Cleveland; Rosalind Rees, soprano;
    Gregg Smith Singers.

W148. O MAGNUM MYSTERIUM. (1976; Boosey & Hawkes; 2 min.)

SATB chorus a cappella.
Text traditional (Latin).
Commissioned by St. Stephen's Church, New York City.
Composed: New York City, February 19, 1978.

Premiere:

1978 (Dec 25): New York City; St. Stephen's
    Church.

W149. THE OXEN. (1978; Boosey & Hawkes; 2 min.)

SATB chorus a cappella.
Text by Thomas Hardy.
"Commissioned for the Choir of Christ and Saint
    Stephen's Episcopal Church, New York City, by Mary
    V. Molleson and Jane M. Wolf in memory of their
    mother, Mabel Sale Molleson."
Composed: New York City, March 5, 1978.

Premiere:

1978 (Dec 15): New York City; St. Stephen's
    Church.

W150. PILGRIM STRANGERS. (1984; Boosey & Hawkes; 20 min.)
    See: B135, B136, B235, B424, B426, B682

Six male voices (AATBarBarB).
Text by Walt Whitman.
Commissioned by the King's Singers.
Composed: 1984.

Premiere:

1984 (Nov 16): New York City; Avery Fisher Hall;
    King's Singers.

Selected performance:

1985 (Oct 27): Boston; King's Singers.

W151. THE POETS' REQUIEM. (1976; Boosey & Hawkes; 28 min.)
      See: B39, B202, B306, B307, B390, B466, B780

      Soprano solo, mixed chorus, and orchestra.
      Texts from works by Franz Kafka, Rainer Maria Rilke,
        Jean Cocteau, Stephane Mallarmé, Sigmund Freud,
        Paul Goodman, André Gide; translated and compiled
        by Paul Goodman.
      Dedicated to Margaret Hillis.
      Composed: Hyères and Rome, 1954-1955.

      Premiere:

        1957 (Feb 15): New York City; Town Hall; Ellen
          Faull, soprano; American Concert Choir and
          Orchestra; Margaret Hillis, conductor.

W152. PRAISE THE LORD, O MY SOUL. (1982; Boosey & Hawkes; 3
      min.)

      SATB chorus and organ.
      Text from Psalm 146.
      Dedicated "to James H. Litton, from the Choirs of
        Trinity Church, Princeton, New Jersey."
      Composed: Nantucket, May 29-June 3, 1982.

W153. PRAISES FOR THE NATIVITY. (1971; Boosey & Hawkes; 5
      min.)
      See: B351

      Four solo voices (SATB), mixed chorus and organ.
      Text from The Book of Common Prayer.
      Commissioned by Saint Patrick's Cathedral, New York
        City.
      Dedicated to Henson Markham.
      Composed: New York City, October 2-November 2, 1970.

      Selected performance:

        1982 (Dec 12): New York City; Greek Church of the
          Annunciation; George Tsontakis, conductor.

W154. PRAYER TO JESUS. (1974, 1983; Boosey & Hawkes; 2
      min.)

      SATB chorus a cappella.
      Text by Gerard Manley Hopkins.
      Composed: 1974.

W155. PRAYERS AND RESPONSES. (1969; Boosey & Hawkes; 2
      min.)

      SATB chorus a cappella.
      Composed: Yaddo, June 1960.

W156. PROPER FOR THE VOTIVE MASS OF THE HOLY SPIRIT. (1967;
      Boosey & Hawkes; 9 min.)
      See: B351, B492

      Unison chorus and organ.

Commissioned by the Church Music Association of America.
Composed: Salt Lake City, UT, January 7-10, 1966.

Selected performance:

1972 (Nov 26): New York City; Chapel of the Intercession; Chapel Concert Choir.

W157. A SERMON ON MIRACLES. (1970; Boosey & Hawkes; 6 min.)
See: B780

Solo voices, unison chorus and strings or keyboard.
Text by Paul Goodman.
Composed: Tanglewood, Summer 1947.

Premiere

1947 (Nov 30): Boston; Second Church in Boston; Janet Hayes, Eunice Alberts, Arthur Schoep, and Bernard Barbeau, soloists; Daniel Pinkham, conductor.

Selected performance:

1973 (Oct 28): New York City; Cathedral of St. John the Divine.

W158. SEVEN MOTETS FOR THE CHURCH YEAR. (1986; Boosey & Hawkes; 19 min.)
See: B224

SATB chorus a cappella.
Text from Episcopal liturgy.
Commissioned by All Saints Episcopal Church, Ft. Lauderdale, FL.
Composed: 1986.
Contents: Christmas; Epiphany; Ash Wednesday; Easter; Ascension; Pentecost; All Saints.

W159. THE SEVENTIETH PSALM. (1966; Boosey & Hawkes; 4 min.)
See: B466

Anthem for SATB chorus and wind ensemble.
Also arranged by the composer for SATB and keyboard.
Dedicated to William Strickland.
Composed: Philadelphia, July 1943.
Rorem's first publicly performed work.

Premiere:

1943 (Summer): Library of Congress; William Strickland, conductor.

W160. SHOUT THE GLAD TIDINGS. (1978; Boosey & Hawkes; 2 min.)

SATB chorus a cappella.
Text from the Muhlenberg Hymnal, 1826.

Commissioned by St. Stephen's Church, New York City.
Composed: New York City, March 1978.

Premiere:

1978 (Dec 25): New York City; St. Stephen's
Church.

W161. SING MY SOUL, HIS WONDROUS LOVE. (1962; Henmar Press;
C. F. Peters; 3 min.)

SATB chorus a cappella.
Text from the Episcopal Hymnal, U.S.A. (1841).
Dedicated to Paul Callaway.
Composed: Hyères, August 15-17, 1955.

W162. TE DEUM. (1987; Boosey & Hawkes; 10 min.)

SATB chorus, 2 trumpets, 2 trombones, and organ.
Text traditional (Latin).
Commissioned by Christ Church Cathedral, Indianapo-
lis, for the opening service of the 150th anniver-
sary year.
Composed: 1987.

Premiere:

1987 (Jul 19): Indianapolis, IN; Christ Church
Cathedral; Fred Burgomaster, conductor.

W163. THREE MOTETS ON POEMS OF GERARD MANLEY HOPKINS.
(1974; Boosey & Hawkes; 6 min.)
See: B351, B747

SATB chorus and organ.
Dedicated to St. Luke's Chapel of the parish of
Trinity Church, New York City, on the occasion of
its 150th anniversary.
Composed: New York City and Yaddo, January-February
1973.
Contents: O Deus, ego amo Te; Oratorio Patris Con-
dren; Thee, God.

Premiere:

1974 (Apr 26): New York City; Trinity Church.

Selected performance:

1984 (Mar 23): Chicago; St. James Cathedral;
William Ferris Chorale.

W164. THREE POEMS OF BAUDELAIRE. (1986; Boosey & Hawkes; 15
min.)
See: B408

SATB chorus a cappella.
Text by Charles Pierre Baudelaire; translated by
Richard Howard.

Commissioned by British Broadcasting Corporation for
the BBC Singers.
Composed: 1986.
Contents: Invitation to the Voyage; Cat; Satan's
Litanies.

Premiere:

1987 (Jun 26): Aldeburgh Festival (UK); BBC Singers, John Pode, conductor.

Selected performance:

1988 (Mar 23): New York City; Merkin Hall; Judith
Clurman's New York Chorale.

W165. THREE PRAYERS.   (1976; Boosey & Hawkes; 6 min.)
See: W141

SATB chorus a cappella.
Texts by Paul Goodman.
"These Three Prayers have been taken intact from
Little Prayers wherein they are featured as unac-
companied interludes."
Composed: 1973.
Contents: Creator Spirit, Who Dost Lightly Hover;
Father Guide and Lead Me; Creator Spirit,
Please...

W166. TRUTH IN THE NIGHT SEASON.   (1967; Boosey & Hawkes; 4
min.)
See: B351

SATB chorus and organ.
Text from Psalm 92:1-5a.
Commissioned by and dedicated to the Houston Chapter
of the American Guild of Organists.
Composed: Salt Lake City, Utah, March 31-April 11,
1966.

W167. TWO HOLY SONGS.   (1955, 1970; Southern Music; 4 min.)
See: W15

SATB chorus and organ or piano.
Arrangements by the composer, of the first and last
psalms of the Cycle of Holy Songs for solo voice
and piano.
Texts from Psalms 134 and 150.
Arranged: 1969.

W168. TWO PSALMS AND A PROVERB.   (1965; E. C. Schirmer; 10
min.)
See: B312, B313

SATB chorus and string quintet.
Text from Psalm 133:1-3; Proverbs 23:29-35; Psalms
13:1-6.
"Commissioned under a grant to Daniel Pinkham in
conjunction with the Ford Foundation..."

Dedicated respectively to Elizabeth Ames; Troy Nedda
Harrison; and the composer's parents, Gladys
Miller and C. Rufus Rorem.
Composed: August 18-21, 1962.

Premiere:

1963 (Apr 21): New York City; Museum of Modern
Art; Choir of King's Chapel, Boston; Daniel
Pinkham, conductor.

W169. VIRELAI.   (1965; Novello & Co.; Boosey & Hawkes; 2
min.)
See: B406

SATB chorus a cappella
Text by Geoffrey Chaucer.
Also issued with Musical Times 106 (June 1965) as a
loose accompanying item.
Composed: Paris, May 1961.

W170. WHITMAN CANTATA.   (1983; Boosey & Hawkes; 21 min.)
See: B6, B14, B29, B30, B129, B422, B466, B654

Men's chorus, twelve brass and timpani.
Texts from poems by Walt Whitman.
Commissioned by the Come Out and Sing Together Cho-
ral Festival.
Composed: New York City and Nantucket, November
1982-January 1983.

Premiere:

1983 (Sep 11): New York City; Avery Fisher Hall;
C.O.A.S.T. Choruses; Gregg Smith, director.

Selected performance:

1984 (Mar 25): Seattle, WA; Meany Theater; Seattle
Men's Chorus; Dennis Coleman, conductor.
1984 (April): Los Angeles; Jerry Carlson, director.
1984 (Apr 29): Boston; Jordan Hall; Boston Gay
Men's Chorus; John Bollinger, piano; Lee Ridg-
way, director.
1985 (Apr 28): Minneapolis; Twin Cities Men's
Chorus; Richard Weinberg, director.

IV.   OPERAS

W171. THE ANNIVERSARY.   (unpublished)
See: B312

Incomplete opera in two acts.
Text by Jascha Kessler.
Commissioned by The Ford Foundation, 1961.
Composed: 1961.

W172. BERTHA.   (1973; Boosey & Hawkes; 25 min.)

See: B114, B160, B218, B269, B270, B320, B684, B738, B780

One act opera; piano accompaniment.
Text by Kenneth Koch.
Composed: New York City, September–December 1968.

Premiere:

   1973 (Nov 26): New York City; Alice Tully Hall;
      Beverly Wolff and cast of ten; James Holmes,
      director.

Selected performances:

   1981 (Feb 27): New York City; Theater 22; Golden
      Fleece, Ltd.
   1984 (Oct 13): Vienna, VA; The Barns of Wolf Trap;
      Opera Southwest; Muriel Von Villa, director.

W173.   CAIN AND ABEL.   (unpublished)

   Short opera.
   Text by Paul Goodman.
   Composed: 1946.

W174. A CHILDHOOD MIRACLE.   (1972; Southern Music; 33 min.)
      See: B69, B144, B306, B440

   Opera in one act; scored for thirteen instruments.
   Text by Elliott Stein.
   Dedicated to Guy Ferrand, Edwin Denby, Annette
      Michaelson, Thomas Michaelis, Jeannette and Murry,
      Gladys and Rufus, Henri Fourtine and Marie Laure.
   Composed: Paris and Marrakech, Winter 1952.

Premiere:

   1955 (May 10): New York City; Carl Fischer Hall;
      Punch Opera.

Selected Performance:

   1956 (Feb 12): Philadelphia.

W175. FABLES: Five Very Short Operas.   (1974; Boosey &
      Hawkes; 24 min.)
      See: B160, B318, B397, B429, B447, B718, B780

   Operas; with piano accompaniment.
   Texts by Jean de la Fontaine; translated by Marianne
      Moore.
   Commissioned by the University of Tennessee at Mar-
      tin.
   Composed: Peterborough, NH and New York City, June–
      November 1970.
   Contents: Animals Sick of the Plague; Bird Wounded
      by an Arrow; Fox and Grapes; The Lion in Love; The
      Sun and the Frogs.

Premiere:

> 1971 (May 21): Martin, TN; University of Tennessee; Marilyn Jewett, director.

Selected performance:

> 1971 (Nov 20): Nashville; Belmont College; Opera Theater of the University of Tennessee at Martin; Marilyn Jewett, director.
> 1984 (Oct 13): Vienna, VA; The Barns of Wolf Trap; Opera Southwest; Muriel Von Villa, director.
> 1986 (Mar 20-23): New York City; Actors Outlet Theater Center; Golden Fleece Ltd.; Lou Rodgers, director.

W176. HEARING: A Small Opera for Four Singers and Seven Instrumentalists. (1983; Boosey & Hawkes, 30 min.)
See: B478, B780; W33

Opera in five scenes.
Text by Kenneth Koch.
Commissioned on a grant from the National Endowment for the Arts.
Composed: Nantucket, August 12, 1976.

Premiere:

> 1977 (Mar 15): Gregg Smith Singers (concert version).

W177. LAST DAY. (unpublished)
See: B172, B265

Monodrama for voice, string quartet, woodwind quartet, and piano.
Text by Jay Harrison.
Written for Spoleto Festival.
Composed: 1959.

Premiere:

> 1967 (May 26): New York City; New School Opera Workshop.

W178. MISS JULIE: Opera in Two Acts. (1965, 1968; Boosey & Hawkes; 2 hrs.)
See: B2, B19, B43, B110, B165, B177, B195, B245, B282, B299, B314, B330, B376, B441, B443, B510, B680, B769, B779, B780

Opera; full orchestra.
Text by Kenward Elmslie from the play by August Strindberg.
Commissioned by the New York City Opera Company and The Ford Foundation.
Revised in 1979 for a shortened and improved version for the New York Lyric Opera production.
Dedication "from Kenward to Ruth Yorck and from Ned

to his parents Gladys and Rufus Rorem."
Composed: New York City, 1964-65.

Premiere:

1965 (Nov 4): New York City; New York City Opera;
Marguerite Willauer, soprano; Elaine Bonazzi,
mezzo-soprano; Donald Gramm, bass-baritone;
Robert Zeller, conductor.

Selected performances:

1966 (Apr 6): New York City; New York City Opera;
Judith James, soprano; Ronald Madden, bass-
baritone; Veronica August, mezzo-soprano; Peter
Leonard, conductor; John Margulis, director.
1979 (Apr 4): New York City; New York University
Theatre; New York Lyric Opera; Beverly Morgan,
soprano; Veronica August, mezzo-soprano; Ronald
Madden, bass-baritone.
1979 (Apr 5): New York City; New York University
Theatre; New York Lyric Opera; Judith James,
soprano; William Dansby, bass.

W179. THE ROBBERS. (1956; Boosey & Hawkes; 28 min.)
See: B187, B308, B355, B453, B659, B780

Melodrama in one scene; scored for thirteen instru-
ments.
Libretto by the composer.
Composed: Hyères, Summer 1956.

Premiere:

1958 (Apr 14): New York City; Kaufmann Auditorium
of the YMHA; Opera Workshop and Orchestra of
Mannes College; Carl Bamberger, conductor.

W180. THREE SISTERS WHO ARE NOT SISTERS. (1974; Boosey &
Hawkes; 35 min.)
See: B107, B159, B160, B252, B271, B318, B449, B463,
B718, B737, B742, B780

Opera in three brief acts; with piano.
Melodrama by Gertrude Stein.
Composed: 1968.

Premiere:

1971 (Jul 24): Philadelphia; Temple University;
Student Opera Workshop; Henry Butler, director.

Selected performances:

1971 (Jul 27): Lake Placid, NY; Signal Hill Play-
house; After Dinner Opera Company; Richard
Flusser, director.
1971 (Jul 31): Westport, CT; White Barn Theatre;

After Dinner Opera Company; Richard Flusser, director.
1971 (Oct 4): New York City; New York University; After Dinner Opera Company; Richard Flusser, director.
1978 (Apr 1-2): New York City; Three Muses Theater; Golden Fleece Ltd.
1984 (Oct 13): Vienna, VA; The Barns of Wolf Trap; Opera Southwest; Muriel Von Villa, director.
1985 (Apr 9): New York City; Center for Contemporary Opera; Patricia Heuermann, director.
1985 (Nov 24): New York City; American Chamber Opera Company.
1986 (Feb 4 & 6): Charlotte, NC; University of North Carolina, Charlotte; Performing Arts Department.

W181. THE TICKLISH ACROBAT: (unpublished)

Musical comedy; book by Kenward Elmslie.
Composed: 1958.

V.   KEYBOARD MUSIC

W182. BARCAROLLES.   (1963; Henmar Press; C. F. Peters; 9 min.)
See: B228, B229, B260, B740

Piano.
Dedicated to Leon Fleisher, Shirley Rhoads, Jean Pierre Marty.
Composed: Fez, Morocco, November 24-26, 1949.

Premiere:

1950 (May 4): Paris; American Embassy; Leon Fleisher, piano.

Selected performance:

1981 (Sep 23): Washington, DC; Kennedy Center Terrace Theater; Jerome Lowenthal, piano.

W183. A BIRTHDAY SUITE.   (unpublished)
See: W110, W214, W223, W239, W242

Piano, four hands, in 12 movements.
Five movements were orchestrated and incorporated into instrumental works: Winter Pages; Remembering Tommy; The Santa Fe Songs; Sunday Morning; and Septet.
Composed: 1967.

W184. BURLESQUE.   (unpublished)

Piano.
Dedicated to Eugene Istomin.
Theme later used in A Quaker Reader.
Composed: 1955.

Premiere:

1956: Honolulu; Eugene Istomin, piano.

W185. EIGHT ETUDES. (1977; Boosey & Hawkes; 20 min.)
See: B141, B167, B228, B229, B260, B321, B322, B411,
B685, B780

Piano.
"Commissioned by Emanuel Ax on a grant from the
Edyth Bush Charitable Foundation, Inc., for the
Bicentennial Piano Series of the Washington Per-
forming Arts Society and dedicated to the memory
of Edyth Bush."
Composed: Nantucket, 1975.

Premiere:

1976 (Mar 13): Washington, DC; Kennedy Center;
Emanuel Ax, piano.

Selected performances:

1976 (May 6): New York City; Columbia University;
Emanuel Ax, piano.
1981 (Sep 23): Washington, DC; Kennedy Center;
Jerome Lowenthal, piano.
1984 (Feb 4): Pasadena, CA; California Institute
of Technology; Beckman Auditorium; Reymond
Berney, piano.

W186. FANTASY AND TOCCATA. (unpublished; 5 min.)

Organ.
Composed: 1947.

Selected performance:

1988 (May 11): New York City; 65th anniversary
year of the composer; Church of St. Matthew and
St. Timothy; Leonard Raver, organ; James Holmes,
music director.

W187. FOUR-HAND PIANO SONATA. (unpublished)
See: B37, B205

Composed: 1943.

Premiere:

1944: New York City; Statler Hotel; Betty Crawford
and Ned Rorem, pianos.

Selected performance:

1949 (May 19): New York City; McMillan Theatre;
Eugene Istomin and Byron Hardin, pianos.

W188. PASTORALE. (1953: Southern Music)

See: B433; W243

Andantino from Symphony No. 1, arranged for organ by
the composer.
Dedicated to Henri Fourtine.
Composed: Fez, Morocco, December 1949.

W189. A QUAKER READER: Eleven Pieces for Organ.   (1977;
Boosey & Hawkes; 35 min.)
See: B2, B61, B64, B101, B117, B229, B250, B254,
B257, B296, B323, B334, B335, B348, B362, B493,
B494, B609, B780; W238

Commissioned by and dedicated to Alice Tully.
Composed for Leonard Raver.
Composed: Nantucket, Summer 1976.

Premiere:

1977 (Feb 2): New York City; Alice Tully Hall;
Leonard Raver, organ.

Selected performances:

1977 (Aug 1): Philadelphia; Old Christ Church;
International Congress of Organists; Leonard
Raver, organ.
1979 (Jun 4): New York City; Alice Tully Hall;
Catharine Crozier, organ.
1979 (Jun 12): Hartford, CT; Trinity Church; Paul
Callaway, organ.
1979 (Oct 21): Washington, DC; Washington Cathedral; Paul Callaway, organ.
1981 (Oct 4): Bethesda, MD; Bradley Hills Presbyterian Church; Donald Sutherland, organ.
1981 (Dec 6): Whittier, CA; Whittier College;
Quaker Festival; Catharine Crozier, organ.
1982 (Jun 29): Washington, DC; A.G.O. National
Convention; Church of the Epiphany; Catharine
Crozier, organ.
1982 (Jul 29): Aspen, CO; Aspen Music Festival.

W190. A QUIET AFTERNOON. (1951; Peer International)
See: B27, B228, B229

Piano.
Dedicated to "Rosemary's children."
Composed: 1948.

W191. SECONDE SONATE POUR PIANO.   (1953; Gerard Billaudot;
14 min.)
See: B228, B229, B719

Dedicated to Guy Ferrand.
Composed: 1949; new version with last movement Toccata added in 1950 for Julius Katchen.

Premiere:

1950 (May 4): Paris; American Embassy; Leon Fleisher, piano.

Selected performance:

1951 (Feb 28): New York City; Town Hall; Julius
Katchen, piano.

W192. SICILIENNE. (1955; Southern Music; 4 min.)
See: B25, B228, B230, B660

2 pianos, 4 hands.
Dedicated to Pino Fasani.
Composed: Fez, Morocco, June 28-30, 1950.

Premiere:

Early 1950s; New York City; "Today Show";
Whitemore and Lowe, duo-pianos.

Selected performance:

1960 (Feb 25): Buffalo, NY; Buffalo University;
Allen Giles and Ned Rorem, pianos.

W193. SLOW WALTZ: for Piano.   (1958, 1976; H. Branch Publishing)
See: B161

Dedicated to Perry O'Neil.
Composed: New York City, May 1958.
Published in: 4 Short Piano Pieces.

W194. SONATA I: for Piano. (1971; Henmar Press; C. F. Peters; 13 min.)
See: B75, B228, B229, B243, B460; W198

Last movement published separately by Henmar Press
under the title Toccata.
Dedicated to William Masselos.
Composed: New York City, May 1948.

Premiere:

1949 (Oct 6): New York City; Town Hall; David
Stimer, piano.

W195. SONATA III: for Piano. (1971: Henmar Press; C. F. Peters; 15 min.)
See: B75, B228, B229, B452; W240

First and third movements orchestrated to comprise
the first and fourth movements of Sinfonia.
Composed: Hyères, September 1954.

Premiere:

1955 (Jun 7): Paris; Foyer de la Musique Contempo-
raine; John Moriarty, piano.

Selected performance:

> 1963 (Feb 9): New York City; Town Hall; Herbert
> Rogers, piano.

W196. SONG & DANCE. (1987; Boosey & Hawkes; 4 min.)

Piano.
Commissioned by the Friends of the Maryland Summer
Institute for the Creative and Performing Arts for
the University of Maryland International Piano
Festival and William Kapell Competition.
Composed: Nantucket and New York City, October 2–18,
1986.

Premiere:

> 1987 (June): College Park, MD; University of Mary-
> land Piano Festival; William Kapell Competition;
> 13 different pianists.

W197. SPIDERS: for Harpsichord. (1969; Boosey & Hawkes; 2
min.)

Dedicated to Igor Kipnis.
Composed: New York City, July 1968.

W198. TOCCATA. (1961; Henmar Press; C. F. Peters; 4–1/2
min.)
See: B260; W194

Piano.
From third movement of Sonata I, for piano.
Dedicated to William Masselos.
Composed: New York City, 1948.

Selected performance:

> 1981 (Sep 23): Washington, DC: Kennedy Center;
> Jerome Lowenthal, piano.

W199. VIEWS FROM THE OLDEST HOUSE. (1981; Boosey & Hawkes;
22 min.)
See: B5, B61, B348, B494

Suite in six movements for organ.
Commissioned by the 1982 American Guild of Organists
National Convention.
Composed: Nantucket, June–October 1981.

Premiere:

> 1982 (Jun 29): Washington, DC; The AGO Convention;
> All Souls' Unitarian Church; John Obetz, organ.

Selected performance:

> 1983 (Mar 7): New York City; Ascension Church;
> Leonard Raver, organ.

VI.   SOLO INSTRUMENTAL AND CHAMBER MUSIC

W200. AFTER READING SHAKESPEARE: Suite in Nine Movements for
      Solo Cello. (1981; Boosey & Hawkes; 21 min.)
      See: B4, B147, B232, B260, B421, B691, B701

      Commissioned by and dedicated to Sharon Robinson.
      Composed: Nantucket, July 1979.

      Premiere:

         1981 (Feb 22): Philadelphia; Sharon Robinson,
         cello.

      Selected performances:

         1981 (Mar 15): New York City; Alice Tully Hall;
         Sharon Robinson, cello.
         1981 (Sep 23): Washington, DC; Kennedy Center Ter-
         race Theater; Sharon Robinson, cello.

W201. BOOK OF HOURS: Eight Pieces for Flute and Harp. (1978;
      Boosey & Hawkes; 20 min.)
      See: B213, B321, B322, B759, B780

      Flute and harp.
      Commissioned by A. Dingfelder.
      Dedicated to Ingrid Dingfelder and Martine Geliot.
      Composed: Yaddo and Nantucket, March-July 1975.

      Premiere:

         1976 (Feb 29): New York City; Alice Tully Hall;
         Ingrid Dingfelder, flute; Martine Geliot, harp.

      Selected performance:

         1982 (Apr 30): New York City; Third Street Music
         School Settlement; John Ranck, flute; Barbara
         Allen, harp.

W202. BRIGHT MUSIC. (1988; Boosey & Hawkes)
      See: B408

      5-movement piece for flute, 2 violins, cello and
      piano.
      Commissioned by the Bridgehampton Chamber Music
      Associates for the Bridgehampton Quintet.
      Composed: 1988.

      Premiere:

         Anticipated 1988 (Aug 6): Bridgehampton, NY;
         Bridgehampton Quintet.

      New York Premiere:

         Anticipated 1989 (Mar 10-12); New York City;

Alice Tully Hall; Lincoln Center Chamber Music
Society.

W203. CONCERTINO DA CAMERA. (unpublished)
        See: B312

        Harpsichord and 7 instruments.
        Composed: 1946.

W204. DANCES: For Cello and Piano. (1984; Boosey & Hawkes;
        15 min.)
        See: B7, B423, B652

        Commissioned by the Music Study Club of Metropolitan
            Detroit.
        Composed: 1983.

        Premiere:

            1984 (May 6): Detroit; Jonathan Spitz, cello;
            Frederich Moyer, piano.

        Selected performance:

            1984 (Dec 4): New York City; Alice Tully Hall;
            Sharon Robinson, cello; Margo Gerritt, piano.

W205. DAY MUSIC: For Violin and Piano. (1973; Boosey &
        Hawkes; 24 min.)
        See: B33, B66, B218, B229, B319, B320, B374, B475,
        B608, B684, B699, B767, B780

        Commissioned by Iowa State University for Ilza
            Niemack under a grant from the J. W. Fisher Trust.
        Composed: New York City, September 29–October 10,
            1971.

        Premiere:

            1972 (Oct 15): Ames, IA; Iowa State University;
            Great Hall of Memorial Union; Ilza Niemack, vio-
            lin; William David, piano.

        Selected performances:

            1973 (Aug 4): Marlboro, VT; Jaime Laredo, violin;
            Ruth Laredo, piano.
            1973 (Nov 25): New York City; Alice Tully Hall;
            Sergiu Luca, violin; Jerome Lowenthal, piano.
            1980 (Aug 16): Seattle; Meany Theater; Ani Kava-
            fian, violin; Edward Auer, piano.
            1980 (Aug 25): New York City; Alice Tully Hall;
            Franco Gulli, violin; Enrica Cavallo, piano.
            1981 (Nov 18): New York City; Miriam Fried; Gar-
            rick Ohlsson, piano.
            1982 (Jul 27): Aspen, CO; Aspen Music Festival.

W206. ELEVEN STUDIES FOR ELEVEN PLAYERS. (1962; Boosey &
        Hawkes)

See: B33, B81, B310, B311, B316, B389, B663, B722, B764, B780; W248, W250, W251, W254, W255, W256, W258, W260, W278

For flute, oboe, clarinet, trumpet, percussion, harp, piano and three strings.
Source for the following ballets: Early Voyagers; Eleven by Eleven; Antics for Acrobats; Excursions; Lovers; Progressions; Competitions; and Dancing Ground.
Commissioned by the Slee Foundation, Buffalo University.
Dedicated to Cameron Baird.
Composed: Buffalo, October 1959-March 1960.

Premiere:

1960 (May 17): Buffalo, NY; Baird Hall, Buffalo University; Ned Rorem, conductor.

Selected performances:

1961 (Oct 12): New York City; Town Hall; Arnold Gamson, conductor.
1961 (Nov 3): Paris; Salle Gaveau; Antonio De-Almeida, conductor.
1965 (Jun 18): Washington, DC; White House Festival of the Arts; Louisville Orchestra.
1979 (Jan 29): Philadelphia; Curtis Institute; Glenn Dodson, conductor.
1987 (Nov): New York City; Merkin Hall; Chamber Symphony; Gerard Schwarz, conductor.

W207. END OF SUMMER: Remembrance of Things Past. (1986; Boosey & Hawkes)
See: B87, B212, B261, B467, B516, B666, B755

For clarinet, violin, and piano.
Commissioned by the Verdehr Trio.
Composed: 1985.

Premiere:

1986 (Mar 31): Bombay; Patkar Hall; Verdehr Trio.

Selected performances:

1986 (Nov 3): Cleveland; Cleveland Institute of Music; Verdehr Trio.
1986 (Nov 20): Terre Haute, IN; Indiana State University; Verdehr Trio.
1986 (Dec 10): New York City; Alice Tully Hall; Verdehr Trio.
1987 (Mar 30): London; St. John's; Smith Square; Verdehr Trio.

W208. LOVERS: A Narrative in Ten Scenes. (1966; Boosey & Hawkes; 17 min.)
See: B229, B517, B710, B780

Harpsichord, oboe, cello and percussion.
Dedicated to Sylvia Marlowe.
Composed: Yaddo, February-March 1964.

Premiere:

> 1964 (Dec 15): New York City, Carnegie Recital
> Hall; Sylvia Marlowe, harpsichord; Samuel Baron,
> flute; Ronald Roseman, oboe; Harold Farberman,
> percussion.

W209. MOUNTAIN SONG. (1950; Peer International)
See: B37, B205, B369, B414, B665; W265

Flute (or oboe, or violin or cello) and piano.
Originally used as the incidental music for the play
  Cock-A-Doodle-Doo, by Iris Tree.
Composed: New York City, 1948.

Selected performance:

> 1949 (May 19): New York City; McMillan Theatre;
> Seymour Barab, cello; Byron Hardin, piano.

W210. NIGHT MUSIC. (1973; Boosey & Hawkes; 20 min.)
See: B91, B218, B229, B319, B320, B475, B684, B738,
B780

Violin and piano.
Commissioned by the McKim Fund in the Library of
  Congress.
Composed: New York City and Saratoga Springs, Febru-
ary-May 1972.

Premiere:

> 1973 (Jan 12): Washington, DC; Library of Con-
> gress; Coolidge Auditorium; Earl Carlyss, vio-
> lin; Ann Schein, piano.

Selected performances:

> 1973 (Apr 14): Albuquerque; University of New Mex-
> ico; Leonard Felberg, violin; George Robert,
> piano.
> 1973 (Nov 26): New York City; Alice Tully Hall;
> Zvi Zeitlin, violin; Jerome Lowenthal, piano.

W211. PICNIC ON THE MARNE: Seven Waltzes. (1984; Boosey &
Hawkes; 17 min.)
See: B422, B450

Alto saxophone and piano.
Commissioned by the Concert Artists Guild for John
  Harle.
Composed: Nantucket, September-October 1983.

Premiere:

1984 (Feb 14): New York City; Carnegie Recital Hall; John Harle, saxophone; John Lenehan, piano.

W212. PRAISING CHARLES: Fanfare and Flourish. (1988; Boosey & Hawkes)

2 trumpets, 2 trombones and organ.
Premiered under the title: Fanfare and Flourish.
In honor of the 20th anniversary of Lincoln Center.
Commissioned by the Chamber Music Society of Lincoln Center in honor of Charles Wadsworth.
Composed: 1988.

Premiere:

1988 (Oct 16): New York City; Alice Tully Hall; Chamber Music Society of Lincoln Center.

W213. ROMEO AND JULIET. (1978; Boosey & Hawkes; 20 min.)
See: B215, B323, B324, B354, B678, B743, B780

Nine pieces for flute and guitar.
Commissioned by and dedicated to Ingrid Dingfelder.
Composed: Nantucket and Yaddo, May-August 1977.

Premiere:

1978 (Mar 1): New York City; Alice Tully Hall; Ingrid Dingfelder, flute; Herbert Levine, guitar.

W214. SEPTET: Scenes from Childhood. (1985; Boosey & Hawkes; 22 min.)
See: B7, B42, B131, B132, B133, B192, B193, B326, B427, B489; W56, W183

For oboe, horn, piano and string quartet.
Fifth movement adapted from O Do Not Love Too Long; other material from A Birthday Suite.
Composed: 1984-1985.

Premiere:

1985 (Aug 11): Santa Fe; Santa Fe Chamber Music Festival; Allan Vogel, oboe; Robert Routch, horn; Mendelssohn String Quartet; Ned Rorem, piano.

W215. SKY MUSIC: Ten Pieces for Solo Harp. (1976; Boosey & Hawkes; 18 min.)
See: B322, B780

Commissioned by the American Harp Society, Inc.
Composed: Nantucket and Manhattan, January-February 1976.

Premiere:

1976 (Jun 24): Albuquerque; University of New Mexico; Marcella DeCray, harp.

W216. <u>SOLEMN PRELUDE</u>. (unpublished; 2 min.)

Fanfare for eleven brass instruments.
Composed: 1973.

Premiere:

1973 (May 21): New York City; Metropolitan Opera:
Sol Hurok's 60th birthday gala; Robert Irving,
conductor.

W217. <u>SONATA</u>: for Violin and Piano in Four Scenes.   (1961;
Henmar Press; C. F. Peters; 19 min.)
See: B405

Dedicated to Edward Albee and Bessie Smith.
Composed: New York City and Fez, Morocco, 1948-49.

Premiere:

1950: Washington, DC; Maurice Wilk, violin.

W218. <u>STRING QUARTET NO. 1</u>. (unpublished)

Composed: 1947.

W219. <u>STRING QUARTET NO. 2</u>. (1971; Southern Music)

Dedicated to the memory of Lili Boulanger.
Composed: Fez, Morocco, July 8-16, 1950.
Final movement also for string orchestra, entitled
<u>Lento for Strings</u> and <u>In Memoriam</u>.

Premiere:

1951: Paris.

W220. <u>SUITE FOR GUITAR</u>. (1980; Boosey & Hawkes; 12 min.)
See: B3, B55, B80, B277, B353, B451, B678

Commissioned by the Cleveland Orchestra.
Composed: 1980.

Premiere:

1980 (Jul 25): Blossom Music Center; Joseph Breznikar, guitar.

Selected performances:

1982 (May 4): New York City; Merkin Hall; David
Leisner, guitar.
1984 (Oct 9): New York City; Carnegie Recital
Hall; Lawrence Ferrara, guitar.

W221. <u>THREE SLOW PIECES</u>. (1978; Boosey & Hawkes)

Cello and piano.
Composed: 1950, 1959, 1970.

W222. TRIO: Flute, Violoncello and Piano.   (1966; Henmar
Press; C. F. Peters; 18 min.)
See: B85, B91, B130, B148, B218, B229, B310, B311,
B320, B396, B442, B482, B502, B684, B766

Commissioned by Bernard Goldberg for the Musica Viva
Trio.
Dedicated to Bernard Goldberg.
Composed: Yaddo, June-July 1960.

Premiere:

1960 (Jan 7): Pittsburgh; Musica Viva Trio.

Selected performances:

1960 (Dec 19): New York City; Carnegie Recital
Hall; Murray Panitz, flute; Alexander Kouguell,
cello; Douglas Nordli, piano.
1961 (Dec): Paris; Radiodiffusion broadcast.
1966 (Jan 30): Salt Lake City; University of Utah;
Annual Chamber Music Festival.
1968 (Aug 23): Aspen, CO: Aspen Music Festival.
1969 (Feb 2): Upper Montclair, NJ; Montclair State
College; New York Camerata.
1969 (May 25): Upper Montclair, NJ; Montclair
State College; Trio de l'Academic.
1969 (Nov 9): Trenton, NJ; New Jersey State Museum; Jeanne Patterson, flute; Daniel Rothmueller,
cello; Francis Lumpkin, piano.
1973 (Apr 14): Albuquerque; University of New
Mexico; Frank Bowen, flute; Joanna de Keyser,
cello; George Robert, piano.
1973 (Nov 26): New York City; Alice Tully Hall;
Eugenia Zuckerman, flute; Jeffry Solow, cello;
Jerome Lowenthal, piano.
1975 (Mar 24): same as Nov 26, 1973.
1984 (Apr 4): Boston; Boston University; September
Payne, flute; Jeffrey Butler, cello; Benjamin
Pasternak, piano.
1986 (Nov 17): Philadelphia; David Cramer, flute;
Gloria Johns, cello; Andrew Willis, piano.

W223. WINTER PAGES.   (1987; Boosey & Hawkes; 33 min.)
See: B4, B5, B138, B247, B284, B305, B331, B342,
B363, B408, B519, B674, B765, B781; W183

Quintet in 12 movements for clarinet, bassoon,
piano, violin and violoncello.
Commissioned by and dedicated to the Chamber Music
Society of Lincoln Center.
Some material from A Birthday Suite has been used in
this work.
Composed: New York City and Nantucket, January-May
1981.

Premiere:

    1982 (Feb 14): New York City; Alice Tully Hall;
    Gervaise de Peyer, clarinet; Loren Glickman,
    bassoon; Charles Wadsworth, piano; James Bus-
    well, violin; Leslie Parnas, cello.

Selected performances:

    1982 (June): Miami; New World Festival of the
    Arts; Lincoln Center Players.
    1982 (Jul 25-26): Santa Fe; Santa Fe Chamber Music
    Festival; Ida Kavafian, violin; Carter Brey,
    cello; Edward Auer, piano; Kenneth Munday, bas-
    soon, Franklin Cohen, clarinet.
    1983 (May 29-30): Charleston, SC; Spoleto Festi-
    val; Charles Wadsworth, conductor.
    1986 (Jan 8): New York City; Cooper Union; Musical
    Elements Concert.
    1988 (Jun 21): New York City; New York Interna-
    tional Festival; Chamber Music Society of Lin-
    coln Center.

VII. ORCHESTRA AND BAND MUSIC

W224. AIR MUSIC. (1977; Boosey & Hawkes; 32 min.)
    See: B26, B115, B275, B298, B321, B322, B378, B407,
    B459, B480, B487, B587, B651, B676, B681, B695,
    B774, B776, B780; W276

    Ten variations for orchestra.
    Pulitzer Prize, 1976.
    Commissioned by the Cincinnati Symphony Orchestra,
    assisted by a grant from the National Endowment
    for the Arts.
    Some material from the film music Panic in Needle
    Park has been used in this work.
    Composed: Saratoga Springs and New York City, 1974.

Premiere:

    1975 (Dec 5): Cincinnati; Cincinnati Symphony;
    Thomas Schippers, conductor.

Selected performances:

    1975 (Dec 11): New York City; Carnegie Hall; Cin-
    cinnati Symphony; Thomas Schippers, conductor.
    1977 (Jan 6-7): Chicago; Chicago Symphony Orches-
    tra; Guido Ajmone-Marsan, conductor.

W225. ASSEMBLY AND FALL. (1975; Boosey & Hawkes; 25 min.)
    See: B142, B241, B275, B321, B395, B479, B499, B697,
    B780

    Orchestra with solo oboe, trumpet, timpani, and
    viola.
    Commissioned by the North Carolina Symphony with a

matching grant from the North Carolina Bicentennial Commission.
Composed: New York City and Yaddo, January-March
1975.

Premiere:

1975 (Oct 11): Raleigh, NC; Raleigh Memorial Auditorium; Ronald Weddle, oboe; Douglas Myers,
trumpet; John Fedderson, timpani; Robert Glazer,
viola; North Carolina Symphony; John Gosling,
conductor.

Selected performances:

1976 (Oct 12): Greensboro, NC; North Carolina Symphony; John Gosling, conductor.
1977 (Mar 9): New York City; Carnegie Hall; North
Carolina Symphony; John Gosling, conductor.

W226. CONCERTO FOR PIANO, NO. 1.   (unpublished; withdrawn)

For Eugene Istomin.
Composed: 1948.

W227. CONCERTO IN SIX MOVEMENTS.   (1974; Boosey & Hawkes; 26
min.)
See: B5, B6, B28, B99, B128, B211, B229, B231, B275,
B317, B318, B319, B347, B417, B474, B775, B780

For piano and orchestra; two-piano version avail-
able.
Commissioned by the Music Associates of Aspen, Inc.
Dedicated to Jerome Lowenthal.
Composed: 1969.

Premiere:

1970 (Dec 3): Pittsburgh; Syria Mosque; Jerome
Lowenthal, piano; Pittsburgh Symphony; William
Steinberg, conductor.

Selected performances:

1971: Blossom Music Festival; Jerome Lowenthal,
piano; Cleveland Orchestra; Louis Lane, conductor.
1972 (Jun 15): Chicago; Chicago Symphony; Irwin
Hoffman, conductor.
1972 (Dec 13-14): Philadelphia; Philadelphia
Orchestra; Eugene Ormandy, conductor.
1983 (May 1): New York City; Carnegie Hall; Rita
Bouboulidi, piano; American Symphony Orchestra;
Moshe Atzmon, conductor.
1983 (Nov 7): New York City; Alice Tully Hall;
Jerome Lowenthal, piano; American Composers
Orchestra; Dennis Russell Davies, conductor.

W228. CONCERTO NO. 2: For Piano and Orchestra.   (1970;
      Southern Music)
      See: B229, B231, B727

      Dedicated to Julius Katchen.
      Composed: Fez, Morocco, October 20-December 26,
      1950.

      Premiere:

          1954 (May): Paris; Julius Katchen, piano; Orches-
          tre de la Radiodiffusion; Jean Giardino, conduc-
          tor.

W229. DESIGN. (1958; Boosey & Hawkes; 18 min.)
      See: B89, B307, B309, B780

      Orchestra.
      Commissioned by the Louisville Orchestra.
      Dedicated to Robert Whitney and the Louisville
      Orchestra.
      Composed: Paris, March-April 1953.

      Premiere:

          1955 (May 29): Louisville, KY; Louisville Orches-
          tra; Robert Whitney, conductor.

      Selected performances:

          1957 (Nov 28-29): Philadelphia; Philadelphia
          Orchestra; Eugene Ormandy, conductor.
          1959 (Nov 12-13): Chicago; Chicago Symphony; Fritz
          Reiner, conductor.
          1959 (Nov 17): Harrisburg, PA; Harrisburg Sym-
          phony; Edwin McArthur, conductor.

W230. EAGLES. (1962; Boosey & Hawkes; 9 min.)
      See: B119, B309, B310, B311, B313, B322, B346, B358,
      B780

      Orchestra.
      Dedicated to Eugene Ormandy and the Philadelphia
      Orchestra.
      Composed: New York City and Peterborough, July-
      September 1958.

      Premiere:

          1959 (Oct 23): Philadelphia; Philadelphia Orches-
          tra; Eugene Ormandy, conductor.

      Selected performances:

          1964 (Mar 10): Boston; Boston Symphony Orchestra;
          Leopold Stokowski, conductor.
          1975 (Sep 19-20): Philadelphia; Philadelphia
          Orchestra; Eugene Ormandy, conductor.

1976 (May 20): Washington, DC; Kennedy Center Concert Hall; Philadelphia Orchestra; Eugene Ormandy, conductor.

W231. FROLIC: Fanfare for Orchestra.   (1986; Boosey & Hawkes; 2-1/2 min.)
See: B428, B470, B758

Commissioned by the Houston Symphony Orchestra for Citicorp-Houston Fanfare Project.
Composed: 1986.

Premiere:

1986 (Apr 12): Houston; Jones Hall; Houston Symphony Orchestra; Sergiu Comissiona, conductor.

W232. IDEAS FOR EASY ORCHESTRA.   (1967; Boosey & Hawkes; 13 min.)
See: B240, B780

Composed: Rabat, Morocco; Summer 1961.

Premiere:

1968: Oakland, CA; Oakland Youth Orchestra; Robert Hughes, conductor.

W233. LIONS: (A Dream).   (1967; Boosey & Hawkes; 14 min.)
See: B5, B51, B54, B140, B244, B267, B292, B314, B339, B409, B483, B496, B650, B688, B732, B779, B780; W275

Orchestra and jazz combo.
Some material from the incidental music for The Nephew has been incorporated into this work.
Composed: New York City, October 1963.

Premiere:

1965 (Oct 28): New York City; Carnegie Hall; Detroit Symphony; Sixten Ehrling, conductor.

Selected performances:

1967 (Jan 24-25): Salt Lake City; Utah Symphony Orchestra; Maurice Abravanel, conductor.
1969 (Nov 17-18): Phoenix, AZ; Phoenix Symphony Orchestra; Maurice Abravanel, conductor.
1976 (May 7): Detroit; Detroit Symphony Orchestra; Lukas Foss, conductor.
1982 (July 4): Aspen, CO; Leonard Slatkin, conductor.
1983 (Oct 25): New Haven, CT; New Haven Symphony Orchestra.
1987 (Mar 26, 1987): Long Beach, CA; Long Beach Symphony; Murry Sidlin, conductor.

W234. ORGAN CONCERTO. (1985; Boosey & Hawkes; 30 min.)
      See: B7, B9, B11, B56, B225, B275, B425, B426, B471

      Organ and orchestra.
      Commissioned by the Portland Symphony Orchestra.
      Dedicated to Leonard Raver and Bruce Hangen.
      Composed: 1984.

      Premiere:

          1985 (Mar 19): Portland, ME; Leonard Raver, organ;
          Portland Symphony Orchestra; Bruce Hangen, con-
          ductor.

      Selected performances:

          1986 (May 22): Omaha, NE; Strauss Center for the
          Performing Arts; Contemporary Music Festival;
          Leonard Raver, organ; Omaha Symphony Orchestra;
          Bruce Hangen, conductor.
          1987 (Oct 21): New York City; Alice Tully Hall;
          Leonard Raver, organ; Little Orchestra; Dino
          Anagnost, conductor.

W235. OVERTURE FOR G.I.'S. (unpublished)

      Military band.
      Composed: 1944 or 1945; read but not publicly per-
          formed, by the Army Music School Band, Washington,
          DC; William Strickland, conductor.

W236. OVERTURE IN C. (unpublished)
      See: B183, B242, B412, B709

      Orchestra.
      Gershwin Award 1949.
      Composed: 1949.

      Premiere:

          1949 (May 7): New York City; Carnegie Hall; Sym-
          phonette Orchestra; Mishel Piastro, conductor.

W237. PILGRIMS. (1970; Boosey & Hawkes; 6 min.)
      See: B323, B780

      String orchestra.
      Composed: New York City and Peterborough, NH, July-
          September 1958.

      Premiere:

          1959 (Jan 30): New York City; Cooper Union; Music
          in the Making Series; Howard Shanet, conductor.

      Selected performance:

          1977 (Oct): Philadelphia; Philadelphia Orchestra;

Eugene Ormandy, conductor.
1984 (Feb 25-26): New York City; Chamber Orchestra
of Y.M.H.A.; Gerard Schwarz, conductor.

W238. QUAKER READER (Orchestral version)   (1988; Boosey &
Hawkes)
See: B408; W189

Orchestra.
Arranged: 1988; from the organ version.

Premiere:

1988 (Oct 7): New York City; Tilles Center; New
York Chamber Symphony; Gerard Schwarz, conductor.

W239. REMEMBERING TOMMY.   (1979; Boosey & Hawkes; 28 min.)
See: B4, B5, B77, B78, B275, B364, B484, B514, B781;
W183

Ten movements for piano, cello and orchestra.
Other titles used for this work: Green Music; Double
Concerto.
Some material from A Birthday Suite has been incor-
porated into this work.
Commissioned by Jeanne and Jack Kirstein.
Dedicated to Thomas Schippers.
Composed: 1979.

Premiere:

1981 (Nov 13-14): Lee Luvisi, piano; Peter Wiley,
cello; Cincinnati Symphony; Jorge Mester, conductor.

Selected performances:

1982 (Jan 29): New York City; Alice Tully Hall;
Jon Parker, piano; John Sharp, cello; Juilliard
Symphony; Jorge Mester, conductor.
1982 (Aug 1): Aspen, CO; Lee Luvisi, piano; Laszlo
Varga, cello; Edo de Waart, conductor.

W240. SINFONIA: in Four Movements.   (1957; Henmar Press;
C. F. Peters; 9 min.)
See: B307, B308, B314; W20, W195

Fifteen wind instruments and optional percussion.
First and fourth movements are orchestrated versions
of the first and third movements of Sonata III for
piano; other material drawn from unpublished song
cycle, Eclogues.
Dedicated to Mr. and Mrs. H. J. Heinz II and the
Howard Heinz Endowment.
Composed: 1956-1957.

Premiere:

1957 (Jul 14): Pittsburgh; Robert Boudreau, conductor.

Selected performances:

1957 (Nov 10): New York City; New York Philharmonic; Dimitri Mitroupoulos, conductor.
1965 (Nov 16): Vancouver, BC; Canadian Broadcasting Co.

W241. STRING SYMPHONY. (1986; Boosey & Hawkes; 23 min.)
See: B221, B222, B337, B398, B408, B466, B652, B679

In five movements.
Commissioned by the Atlanta Symphony Orchestra.
Composed: 1985.

Premiere:

1985 (Oct 31): Atlanta, GA; Atlanta Symphony Orchestra; Robert Shaw, conductor.

Selected performances:

1986 (Apr 4): Washington, DC; Kennedy Center; Atlanta Symphony Orchestra; Robert Shaw, conductor.
1986 (Apr 6): New York City; Carnegie Hall; Atlanta Symphony Orchestra; Robert Shaw, conductor.
1986 (Jun 8): Paris; Atlanta Symphony, Robert Shaw, conductor.
1988 (Mar 4): Grand Rapids, MI; Grand Rapids Symphony; Catherine Comet, conductor.
1988 (Apr 15, 16, 18): Milwaukee, WI; Milwaukee Symphony; Zdenek Macal, conductor.

W242. SUNDAY MORNING. (1978; Boosey & Hawkes; 19 min.)
See: B3, B4, B280, B324, B378, B418, B481, B780, B782; W183

Poem in eight parts for orchestra.
All movement titles are from Wallace Steven's poem Sunday Morning.
Commissioned by the Saratoga Performing Arts Center, Inc. for the Philadelphia Orchestra.
Some material from A Birthday Suite has been incorporated into this work.
Composed: Nantucket and New York City, Summer/Fall 1977.

Premiere:

1978 (Aug 25): Saratoga, NY; Saratoga Performing Arts Center; Philadelphia Orchestra; Eugene Ormandy, conductor.

Selected performances:

1978 (Sep 23): Philadelphia; Academy of Music;

Philadelphia Orchestra; Eugene Ormandy, conductor.
1981 (Feb 4-7, 10): New York City; Avery Fisher Hall; New York Philharmonic; Leonard Bernstein, conductor.
1983 (Oct 1-3): Terre Haute, IN; Indiana State University; Indianapolis Symphony; William Henry Curry, conductor.

W243. SYMPHONY NO. 1. (1972; Southern Music; 27 min.)
    See: B306, B307, B325, B399, B675; W188

Orchestra.
Andantino arranged by the composer for organ and published under the title Pastorale.
Composed: Fez, Morocco, December 1949-January 1950.

Premiere:

1951 (Feb): Vienna, Austria; Vienna Philharmonic; Jonathan Sternberg, conductor.

Selected performances:

1956 (Feb 18): New York City; Carnegie Hall; American Music Festival; New York Philharmonic; Alfredo Antonini, conductor.
1956 (Sep 17): Oslo, Norway; Alfredo Antonini, conductor.
1957 (Nov 19): Harrisburg, PA; Harrisburg Symphony Orchestra; Edwin McArthur, conductor.
1971 (June): New York City; Carnegie Hall; Utah Symphony Orchestra; Maurice Abravanel, conductor.

W244. SYMPHONY NO. 2. (1956; Boosey & Hawkes; 18 min.)
    See: B306, B309, B647, B780

Orchestra.
Commissioned by and dedicated to Nikolai Sokoloff and the Musical Arts Society of La Jolla, California.
Composed: New York City, January-March 1956.

Premiere:

1956 (Aug 5): La Jolla, CA; Musical Arts Society of La Jolla; Nikolai Sokoloff, conductor.

Selected performance:

1959 (May 3): New York City; Town Hall; New York Chamber Players; Arthur Leif, conductor.

W245. SYMPHONY NO. 3. in Five Movements. (1960; Boosey & Hawkes; 24 min.)
    See: B45, B143, B308, B309, B310, B311, B317, B318, B409, B780

Orchestra.
Dedicated to Robert Holton.
Composed: Hyères and New York, July 1957–April 4,
    1958; 2nd movement originally for 2-pianos, com-
    posed in Fez, Morocco, August 23–26, 1949.

Premiere:

> 1959 (Apr 18): New York City; Carnegie Hall; New
> York Philharmonic; Leonard Bernstein, conductor.

Selected performances:

> 1959 (Aug 3): Ravinia; Chicago Symphony; Alfred
> Wallenstein, conductor.
> 1959 (Sep 8): Hamburg, Germany; Moritz Bomhard,
> conductor.
> 1959 (Nov 15): Denver; Denver Symphony.
> 1960 (Nov 10–12): Detroit; Detroit Symphony; Paul
> Paray, conductor.
> 1961 (Dec 16–18): Pittsburgh; Pittsburgh Symphony;
> William Steinberg, conductor.
> 1962 (Jan): Paris; Manuel Rosenthal, conductor.
> 1970 (Nov 28): Salt Lake City, UT; Utah Symphony
> Orchestra; Maurice Abravanel, conductor.
> 1971 (Jun 2): New York City; Carnegie Hall; Utah
> Symphony Orchestra; Maurice Abravanel, conduc-
> tor.

W246. VIOLIN CONCERTO. (1984; Boosey & Hawkes; 22 min.)
    See: B7, B275, B425, B439; W8

Violin and orchestra.
Third movement is drawn from unpublished song, Boy
    with a Baseball Glove.
Composed: 1984.

Premiere:

> 1985 (Mar 30): Springfield, MA; Jaime Laredo,
> violin; Springfield Symphony Orchestra; Robert
> Gutter, conductor.

Selected performances:

> 1986 (Dec 2–3): Hartford, CT; Jaime Laredo, vio-
> lin; Hartford Symphony Orchestra; Michael
> Lankester, conductor.
> 1988 (Nov 23, 25–26, 29): New York City; Gidon
> Kremer, violin; New York Philharmonic; Leonard
> Bernstein, conductor.

W247. WATER MUSIC. (1970; Boosey & Hawkes; 17 min.)
    See: B74, B96, B315, B711, B780

Clarinet and violin with orchestra.
Commissioned by the Youth Chamber Orchestra of the
    Oakland Symphony.

Composed: Yaddo and New York City, September–December 1966.

Premiere:

1967 (Apr 9): Oakland, CA; Thomas Halpin, violin; Larry London, clarinet; Oakland Youth Orchestra; Robert Hughes, conductor.

Selected performances:

1968 (Sep 2): New York City; Town Hall; Gerald Tarack, violin; George Silfies, clarinet; Clarion Society; Newell Jenkins, conductor.
1979 (Mar 2): New York City; MacMillan Theater; Anahid Ajemian, violin; Stanley Drucker, clarinet; Howard Shanet, conductor.

VIII. BALLETS

W248. ANTICS FOR ACROBATS. (unpublished)
See: W206

Ballet based on Eleven Studies for Eleven Players. Choreographed by J. Marks, 1964.

W249. BALLET FOR JERRY. (unpublished)

Choreographed by Jerome Robbins.
Composed: 1951.

W250. COMPETITIONS. (unpublished)
See: B722; W206

Ballet based on Eleven Studies for Eleven Players. Choreographed by Stuart Sebastian for the Summer Festival of the Forest Meadows Center of the Arts, 1977.

Premiere:

1977 (Summer): San Rafael, CA; Dominican College; Meadows Center of the Arts; Marin Civic Ballet.

W251. DANCING GROUND. (unpublished)
See: B315, B352, B365; W206

Ballet based on Eleven Studies for Eleven Players. Choreographed by Martha Graham, 1967.

Premiere:

1967 (Feb 24): New York City; Mark Hellinger Theater; Martha Graham Dance Company.

W252. DEATH OF THE BLACK KNIGHT. (unpublished)

Ballet; in collaboration with Paul Goodman.

Commissioned by Alfonso Ossorio.
Composed: 1948.

W253. <u>DORIAN GRAY</u>. (unpublished)

Ballet; in collaboration with Jean Marais.
Choreographed by Paul Goube.
Composed: 1952.

<u>Premiere</u>:

1952 (May): Barcelona; Les Etoiles de la Danse;
Yvonne Alexander and Michelle Rayne.

W254. <u>EARLY VOYAGERS</u>. (unpublished)
<u>See</u>: B313, B733; W206

Ballet based on <u>Eleven Studies for Eleven Players</u>,
and excerpts from other works.
In collaboration with Truman Capote.
Choreographed by Valerie Bettis, 1959.

<u>Premiere</u>:

1960 (Aug 2): Lee, MA; Jacob's Pillow Festival;
Valerie Bettis Dance Theatre.

<u>Selected performances</u>:

1963 (Feb 16): New York City; Brooklyn College;
National Ballet.
1973 (Jan 30): Philadelphia; Academy of Music.

W255. <u>ELEVEN BY ELEVEN</u>. (unpublished)
<u>See</u>: B313; W206

Ballet based on <u>Eleven Studies for Eleven Players</u>.
Choreographed by Norman Walker, 1963.

W256. <u>EXCURSIONS</u>. (unpublished)
<u>See</u>: W206

Ballet based on <u>Eleven Studies for Eleven Players</u>.
Choreographed by Marvin Gordon, 1964.

W257. <u>LOST IN FEAR</u>. (unpublished)

Ballet.
Choreographed by Marie Marchowsky.
Composed: 1945.

W258. <u>LOVERS</u>. (unpublished)
<u>See</u>: W206

Ballet based on <u>Eleven Studies for Eleven Players</u>.
Choreographed by Glen Tetley, 1966.

<u>Premiere</u>:

1966 (?): New York City; Hunter College.

Selected performance:

1966: National Educational Television; Jac Venza and Virginia Kassel, producers.

W259. MÉLOS. (unpublished)

Ballet; in collaboration with Marie Laure de Noailles.
Prix de Biarritz, 1951.
Composed: 1951.

W260. PROGRESSIONS. (unpublished)
See: W206

Ballet based on Eleven Studies for Eleven Players.
Choreographed for the Orchesis Dance Repertory in Salt Lake City, UT, 1967.

W261. SCULPTURES. (unpublished)

Ballet.
Choreographed by Shirley Ririe and Joanne Woodbury.
Composed: 1967.

Premiere:

1967: Salt Lake City; Joanne Woodbury and Shirley Ririe.

IX.   INCIDENTAL MUSIC

W262. AT NOON UPON TWO. (unpublished)

Puppet show; with Charles Henri Ford.
Composed: 1947.

W263. CALIGULA. (unpublished)

Incidental music for a play by Albert Camus.
Composed: 1962.

Premiere:

Buffalo, NY: Albright Theater.

W264. THE CAVE AT MACHPELAH. (unpublished)

Incidental music for a drama in verse by Paul Goodman.
Composed: 1959.

Premiere:

1959 (July): New York City; The Living Theatre; Julian Beck, director.

W265. <u>COCK-A-DOODLE-DOO</u>. (unpublished)

    Incidental music for a play by Iris Tree.
Some material from this work was published as <u>Mountain Song</u>.
Composed: 1949.

    <u>Premiere</u>:

        New York City; ANTA Theater; Charlton Heston and
Darren McGavin.

W266. <u>COLOR OF DARKNESS: AN EVENING IN THE WORLD OF JAMES
PURDY</u>. (unpublished)
<u>See</u>: B179, B313

    Incidental music for a dramatization of James Purdy's works; adapted by Ellen Violett.

    <u>Premiere</u>:

        1963 (Sep 30): New York City; Writers' Stage;
Harvest Productions; Margaret Barker, director.

W267. <u>DUSK</u>. (unpublished)

    Incidental music; text by Paul Goodman.
Composed: 1948.

    <u>Premiere</u>:

        1948 or 9: New York City; <u>The Poet's Theater</u> production by Marie Piscator; Y.M.H.A.

W268. <u>THE EMPEROR</u>. (unpublished)

    Incidental music for a play by Luigi Pirandello.
Composed: 1963.

W269. <u>FIRE BOY</u>. (unpublished)
<u>See</u>: W87

    Puppet show; with John Myers.
Text by Charles Boultenhouse.
Some material from this work was later incorporated
into <u>Three Incantations from a Marionette Tale</u>.
Composed: 1947.

W270. <u>HIPPOLYTUS</u>. (unpublished)

    Incidental music for Leighton Rollins' adaptation
from Euripides; with Muriel Smith and Donald Buka.
Composed: 1948.

    <u>Premiere</u>:

        1948 (Nov): New York City; Lenox Hill Playhouse.

W271. <u>IL N'Y A PLUS RIEN A VIVRE</u>. (unpublished)

> Incidental music for a play by Daniel Mauroc.
> Composed: Paris, 1950.

W272. <u>THE LADY OF THE CAMELLIAS</u>. (unpublished)
   <u>See</u>: B313

> Incidental music for the play by Alexandre Dumas;
>   Franco Zeferelli, director.
> Composed: 1963.

> <u>Premiere</u>:

>> 1963 (Mar 20): New York City;· Winter Garden The-
>> atre.

W273. <u>THE MILK TRAIN DOESN'T STOP HERE ANYMORE</u>.   (unpublished)
   <u>See</u>: B720

> Incidental music for the play by Tennessee Williams;
>   Tony Richardson, director.
> Composed: 1964.

> <u>Premiere</u>:

>> 1964 (Jan 1): New York City; Brooks Atkinson The-
>> atre.

W274. <u>MOTEL</u>. (unpublished)

> Incidental music for the play; with Siobhan McKenna;
>   Herbert Machiz, director.
> Composed: 1960.

W275. <u>THE NEPHEW</u>. (unpublished)
   <u>See</u>: B318; W233

> Incidental music for a play based on a novel by
>   James Purdy.
> Some material was later used in <u>Lions</u>.
> Composed: 1971.

> <u>Premiere</u>:

>> 1971 (Mar 24): Buffalo, NY: Arena Theater.

W276. <u>PANIC IN NEEDLE PARK</u>. (unpublished)
   <u>See</u>: W224

> Incidental music written for the movie directed by
>   Jerry Schatzberg; recorded under the direction of
>   the composer. The recording was not used when the
>   film was finally released. Some material was
>   later used in <u>Air Music</u>.
> Composed: 1971.

W277. <u>SETTINGS FOR WHITMAN</u>. (unpublished)

    Spoken voice and piano.
    Text by Walt Whitman.
    Commissioned by Inga and Maxim Shur.
    Composed: 1957.

    <u>Premiere</u>:

        1957 (Oct 30): New York City; Town Hall; Inga and
        Maxim Shur.

W278. <u>SUDDENLY LAST SUMMER</u>. (unpublished)
      See: B308; W206

    Incidental music for a play by Tennessee Williams.
    Some material was later used in <u>Eleven Studies for</u>
    <u>Eleven Players</u>.
    Composed: 1957.

    <u>Premiere</u>:

        1958 (Jan 7): New York City; York Playhouse.

W279. <u>THAT WE MAY LIVE</u>. (unpublished)

    Incidental music for a pageant, with Milton Robert-
    son.
    Composed: 1946.

W280. <u>THE YOUNG DISCIPLE</u>. (unpublished)

    Incidental music; text by Paul Goodman.
    Composed: 1955.

X.   <u>ARRANGEMENTS</u>

W281. <u>POLISH SONGS, OP. 74</u>, by Frederic Chopin.   (unpub-
      lished)
      See: B58

    Orchestrated by Ned Rorem, 1960.

    <u>Premiere</u>:

        1960 (Apr 18) New York City; Carnegie Hall; Alfred
        Zega, baritone; Ars Nova Orchestra.

XI.   <u>PLAYS</u>

W282. <u>THE PASTRY SHOP</u>. (unpublished)
      See: B201

    One-act play.
    Text and incidental music by Ned Rorem.
    Written and composed: 1970.

    <u>Premiere</u>:

1970 (June): New York City; The Extension Theatre.

W283. THE YOUNG AMONG THEMSELVES.   (unpublished)
 See: B201

 One-act play.
 Text and incidental music by Ned Rorem.
 Written and composed: 1970.

 Premiere:

1970 (June): New York City: The Extension Theatre.

XII.   BOOKS

W284. AN ABSOLUTE GIFT: A NEW DIARY.   New York: Simon and
 Schuster, 1978.
 See: B162, B268, B333, B336, B356, B378, B403, B705,
 B754

W285. CRITICAL AFFAIRS - A COMPOSER'S JOURNAL.   New York:
 George Braziller, 1970.
 See: B46, B48, B97, B145, B188, B505, B552

W286. THE FINAL DIARY, 1961-1972.   New York: Holt, Rinehart
 and Winston, 1974.
 See: B24, B92, B103, B290, B341, B361, B704, B707,
 B721; W287

W287. THE LATER DIARIES OF NED ROREM, 1961-1972.   San Francisco: North Point Press, 1983.
 See: B53, B164, B464, B671, B694; W286

 Originally published as The Final Diary, 1961-1972.

W288. MUSIC AND PEOPLE.   New York: George Braziller, 1968.
 See: B163, B171, B240, B287, B332, B344, B409, B504,
 B599, B723

W289. MUSIC FROM INSIDE OUT.   New York: George Braziller,
 1967.
 See: B1, B49, B155, B262, B301, B400, B557, B724

W290. THE NANTUCKET DIARY OF NED ROREM, 1973-1985.   San
 Francisco: North Point Press, 1987.
 See: B38, B122, B126, B149, B152, B408, B454, B500,
 B614, B696

W291. THE NEW YORK DIARY OF NED ROREM.   New York: George
 Braziller, 1967.
 See: B50, B100, B263, B508, B569, B725; W292

W292. THE PARIS AND NEW YORK DIARIES OF NED ROREM 1951-1961.
 San Francisco: North Point Press, 1983.
 See: B23, B32, B60, B279, B295, B464, B721; W291,
 W293

 Originally published separately as The Paris Diary
 of Ned Rorem and The New York Diary of Ned Rorem.

W293. THE PARIS DIARY OF NED ROREM. New York: George Bra-
        ziller, 1966.
        See: B175, B210, B278, B301, B327, B349, B549, B606;
        W292

W294. PAUL'S BLUES. New York: Red Ozier Press, 1984.
        See: W7, W38, W53

        Limited edition.
        Notes about Paul Goodman, with reproductions of the
        manuscripts of three songs by Ned Rorem on texts
        by Paul Goodman: Bawling Blues; Jail-Bait Blues;
        Near Closing Time.

W295. PURE CONTRAPTION: A COMPOSER'S ESSAYS.   New York:
        Holt, Rinehart and Winston, 1974.
        See: B52, B95, B611, B736

W296. SETTING THE TONE: ESSAYS AND A DIARY.   New York:
        Coward, McCann, 1983.
        See: B47, B60, B113, B134, B184, B279, B416, B446,
        B464, B488, B687, B693, B713, B721, B746

W297. SETTLING THE SCORE: Essays on Music.   New York;
        Harcourt Brace, 1988.

XIII. IN PREPARATION

W298. Choral work as yet untitled. (in preparation, 1988)

        Commissioned by the Gay Men's Chorus of New York.

W299. GOODBYE MY FANCY. (in preparation, 1988)

        Oratorio for mezzo-soprano, baritone, mixed chorus
        and orchestra.
        Text by Walt Whitman.
        Commissioned for the Chicago's Symphony's 100th
        anniversary 1990-1991.

W300. SOCIETY OF FRIENDS. (in preparation, 1988)

        Large orchestra and chorus.
        Commissioned by WCRB Radio, Boston; to be completed
        in 1991.

Publisher Directory

MUSIC PUBLISHERS

Associated Music Publishers
24 E. 22 St.
New York, NY 10010

Belwin Mills
15800 NW 48 Ave.
Miami, FL 33014

Boosey & Hawkes, Inc.
24 W. 57th St.
New York, NY 10019

Harold Branch Publishing Inc.
87 Eads St.
West Babylon, NY 11704

Elkan-Vogel Inc. (see Theodore Presser)

Hargail Music
P. O. Box 118
Saugerties, NY 12477

Henmar Press (see C. F. Peters)

Mercury Music Corp. (see Theodore Presser)

Peer-Southern Organization
1740 Broadway
New York, NY 10019

C. F. Peters Corp.
373 Park Ave., S.
New York, NY 10016

Theodore Presser Co.
Presser Place
Bryn Mawr, PA 19010

E. C. Schirmer Music Co.
138 Ipswich St.
Boston, MA   02215

BOOK PUBLISHERS

George Braziller
1 Park Avenue
New York, NY   10016

Coward McCann
51 Madison Ave.
New York, NY   10010

Harcourt Brace
1250 6th Avenue
San Diego, CA   92101

Holt, Rinehart, Winston
383 Madison Ave.
New York, NY   10017

North Point Press
P. O. 6275
Berkeley, CA   94706

Red Ozier Press
636 W. Washington
Madison, WI   53701

Simon and Schuster
1230 Avenue of the Americas
New York, NY   10020

Discography

This is a listing of commercially-produced recordings. The "See" references, e.g., See: B52 or D5, refer to citations found in the "Bibliography" or "Discography" sections.

D1. American Wind Symphony Orchestra SWS-106. 1986.

Contents: Sinfonia.
American Wind Symphony Orchestra; Robert Austin Boudreau, conductor.
Includes works by William Steffe, Colin McPhee, and Robert Russell Bennett.

D2. Boosey & Hawkes SNBH-5001. 1978.

Contents: Blessed Art Thou; Canticle of the Lamb; He Shall Rule from Sea to Sea; Lift Up Your Heads; Love Divine, All Loves Excelling; Virelai.
North Texas State University A Cappella Choir; Frank A. McKinley, conductor.
Album title: Binkerd/Rorem Works.

D3. Cambridge CRM-414/CRS-1416. 1964.

Contents: Two Psalms and a Proverb.
King's Chapel Choir of Boston; Cambridge Festival Strings; Daniel Pinkham, conductor.
Album title: 4 Contemporary Choral Works.
Includes works by Charles Wuorinen, Ulysses Kay, and William Flanagan.

D4. Columbia ML-5961/MS-6561. 1964.

Contents: The Call; A Christmas Carol; Cycle of Holy Songs; Early in the Morning; Echo's Song; Flight for Heaven (Upon Julia's Clothes; To the Willow Tree); I Am Rose; Lordly Hudson; Lullaby of the Woman of the Mountain; My Papa's Waltz; The Nightingale; O You

Whom I Often and Silently Come; Rain in Spring; Requiem; Root Cellar; Sally's Smile; See How They Love Me; The Silver Swan; Snake; Pippa's Song; In a Gondola; Song for a Girl; Spring; Spring and Fall; Such Beauty as Hurts to Behold; To You; Visits to St. Elizabeths; What If Some Little Pain; Youth, Day, Old Age, and Night.
Phyllis Curtin and Gianna d'Angelo, sopranos; Regina Sarfaty, mezzo-soprano; Charles Bressler, tenor; Donald Gramm, bass-baritone; Ned Rorem, piano.
Reissued in 1968 on Odyssey label, and in part, on New World Records label in 1978.
   See: B380, B445; D37, D40

D5.   Coronet LPS-3115. 1980?

Contents: Suite for Guitar.
Joseph Breznikar, guitar.
Album title: The Contemporary Classical Guitar.
Includes works by James Marshall, Abel Carlevaro, Francisco Mignone, and Guido Santorsola.

D6.   CRI 202. 1965.

Contents: Poems of Love and the Rain (Regina Sarfaty, mezzo-soprano; Ned Rorem, piano); Second Piano Sonata (Julius Katchen, piano).
2nd title is a reissue of the London/Decca recording, 1952.
   See: B82, B158, B384, B779

D7.   CRI 238 USD/CAS-238. 1969.

Contents: Some Trees; Little Elegy; Night Crow; The Tulip Tree; Look Down, Fair Moon; What Sparks and Wiry Cries; For Poulenc.
Phyllis Curtin, soprano; Beverly Wolff, contralto; Donald Gramm, bass-baritone; Ned Rorem, piano.
Includes work by David Ward-Steinman.
   See: B82, B386, B506

D8.   CRI 362 SD. 1977.

Contents: Book of Hours.
Ingrid Dingfelder, flute; Martine Geliot, harp.
Recorded March 2, 1976.
Album title: Ingrid Dingfelder Plays Flute Music.
Includes work by Bohuslav Martinu.
   See: B82, B170, B392, B744

D9.   CRI 394 SD. 1978.

Contents: Romeo and Juliet.
Ingrid Dingfelder, flute; Herbert Levine, guitar.
Includes works by Walter Piston and Jean Francaix.

D10.   CRI 396 SD. 1978.

Contents: A Quaker Reader.

Leonard Raver, organ.
Recorded June 7, 1978 on the Kuhn tracker organ; Alice
Tully Hall, Lincoln Center, New York City.

D11.   CRI 485 SD. 1983.

Contents: The Nantucket Songs (Phyllis Bryn-Julson,
soprano; Ned Rorem, piano); Women's Voices
(Katherine Ciesinski, mezzo-soprano; Ned Rorem,
piano).
Nantucket Songs recorded at the Library of Congress,
October, 1979; Women's Voices recorded in New York,
June 1982.
Album title: Vocal Music by Ned Rorem.
See: B173, B199, B360, B381, B669

D12.   CRI 533 SD. 1986.

Contents: Spiders.
Carole Terry, harpsichord.
Album title: 20th Century Harpsichord Works.
Includes works by Henry Cowell, Vincent Persichetti,
and William Albright.

D13.   CRI 6007 ACS. 1985.

Contents: Piano Sonata No. 2, (Julius Katchen, piano);
Nantucket Songs (Phyllis Bryn-Julson, soprano; Ned
Rorem, piano); Some Trees and other songs (Phyllis
Curtin, soprano; Beverly Wolff, mezzo-soprano;
Donald Gramm, bass-baritone; Ned Rorem, piano);
Romeo and Juliet (Ingrid Dingfelder, flute; Herbert
Levine, guitar).
Previously released on CRI 202; 485; 238; and 394.
Album title: Music of Ned Rorem.
See: D6, D7, D9, D11

D14.   Decca DL-101108/DL-710,108. 1965.

Contents: Lovers (selections).
Sylvia Marlowe, harpsichord; Ronald Roseman, oboe;
Alexander Kouguell, cello; Harold Farberman, percus-
sion.
Includes works by Elliott Carter, Henri Sauguet, and
Manuel de Falla.
See: B206; D46

D15.   Desto D-411-412/DST-6411-6412. 1964. 2 discs.

Contents: Visits to St. Elizabeths; Alleluia.
Mildred Miller, mezzo-soprano (1st work); Eleanor
Steber, soprano (2nd work); Edwin Biltcliffe, piano.
Album title: Songs of American Composers.
Includes works by David Diamond, Vincent Persichetti,
Otto Luening, Irving Fine, William Flanagan, Charles
Ives, Douglas Moore, Jack Beeson, John Edmunds, John
Alden Carpenter, Edward MacDowell, Theodore Chanler,
Aaron Copland, Robert Ward, John Gruen, Daniel Pink-
ham, Ben Weber, Henry Cowell, Ernst Bacon, Samuel

Barber, William Bergsma, Charles T. Griffes, John LaMontaine, and Virgil Thomson.
<u>See</u>: B82

D16.   Desto DC-6443. 1975.

Contents: <u>King Midas</u>.
Sandra Walker, mezzo-soprano; John Stewart, tenor; Ann Schein, piano.
Recorded April 29, 1975.
Includes work by Dominick Argento.
<u>See</u>: B82, B272

D17.   Desto DC-6462. 1968.

Contents: <u>Water Music</u>; <u>Ideas for Easy Orchestra</u>; <u>Trio for Flute, Cello and Piano</u>.
Thomas Halpin, violin and Larry London, clarinet (1st work); The Oakland Youth Orchestra; Robert Hughes, conductor (1st and 2nd works); New York Camerata (3rd work).
<u>See</u>: B82, B163, B385, B409

D18.   Desto DC-6480. 1969.

Contents: <u>Poems of Love and the Rain</u>; <u>Four Madrigals</u>; <u>From an Unknown Past</u>.
Beverly Wolff, mezzo-soprano, Ned Rorem, piano (1st work); Modern Madrigal Quartet (2nd and 3rd works).
<u>See</u>: B82, B386

D19.   Desto DC-7101. 1970.

Contents: <u>War Scenes</u> (Donald Gramm, bass-baritone; Eugene Istomin, piano); Five Songs: <u>As Adam Early in the Morning</u>; <u>O You Whom I Often and Silently Come</u>; <u>Look Down, Fair Moon</u>; <u>Gliding o'er All</u> (Donald Gramm, bass-baritone; Eugene Istomin, piano); <u>Four Dialogues for Two Voices and Two Pianos</u> (Anita Darian, soprano; John Stewart, tenor; Richard Cumming and Ned Rorem, pianos).
<u>See</u>: B82, B214, B388, B507, B648

D20.   Desto DC-7147. 1973.

Contents: <u>Ariel</u> (Phyllis Curtin, soprano; Joseph Rabbai, clarinet; Ryan Edwards, piano; <u>Gloria</u> (Phyllis Curtin, soprano; Helen Vanni, mezzo-soprano; Ned Rorem, piano).
<u>See</u>: B82, B169

D21.   Desto DC-7151. 1973.

Contents: <u>Day Music</u>.
Jaime Laredo, violin; Ruth Laredo, piano.
Includes work by Leon Kirchner.
<u>See</u>: B63, B667, B729, B739

D22.   Desto DC-7174.   1974.

Contents: <u>Night Music</u>.
Earl Carlyss, violin; Ann Schein, piano.
Recorded January 13, 1973.
Includes work by Benjamin Lees.
   <u>See</u>: B82

D23.   Duke University Press DWR-7306.   1974.

Contents: <u>A Christmas Carol</u>; <u>Guilt</u>; <u>For Susan</u>; <u>Clouds</u>;
   <u>What Sparks and Wiry Cries</u>.
Album title: <u>The Art Song in America</u>, Vol. 2.
Includes works by Vincent Persichetti, John Duke,
   Richard Cumming, Lester Trimble and Paul Earls.
   <u>See</u>: B82, B302

D24.   Epic BC-1262/LC-3862.   1963.

Contents: <u>Barcarolles</u>.
Leon Fleisher, piano.
Includes works by Aaron Copland, Roger Sessions and
   Leon Kirchner.

D25.   GAMUT UT-7501.   1980.

Contents: <u>Three Motets on Poems of Gerard Manley
   Hopkins</u> (O Deus, ego amo Te; Oratorio Patris Con-
   dren; Thee, God).
Choir of Trinity Church, Princeton, N.J.
Recorded in New College Chapel, Oxford, August 1980.
Album title: <u>Rejoice, Give Thanks and Sing</u>.
Includes works by Leo Sowerby, Alec Wyton, A. C. Fur-
   nivall, W. L. Dawson, Aaron Copland, L. H. Bristol,
   Jr., Charles Ives and R. Dirksen.
   <u>See</u>: B125, B438

D26.   Gothic D-87904.   1980.   2 discs.

Contents: <u>Quaker Reader</u> (selections).
Catharine Crozier, performing on the Kuhn tracker
   organ; Alice Tully Hall, Lincoln Center, New York
   City.
Album title: <u>Catharine Crozier in Recital</u>.
Includes works by J. S. Bach, Hugo Distler, Paul Hin-
   demith, Milos Sokola.
   <u>See</u>: B204, B368, B436, B689

D27.   Grenadilla GS-1031.   1980.

Contents: <u>Serenade on Five English Poems</u>.
Elaine Bonazzi, mezzo-soprano; The Cantilena Chamber
   Players.
Recorded at Rutgers Presbyterian Church, New York
   City, December 21, 1977 and March 6, 1978.
Includes work by Robert Starer.
   <u>See</u>: B393, B394, B670, B698

D28.   Grenadilla 1065 (cassette).   1982.

Contents: After Reading Shakespeare.
Sharon Robinson, cello.
Includes works by Claude Debussy and Gabriel Fauré.

D29.   GSS 104.   1984.

Contents: Alleluia; Two Poems of Edith Sitwell (The
Youth with the Red-Gold Hair; You the Young Rain-
bow); Root Cellar; Snake; The Serpent; Poems of
Tennyson (Ask Me No More; Now Sleeps the Crimson
Petal; Far, Far, Away); Conversation; Visits to St.
Elizabeths; Rain in Spring; For Susan; Such Beauty
as Hurts to Behold; Clouds; Sally's Smile; What
Sparks and Wiry Cries; The Lordly Hudson; The Night-
ingale; A Christmas Carol; Sometimes with one I
Love; O You Whom I Often and Silently Come; I Am
Rose; A Journey; Let's Take a Walk; See How They
Love Me; Early in the Morning.
Rosalind Rees, soprano; Ned Rorem, piano.
Recorded February-March, 1983 at the Episcopal Church
of the Holy Trinity, New York City.
Album title: Rosalind Rees Sings Ned Rorem.
   See: B383, B763

D30.   Leonarda LPI-116.   1983.

Contents: Last Poems of Wallace Stevens.
Rosalind Rees, soprano; Sharon Robinson, cello; Jerome
Lowenthal, piano.
Recorded at Holy Trinity Church, New York City, 1982.
Album title: Poems and Magic: Music by Ned Rorem and
Judith Lang Zaimont.
   See: B173, B382, B763

D31.   London LL-759.   1952?

Contents: Sonata for Piano, No. 2.
Julius Katchen, piano.
Includes work by Bartok.

D32.   Louisville L-57-5.   1959.

Contents: Design for Orchestra.
Louisville Orchestra; Robert Whitney, conductor.
Includes work by Bernard Reichel.
   See: B82

D33.   Louisville L-644/LS-644.   1964.

Contents: Eleven Studies for Eleven Players.
Members of the Louisville Orchestra.
Includes work by William Sydeman.
   See: B82

D34.   Louisville LS-733.   1974.

Contents: <u>Concerto in Six Movements for Piano</u>.
Jerome Lowenthal, piano; Louisville Orchestra; Jorge
    Mester, conductor.
Includes works by Thomas Briccetti and Paul Turok.
    <u>See</u>: B82, B703

D35.   Louisville LS-787.   1987.

Contents: <u>Air Music</u>; <u>Eagles</u>.
Louisville Orchestra; Peter Leonard, conductor (1st
    work); Gerhardt Zimmerman, conductor (2nd work).
Recorded in Macauley Theatre, Louisville, KY, May 30,
    1981 (1st work) and November 13, 1982 (2nd work).

D36.   Musique Circle 45567.   1978.

Contents: <u>Visits to St. Elizabeths</u>.
Judith Vaccaro, soprano; Jack Reidling, piano.
Recorded September 1978, Irving, CA.
Album title: <u>Caprice by Musique</u>.
Includes works by Jack Reidling, Alessandro Scarlatti,
    and Richard Cumming.

D37.   New World Records NW-229.   1978.

Contents: <u>Early in the Morning</u>; <u>I Am Rose</u>; <u>To You</u>;
    <u>Pippa's Song</u>; <u>Spring</u>; <u>Spring and Fall</u>; <u>Upon Julia's
    Clothes</u>; <u>To the Willow Tree</u>; <u>Lullaby of the Woman of
    the Mountain</u>; <u>Snake</u>; <u>Root Cellar</u>; <u>My Papa's Waltz</u>.
Phyllis Curtin and Gianna D'Angelo, sopranos; Regina
    Sarfaty, mezzo-soprano; Charles Bressler, tenor;
    Donald Gramm, bass-baritone; Ned Rorem, piano.
Recorded 1962-63 and previously released on Columbia
    ML-5961/JS-6561.
Album title: <u>Songs of Samuel Barber and Ned Rorem</u>.
    <u>See</u>: D4

D38.   New World Records NW-305.   1980.

Contents: <u>Mourning Scene</u>.
William Parker, baritone; Columbia String Quartet.
Recorded February 1, 1980.
Includes works by Charles Griffes, Lee Hoiby, Robert
    Evett, Ernst Bacon, and John Jacob Niles.
    <u>See</u>: B124, B304

D39.   New World Records NW-353.   1988.

Contents: <u>String Symphony</u>; <u>Sunday Morning</u>; <u>Eagles</u>.
The Atlanta Symphony Orchestra; Robert Shaw, conductor
    (in 1st work); Louis Lane, conductor (2nd and 3rd
    works).

D40.   Odyssey 32 16 0274.   1968.

Previously released on Columbia ML-5961/MS-6561, 1964.
Album title: <u>Ned Rorem Songs</u>.
    <u>See</u>: B163, B386; D4

D41.   Opus One 73. 1981?

        Contents: Piano Sonata, No. 1.
        Jeffrey Jacob, piano.
        Includes works by Samuel Adler and Roger Briggs.
        See: B462

D42.   Orion ORS-7268/OC-686.

        Contents: Lions.
        New Orleans Philharmonic-Symphony Orchestra; Werner
        Torkanowsky, conductor.
        Includes works by Carlisle Floyd, Alan Hovhaness, and
        Michael Colgrass.
        See: B730

D43.   Orion ORS-75205. 1975.

        Contents: Sing My Soul.
        King Chorale; Gordon King, director.
        Recorded at All Saints' Episcopal Church, Ft. Worth,
        TX.
        Album title: American Songs for A Cappella Choir.
        Includes works by Samuel Adler, Samuel Barber, Jean
        Berger, John Chorbajian, Michael Hennagin, Peter
        Mennin, Vincent Persichetti, Daniel Pinkham, Halsey
        Stevens, and Randall Thompson.
        See: B168, B345, B437

D44.   Orion ORS-84476. 1984.

        Contents: Two Poems of Theodore Roethke (Orchids; I
        Strolled across an Open Field).
        Theresa Treadway, mezzo-soprano; Marshall Williamson,
        piano.
        Recorded in Glen Falls, NY, December 1983.
        Album title: Blue Moods.
        Includes works by Timothy Cameron Lloyd, Jack Beeson,
        Thomas Pasatieri and Theresa Treadway.

D45.   Painted Smiles PS-1338. 1979.

        Contents: Miss Julie (highlights).
        Revised version; Judith James, soprano; Veronica
        August, mezzo-soprano; Ronald Madden, bass-baritone;
        New York Lyric Opera Company; Peter Leonard, conduc-
        tor; John Margulis, director.
        Recorded April 9-10, 1979.
        See: B174, B303, B372

D46.   Serenus SRS-12056. 1975.

        Contents: Lovers (selections).
        Previously released on Decca DL-101108/DL-710,108,
        1965.
        See: B82; D14

D47.   Turnabout TV S-34447. 1971.

Contents: Symphony No. 3.
Utah Symphony Orchestra; Maurice Abravanel, conductor.
Includes work by William Schuman.
  See: B62, B82, B209, B409, B728, B735

D48. Vox SVBX 5354. 1979. 3 discs.

Contents: Missa brevis.
Rosalind Rees, soprano; Priscilla Magdamo, alto;
  Thomas Bogdan, tenor; Lin Garber, bass-baritone;
  Gregg Smith Singers; Gregg Smith, conductor.
Recorded September-November 1975.
Album title: American Choral Music after 1950.
Includes works by Elliott Carter, Andrew Imbrie, Jacob
  Druckman, William Schuman, Michael Hennagin, Gregg
  Smith, William Mayer, Paul Chihara, William Bergsma,
  Carolyn Madison, Donald Waxman, Ronald Roxbury, Ed-
  mund Najera and Lou Harrison.
  See: B123, B371

D49. Westminster WGS-8239. 1973.

Contents: Trio for Flute, Violoncello and Piano.
Tipton Trio.
Previously released on Westminster WST-17147, 1968.
Album title: Contemporary Trios for Flute, Cello &
  Piano.
Includes works by Jean Michel Damase and Bohuslav
  Martinu
  See: D50

D50. Westminster WST-17147. 1968.

Contents: Trio for Flute, Violoncello and Piano.
Tipton Trio.
Album title: Twentieth Century Trios for Flute, Cello
  & Piano.
Includes works by Jean Michel Damase and Bohuslav
  Martinu.
  See: B386; D49

Bibliography

The "See" references, e.g., See: B52, W49, D57, refer to citations found in the "Bibliography," "Works," and "Discography" sections.

B1.   Adler, Samuel H. "Book Reviews." Review of Music from Inside Out, by Ned Rorem. Music Educators Journal 54 no. 2 (October 1967): 75-77.

"Well-written, easy to read, full of interesting musical tidbits and opinions for the musical layman. There are valuable observations for the musician and the music teacher as well, but this work in its chatty and offhand manner reads a bit too much like a superficial and uncomplicated exposition of the extremely complex and crucial problems facing composition in our age, specifically in the 1960's."
See: W289

B2.   "American Composer Update." Pan Pipes 72 no. 2 (1980): 40.

Contains information about 1979 premieres, performances, recordings, publications, and other news about Rorem compositions. Premieres and performances include: Miss Julie (revised); A Quaker Reader; and Sun. "Ned Rorem was inducted as a full member into the American Academy and Institute of Arts and Letters on May 16, 1979."
See: W115, W178, W189

B3.   _____. Pan Pipes 73 no. 2 (1981): 41.

Contains information about 1980 premieres, performances, recordings, publications, and other news about Ned Rorem. Premieres and performances include: Suite for Guitar; The Santa Fe Songs; Sunday Morning.
See: W110, W220, W242

B4.   _____. Pan Pipes 74 no. 2 (1982): 41.

Contains information about 1981 premieres, performances, recordings, and publications. Premieres and
performances include: After Reading Shakespeare; Give
All To Love; Back to Life; Winter Pages; Double Concerto for Cello and Piano (Remembering Tommy); and
Sunday Morning.
    See: W107, W132, W200, W223, W239, W242

B5.   _____. Pan Pipes 75 no. 2 (1983): 39.

Contains information about 1982 premieres, perfor-
mances, and recent publications. Premieres and per-
formances include: Remembering Tommy; After Long
Silence; Views From the Oldest House; Winter Pages;
Piano Concerto no. 3; Sun; The Santa Fe Songs; and
Lions.
    See: W105, W110, W115, W199, W223, W227, W233,
W239

B6.   _____. Pan Pipes 76 no. 2 (1984): 40.

Contains information about 1983 premieres, performances, recent publications, and recordings. Premieres and performances include: Three Calamus Poems;
Whitman Cantata; and the Third Piano Concerto.
    See: W86, W170, W227

B7.   _____. Pan Pipes 78 no. 2 (1986): 37.

Contains information about 1985 premieres, performances, and recent publications. Premieres and
performances include: An American Oratorio; Organ
Concerto; Violin Concerto; Scenes From Childhood;
Dances for Cello and Piano.
    See: W118, W204, W214, W234, W246

B8.   Anderson, Garland. "The Music of Ned Rorem." Music
Journal 21 no. 4 (April 1963): 34+.

Review of selected published music of Ned Rorem with a
listing of works published to date. Rorem "...has the
gift of writing effectively for the most challenging
of all instruments: the human voice."

B9.   Ansorge, Rick. "Modern Audience Enjoys Modern Music."
Omaha World Herald, May 23, 1986, p. 53.

Review of the May 22, 1986 performance of Rorem's
Organ Concerto during the Contemporary Music Festival
in Omaha. "The Organ Concerto is a gorgeous work...
the first movement was wonderfully dynamic...the second and third movements more subdued, especially the
sweet-tempered second, which evoked a dreamy, nostalgic mood...the fourth and final movement...featured an
organ cadenza written exclusively for foot pedals...a
truly astonishing evening."
    See: W234

B10.   _____.   "'Of Wind and Water' Is Well Received."   Omaha
        World Herald, May 21, 1986, p. 63.

        Review of the May 20, 1986 choral music concert of the
        Contemporary Music Festival.   In Time of Pestilence,
        "...a blend of 16th century madrigals and 20th century
        harmonies--was not an easy piece.   Making it doubly
        difficult was the fact that it was sung without in-
        strumental accompaniment.   Yet the Chamber Choir
        turned in a gorgeous performance of the piece..."
        See: W136

B11.   _____.   "Symphony, UNO Shine Limelight on Contemporary
        Music." Omaha World Herald, May 18, 1986, Entertain-
        ment section, p. 7.

        Background information on the 1986 Contemporary Music
        Festival, including a review of the performance of Ned
        Rorem's Organ Concerto, "...a terrific virtuosic dis-
        play."
        See: W234

B12.   _____.   "Visitor Speaks Up for Modern Composers."   Omaha
        World Herald, May 20, 1986, p. 13.

        Ned Rorem is interviewed on the occasion of the Omaha
        Symphony's Contemporary Music Festival at the Univer-
        sity of Nebraska at Omaha.   In discussing contemporary
        music, Rorem said, "'Music of the present is not even
        hated.   It's simply ignored...Contemporary audiences
        should hear contemporary music...'"

B13.   Anthony, Michael.   "Outspoken Composer-Writer Rorem
        Shotguns Pop and Computer Music."   Minneapolis Star
        and Tribune, April 26, 1985, sec. C, p. 1.

        Interview in which "...Rorem talked insightfully--and
        amusingly--on a flurry of subjects..." in anticipation
        of his visit to Minneapolis/St. Paul for the Twin Cit-
        ies Men's Chorus, April 28, 1985.

B14.   _____.   "Twin Cities Men's Chorus Has Rorem As Spring
        Concert Guest."   Minneapolis Star and Tribune, April
        30, 1985, sec. C, p. 4.

        Review of the April 28, 1985 Twin Cities Men's Chorus
        concert at Ordway Music Theatre.   Under the direction
        of Richard Weinberg, the group sang four of Rorem's
        early songs and the Whitman Cantata.
        See: W170

B15.   Apone, Carl.   "Composer Rorem Melds Love for Words,
        Music in Latest Oratorio."   The Pittsburgh Press,
        December 26, 1984, sec. C, p. 9+.

        Written in anticipation of the January 4, 1985 pre-
        miere of An American Oratorio.   The lengthy article
        contains biographical information and a summary of a

telephone interview in which Mr. Rorem discusses contemporary music; his works in progress; his life-style and his dual role as a composer and writer.
See: W118

B16.   _____ .   "Mendelssohn   Choir: Rorem   'An   American Oratorio.'"   High Fidelity/Musical America 35 no. 5 (May 1985): MA 22.

Review of the January 4, 1985 premiere of Ned Rorem's An American Oratorio.   "Rorem has achieved tender lyricism, dramatic contrasts, and a splendid blending of instrumental and vocal choirs."
See: W118

B17.   _____ .   "Rorem's 'Oratorio' a Disappointment."   The Pittsburgh Press, January 5, 1985, sec. B, p. 8.

Review of the January 4, 1985 premiere of An American Oratorio. A "...40 minute work which had much to commend it, but was largely a disappointment...There was certainly much to admire in Rorem's tender lyricism, dramatic contrasts, splendid blending of instrumental and vocal choirs, bleak and sad moods, explosive fortes...The scoring...was so heavy the inspiring and moving words in the text were largely unintelligible ...when it was over, the feeling was that Rorem's oratorio had promised more than it delivered."
See: W118

B18.   Ardoin, John.   "Alice Esty.......Soprano."   Musical America 80 (May 1960): 41.

Review of the April 3, 1960 Carnegie Recital Hall performance by Alice Esty, soprano, and David Stimer, piano.   The program included the premiere of Eight Poems by Theodore Roethke (I Strolled Across an Open Field; Memory; My Papa's Waltz; Night Crow; Orchids; Root Cellar; Snake; The Waking).   "To one accustomed to Mr. Rorem's usual freshness, these new songs came as a disappointment.   They seemed contrived and each seemed to harp too much on one persistent idea."
See: W47, W51, W54, W70, W75, W95, W97

B19.   _____ .   "America."   Opera 17 (January 1966): 31.

Review of the November 4, 1965 premiere of Miss Julie by the New York City Opera.   "...but in Rorem's static music and Elmslie's stilted libretto this prolonged duologue had no dramatic, or even theatrical, fibre. The opera, comparatively short by the clock, seemed interminable in the house...What a pity that this tenth Ford commission followed in the deadening, dreary footsteps of its predecessors!"
See: W178

B20.   _____ .   "American Song Program."   Musical America 80 (March 1960): 35.

Review of the February 8, 1960 Carnegie Recital Hall performance of works by William Flanagan, Ned Rorem, Aaron Copland, and Noel Lee. "Six songs of Ned Rorem's showed how far tonality can still go when guided by a fresh, distinctive talent. They revealed none of the cliches that often seem to go with the contemporary romantic temperament. Especially fine were 'Pippa's Song'...'A Christmas Carol' and 'Song for a Girl'..."
See: W11, W61, W79

B21.   ____. "Rorem-Flanagan Concert." Musical America 82 (May 1962): 37.

Review of the March 11, 1962 Carnegie Recital Hall performance of American songs, the fourth in the series presented by Ned Rorem and William Flanagan. Ned Rorem's King Midas was premiered by Veronica Taylor, soprano, David Lloyd, tenor, and Ned Rorem, piano. "Rorem's new song group King Midas...began with a dramatic statement...There were several fine songs which followed...but in general there was a pallid sameness which loosened Rorem's grasp on his audience."
See: W40

B22.   "Arts Academy Will Induct 14 New Members May 23." New York Times, April 5, 1979, section C, p. 11.

Announcement that 14 new members, including composer Ned Rorem, would be inducted into the American Academy and Institute of Arts and Letters.

B23.   Atwell, Lee. "In Search of Ned Rorem." Review of The Paris and New York Diaries of Ned Rorem by Ned Rorem. Gay Sunshine 17 (March/April 1973): 5-6.

Review of the 1970 reprint edition of The Paris Diary and The New York Diary. "...this scintillating, indeed cinematic, kaleidoscopic portrait is not only a painful record of auto-criticism, but also a selective index to the gay elite of literary and music circles in Paris and New York." Also includes some selections from the book.
See: W292

B24.   ____. "Ned's 'Dernier Cri.'" Review of The Final Diary by Ned Rorem. Gay Sunshine 25 (Summer 1975): 7.

Lengthy review of The Final Diary by Ned Rorem. His views on work, society and love are summarized by the reviewer in excerpts from the diary. This book "... covering the years 1961 to 1972, is not quite as vibrant as the earlier journals, but there is much here to hold the attention of a reader attuned to Rorem's social calendar."
See: W286

B25.   Austin, William. "Music Reviews." Notes (Music Library
        Association) 12 (September 1955): 650.

        Brief review of the score of Sicilienne for 2 pianos 4
        hands. "Rorem's gently swaying Siciliano might be the
        slow movement of another 'suite champetre.' The lyri-
        cal grace characteristic of Rorem's songs is sustained
        here..."
        See: W192

B26.   "Awards of the 1976 Year." Pan Pipes 69 no. 2 (1977): 8.

        Announcement that Ned Rorem was the recipient of the
        1976 Pulitzer Prize for his composition, Air Music.
        Some program notes and biographical material are in-
        cluded.
        See: W224

B27.   Ballou, Esther Williamson. "Music Reviews." Notes
        (Music Library Association) 9 (June 1952): 499.

        Review of the score of A Quiet Afternoon. "There is a
        certain tenderness and charm in this Rorem Suite, a
        facility in handling the material which becomes almost
        improvisatory at times...this lack of direction and
        shape, produce the impression that these pieces were
        written too casually...It lacks distinction and disci-
        pline."
        See: W190

B28.   Bals, Karen Elizabeth. "The American Piano Concerto in
        the Mid-twentieth Century." D.M.A. diss., University
        of Kansas, 1982.

        Includes an analysis of Concerto in Six Movements.
        See: W227

B29.   Bargreen, Melinda. "Ned Rorem Is Candid about His Life,
        Music." Seattle Times, March 25, 1984, sec. G, p. 1.

        Ned Rorem is interviewed prior to the March 25, 1984
        performance of the Whitman Cantata and four art songs
        for solo voice performed as unison choral pieces. In
        discussing his works, "Rorem says he feels 'like the
        Prodigal Son's brother' in light of the so-called 'new
        romanticism' in which...composers...have earned ex-
        tensive publicity by deserting atonality and returning
        to the world of the C-major scale. Rorem has been
        there all along. A gifted melodist, he ironically
        remarks: 'I'm not getting the attention the others are
        because I've written traditional tonal music all these
        years.'"
        See: W170

B30.   _____. "Resounding Success for Men's Chorus." Seattle
        Times, March 26, 1984, sec. D, p. 4.

        Review of the March 25, 1984 concert by the Seattle
        Men's Chorus at Meany Theater. Conducted by Dennis

Coleman with Ned Rorem as guest artist, the concert included Whitman Cantata and some solo songs performed in unison by the Chorus. Whitman Cantata "...is tuneful and accessible, both introspective and splashy, and it received a convincing performance last night."
See: W170

B31.   Barlow, Wayne.   "Solo Songs."   Notes (Music Library Association) 7 (March 1950): 313.

Review of the score of Alleluia by Ned Rorem.   "The music is organic and tightly put together with tertian and quartal harmonies over a driving accompaniment. The piece works up to a climactic ending, sung 'wildly.' The voice line is quite singable."
See: W2

B32.   Becker, Alida.   "Paperbacks." Review of The Paris and New York Diaries of Ned Rorem, 1951-1961, by Ned Rorem. Philadelphia Inquirer, August 21, 1983, sec. R, p. 4.

"Composer Rorem has also had a distinguished literary career, and these journals, originally published in the mid-'60s, blend his two worlds in a highly absorbing fashion, creating in the process a portrait of a talented, yet self-questioning, man, one whose honesty, candor and wit reveal a good deal not only about the artist but also the society in which he moves."
See: W292

B33.   "Before Brunch."   New York, NY: WNYC Radio.   1988. Sound recording cassette.

February 1988 interview of Ned Rorem by Nancy Shear for WNYC Radio's American Music Week. Mr. Rorem discusses his work as both composer and author.   Three works are played and discussed by the composer: Eleven Studies for Eleven Players; War Scenes; and Day Music.
See: W98, W205, W206

B34.   Belisle, John, ed. American Art-Song Anthology.   New York: Galaxy Music Corporation, 1982.

Contains: The Youth with the Red-Gold Hair.
See: W93

B35.   Belt, Byron.   "Music in the Churches."   Music (AGO) 7 no. 7 (July 1973): 20-23.

Report of the April 30-May 2, 1973 workshop presented by the American Cathedral Organists and Choir Masters Association.   "...Ned Rorem's 'In Christ There Is No East or West' could prove a splendid achievement with a bit of work. Some of the prosody is awkward in the extreme, but the lyric suitability to John Oxenham's text is worth salvaging with a bit of patient effort."
See: W128

B36. Berg, Christopher. "Pleasant Rorem Song Recital 'Clean
      and Clear.'" The New Mexican (Santa Fe, N.M.), July
      30, 1980, sec. B, p. 1.

      Review of the July 27, 1980 premiere of The Santa Fe
      Songs. "The moments of beauty in Rorem's music are
      most often moments which seem to breathe a life of
      their own, to be born at the moment."
      See: W110

B37. Berger, Arthur V. "Composers Forum." New York Herald
      Tribune, May 20, 1949, p. 15.

      Review of the May 19, 1949 Composers Forum concert of
      music by Leon Kirchner and Ned Rorem at McMillan The-
      ater, Columbia University. Included were Rorem's
      Penny Arcade; Mountain Song for Cello and Piano; and
      Sonata for Piano, Four Hands. Concerning Rorem's
      Penny Arcade sung by Nell Tangeman, mezzo-soprano:
      "The first and last songs of 'Penny Arcade' had in-
      triguing figures, with their own validity despite
      ancestry in Poulenc. But too much of Rorem's music
      was square in rhythm and phrase length, and without
      tension."
      See: W59, W187, W209

B38. Bernheimer, Martin. "Ned Rorem: Vindicating His Wicked
      Ways." Los Angeles Times, December 13, 1987, p. 73-74.

      Interview on the occasion of the publication of The
      Nantucket Diary; and a review of the book. The book
      "...offers more than 600 detailed pages of analytical
      profundity, analytical shallowness, churlish criti-
      cism, illuminating criticism, silly gossip, interest-
      ing gossip, narcissistic snobbery, petulant musing,
      elaborate name-dropping, increasingly guarded sexual
      revelation and assorted tales retold."
      See: W290

B39. Berry, Ray,   "Recitals and Concerts (First Perfor-
      mance)." American Organist 40 (April 1957): 26.

      Review of the February 15, 1957 premiere of The Poets'
      Requiem. "...it is also apparent that he is well on
      the way toward producing a compositional idiom dis-
      tinctly his own. Lyricism is his, and rhythmic drive
      --he handles voices graciously..."
      See: W151

B40. Bertsche, Sam. "'They Sang Superbly; Too Bad They Had
      No Voices.'"   Manhattan Mercury (Manhattan, KS),
      March 6, 1974. sec. A, p. 3.

      Review of the May 3, 1974 concert which featured the
      premiere of Ned Rorem's In Time of Pestilence. "At
      first hearing, it was neither overwhelming nor boring
      ...my fleeting first impression was that the first and
      last sections were the most interesting, though they

were not necessarily sung the best by the local
choir."
See: W136

B41.   Blau, Eleanor. "Three Composers Liken Secular to Sacred
Works." New York Times, April 14, 1973, p. 18.

Interviewed separately, composers Ned Rorem, Virgil
Thomson, and Richard Felciano agreed "...there was
virtually no difference between sacred and secular
music, apart from the resources of churches."   Mr.
Rorem continues, "'I set the Psalms of David and
chunks of the Bible not, for God's sake, because they
are religious, but because they are good poetry...'"
Concerning audience participation, Mr. Rorem says, "'I
would like audiences to like my music...but if they're
going to sing with their own wretched voices, I'd prefer to stay home.'"

B42.   Blomster, Wes. "Santa Fe Chamber Music Fest Is More
than a Footnote." Daily Camera (Boulder, CO), August
22, 1985, sec. B, p. 4.

Review of the 1985 Santa Fe Chamber Music Festival
season. There is brief mention that Ned Rorem was
artist-in-residence and his Septet: Scenes from Childhood was given its world premiere during the season.
See: W214

B43.   "Blood and Beds." Newsweek 66 (November 15, 1965): 108.

Review of the November 4, 1965 premiere of Miss Julie
by the New York City Opera. "Rorem goes down fight-
ing. His melodic line flows swiftly, from the atonal
to the tuneful, from nervous fragments to long arias,
duets and one especially lovely quartet which contrasts the loving simplicity of a passing peasant cou-
ple with the dark intricacies of the young noblewoman
and her valet."
See. W178

B44.   Bloomquist, Marvin Robert. "Songs of Ned Rorem: Aspects
of the Musical Settings of Songs in English for Solo
Voice and Piano." D.M.A. diss., University of Mis-
souri-Kansas City, 1970.

Analyses of over 100 songs published prior to 1969.

B45.   Boeringer, James L. "Carnegie Hall." Musical Courier
159 no. 7 (June 1959): 32.

Review of the April 18, 1959 premiere of Ned Rorem's
Symphony No. 3. "The impressions is of a work of ap-
peal, variety and considerable beauty."
See. W245

B46.   "Book Corner." Review of Critical Affairs: a Composer's
Journal, by Ned Rorem. Central Opera Service Bulletin
13 no. 5 (May-June 1971): 12.

"...the composer offers us essays and aphorisms containing his very personal thoughts on diverse subjects
ranging from his own and other composers' music...to
his view of various personalities."
See: W285

B47.   ____. Review of Setting the Tone: Essays and a Diary,
by Ned Rorem. Central Opera Service Bulletin 26 no. 1
(Fall/Winter 1984): 54.

Review of Setting the Tone: Essays and a Diary. "It
is as much his lively, individual style of writing as
the content itself that make Ned Rorem's books such a
pleasure to read...As in most of the previous Rorem
books of collected writings, this too is both entertaining and thought-provoking."
See: W296

B48.   "Book Reviews." Review of Critical Affairs: A Composer's Journal, by Ned Rorem. High Fidelity/Musical
America 20 no. 11 (November 1970): MA 32.

Brief review of Critical Affairs: A Composer's Journal. "A collection of articles on music and further
(reconstructed) extracts from Rorem's name-dropping
journal, the longest of which is an autumnal...de-
scription of his return to Paris..."
See: W285

B49.   ____. Review of Music from Inside Out, by Ned Rorem.
High Fidelity/Musical America 17 no. 7 (July 1967): MA
31.

Brief book review. "...this little collection of odds
and ends will not appreciably add to his stature...
Paradoxically, the writings on music of a practicing
composer read like the meanderings of music-struck
dilettante."
See: W289

B50.   ____. Review of The New York Diary, by Ned Rorem.
High Fidelity/Musical America 19 no. 1 (January 1968):
MA 32.

Brief review. "Continuing the fascinating saga of Our
Very Own Peter Pan in the wonderland of his friends
and acquaintances through the watering spots...of the
Western world."
See: W291

B51.   Botsford, Ward. "Detroit Symphony." High Fidelity/
Musical America 16 no. 1 (January 1966): 139.

Review of the October 28, 1965 Carnegie Hall concert
during the Festival of Visiting Orchestras. The
Detroit Symphony, conducted by Sixten Ehrling, premiered Ned Rorem's Lions. "...the piece has real
charm. A large orchestra is contrasted with a small

jazz combo seated to the left of the stage and the two fabrics are used in a manner of which Ravel would have approved."
See: W233

B52. Boundas, Louise Gooch. "Books Received" Review of Pure Contraption--A Composer's Essays, by Ned Rorem. Stereo Review 33 (August 1974): 16.

"Some of these pieces could qualify as 'essays,' I suppose, but the subtitle of Ned Rorem's latest collection is a little misleading. It's more of a notebook really...It is literate and informed and provocative..."
See: W295

B53. Boyd, Malcolm. "Book Reviews." Review of The Later Diaries of Ned Rorem, by Ned Rorem. Los Angeles Times, December 18, 1983, sec. B, p. 8.

"Rorem is candid, precise, and plays at being alive."
See: W287

B54. Breitner, Bina. "Istomin Brilliant at Keyboard." The Arizona Republic (Phoenix, AZ), November 18, 1969, p. 26.

Review of the November 17, 1969 performance of Lions. "Not only is it a melodious piece, but it is intelligently constructed and concise."
See: W233

B55. "Breznikar Premieres Rorem's Suite for Guitar." Guitar & Lute (October 1980): 35.

Brief review of the July 25, 1980 premiere of Suite for Guitar. "...commissioned under the auspices of the Cleveland Orchestra at Mr. Breznikar's suggestion, saying that Mr. Rorem was the composer that he would most like to see write a piece for the guitar."
See: W220

B56. "Briefly Noted." Omaha World Herald, August 10, 1986, p. 6.

Announcement of the schedule for broadcasting the interviews, discussions and performances of the May 1986 Contemporary Arts Festival held in Omaha. Ned Rorem's In Time of Pestilence was scheduled for August 17; the Organ Concerto and his discussion group for August 31.
See: W136, W234

B57. Briggs, John. "Alice Esty Is Heard in Program of Song." New York Times, April 4, 1960, p. 38.

Brief review of Alice Esty's concert at Carnegie Recital Hall, April 3, 1960, with David Stimer, piano.

Ned Rorem's settings of eight poems by Theodore Roethke were premiered.
<u>See</u>: W47, W51, W54, W70, W75, W95, W97

B58.   ____. "Ars Nova Orchestra at Carnegie Hall." <u>New York
Times</u>, April 19, 1960, p. 40.

Review of the April 18, 1960 Carnegie Hall concert.
"The evening's novelty was Mr. (Alfred) Zega singing
six of the seventeen <u>Polish Songs</u> from Chopin's Op.
74, as newly orchestrated by Ned Rorem...The performance...left no doubt of Mr. Rorem's skill in scoring
for orchestra..."
<u>See</u>: W281

B59.   ____. "Works of Rorem and Ned [sic] Flanagan Sung."
<u>New York Times</u>, February 25, 1959, p. 36.

Brief review of the February 24, 1959 Carnegie Recital
Hall concert of works by Ned Rorem and William Flana-
gan.   Jerold Siena, baritone, sang Rorem's <u>Mourning
Scene</u>; his <u>Cycle of Holy Songs</u> was sung by <u>Patricia</u>
Neway, soprano.
<u>See</u>: W15, W109

B60. Brinnin, John Malcolm.   "A Well-Tempered Ned Rorem."
Review of <u>Setting the Tone: Essays and a Diary</u> and <u>The
Paris and New York Diaries: 1951-1961</u>, by Ned Rorem.
<u>Washington Post Book World</u> (July 24, 1983): 4.

"We deal with a phenomenon--composer never far from a
keyboard who is also a writer seldom out of range of a
mirror.   The keyboard has been the source of sympho-
nies, operas, and scores of the most literate songs of
the century.   From the mirror have come reflections of
the writer's passage from the days in Paris when he
was 'Narcisse incarné' in an illustrious era of 'la
jeunesse dorée' to nowadays Nantucket where, 'eminence
grise malgré lui,' he casts a sage cool eye on the
musical scene and endures the Daumier-like pleasures
of domesticity."
<u>See</u>: W292, W296

B61. Brinson, Doris Parke.   "A Style Critical Study of the
Solo Organ Works of Ned Rorem." D.M.A. diss., Memphis
State University, 1988.

Comprehensive analyses and comparison of <u>A Quaker
Reader</u> and <u>Views from the Oldest House</u>.
<u>See</u>: W189, W199

B62. Brown, Royal S.   "Record Reviews."   <u>High Fidelity/Musi-
cal America</u> 22 no. 12 (December 1972): 104-105.

Review of Turnabout TVS 34447 recording. Ned Rorem's
<u>Symphony No. 3</u> is paired with William Schuman's <u>Sym-
phony No. 7</u>.   About <u>Symphony No. 3</u>: "...an innocuous
work that seems to reach for even greater heights than

the Schuman and gets maybe an nth degree as far."
See: D47

B63.   ____. "Record Reviews." High Fidelity/Musical America
23 no. 8 (August 1973): 86.

Review of Desto DC 7151 recording. Ned Rorem's Day
Music for violin and piano is paired with Leon Kirchner's Sonata Concertante. "...Day Music offers a
fascinating and sometimes dazzling display of instrumental gymnastics in which rhythmic and coloristic
effects are striking in their immediacy."
See: D21

B64.   Browning, Robert. "Ned Rorem: Volleys of Candor, In-
sight from Visiting Composer." Daily News (Whittier,
CA), December 9, 1981, p. 9+.

Interview on the occasion of the Whittier College
Quaker Festival, December 1981, during which Rorem was
present and A Quaker Reader was performed. Mr. Rorem
discusses a wide range of topics including art, composers, commissions, his Quaker heritage and his reasons for composing for organ.
See: W189

B65.   Campbell, Mary. "Leonard Bernstein's Busy Hands."
Philadelphia Inquirer, September 22, 1981, sec. A,
p. 12.

Brief mention that Ned Rorem lectured about Stravinsky
during the Haydn-Stravinsky Celebration by the Chamber
Music Society of Lincoln Center, September 18 and 20,
1981.

B66..   Campbell, R. M. "The Finely Tuned Sounds of Modern
'Santa Fe' Songs." Seattle Post Intelligencer, August
21, 1980, sec. E, p. 9.

Review of the Santa Fe Chamber Music Festival Concerts
at Meany Theater, Seattle, Washington. Performances
included Day Music (August 16, 1980), War Scenes
(August 18, 1980) and the Seattle premiere of Santa Fe
Songs (August 19, 1980). Day Music was described as
"...strong and convincing..." About the Santa Fe
Songs, the reviewer says, "More often than not, Rorem
has been successful in setting the poems...A few of
the songs will enter the lexicon of Rorem's best
works."
See: W98, W110, W205

B67.   Cariaga, Daniel. "Armenian State Choir in U.S. Debut."
Los Angeles Times, September 18, 1987, sec. 6, p. 5.

Review of the September 17, 1987 concert by the State
Choir of Armenia, conducted by Ovannes Tchekidjian.
The program included the world premiere of Ned Rorem's
Armenian Love Songs. "His suite of five songs...have
a bittersweet poignancy and a communicative thrust

that makes any additional written translation into English purely academic."
See: W120

B68.   _____. "Not for Pianists Only: Five Recent Books." Review of The Lives of the Piano, edited by James R. Gaines. Los Angeles Times, December 6, 1981, Calendar sec., p. 67.

Review of a book in which Ned Rorem contributed "... almost intimate reminiscences, titled 'Beyond Playing,' in which he recounts a full and stormy life at the piano, paying homage to many along the path but especially to his once teacher, the late composer Margaret Bonds."
See: B530

B69. "Carl Fischer Hall."   Musical Courier 151 no. 8 (June 1955): 50.

Review of the May 10, 1955 premiere of A Childhood Miracle.   Comparing Rorem's work with The Nightingale by Bernard Rogers which was on the same program, "The Rorem work too is cast in a mold of fantasy; it is more conservative and is perhaps more easily accessible on a single hearing."
See: W174

B70. Carman, Judith E., William K. Gaeddert, and Rita M. Resch.   Art-Song in the United States 1801-1976: an Annotated Bibliography.   n.p.: The National Association of Teachers of Singing, Inc., 1976.

Fifty-five songs by Ned Rorem are listed, with full descriptions of each.

B71. Carr, Jay. "East Lansing." Opera News 46 no. 15 (March 13, 1982): 32-33.

Review of the November 14, 1981 production of Four Dialogues. "The last section captured some mood, but possibilities for atmosphere were plowed under by the unsubtle, full-throttle singing of the principals, who also missed a lot of the pointedness of Frank O'Hara's text."
See: W27

B72. Carson, Leon. "Publishers' Mart." Musical Courier 153 no. 7 (May 1956): 37.

Review of the score of The Nightingale, by Ned Rorem. "A Charming, medium voice...song that ripples along in rapid tempo, and with delicate, supple air."
See: W55

B73. Cartwright, John. "New Works." Music Journal 22 no. 3 (March 1964): 117.

Brief review of the February 8, 1964 recital by Ellen
Faull, soprano. Included was the premiere of Rorem's
Poems of Tennyson.
    See: W28

B74.   _____. "Town Hall."   Music & Artists 1 no. 2 (1968):
        60.

Review of the April 2, 1968 Clarion Concert at Town
Hall.   A featured work was Ned Rorem's Water Music
which received its New York premiere. "The work is a
series of variations which add up to a rather large
scale piece."
    See: W247

B75.   Cerny, William. "Music Reviews." Notes (Music Library
        Association) 29 no. 4 (1973): 815-817.

Review of the scores of Sonata I, for piano and Sonata
III, for piano. "Both works promise a rewarding experience to performer and listener alike, since they
reflect a knowledge of the instrument's potentialities
and a willingness to utilize it toward realization of
undisguised lyricism and effective musical drama."
    See: W194, W195

B76.   Christy, Van A.   Foundations in Singing, 4th ed.   Du-
        buque: Wm. C. Brown Company, Publishers, 1979.

Contains: A Christmas Carol.
    See: W11

B77.   Chute, James. "Cincinnati Symphony: Rorem 'Double Con-
        certo.'"   High Fidelity/Musical America 32 (March
        1982): MA 24-26.

Review of the November 13, 1981 premiere of Remembering Tommy. "The work's emotional impact and immediate appeal should win supporters and help assure the
score a place within the contemporary orchestral repertoire."
    See: W239

B78.   _____. "Premiere Composers: Ned Rorem."   Cincinnati
        Post, November 12, 1981, sec. C, p. 1.

Interview with Rorem on the occasion of the November
13, 1981 premiere of Remembering Tommy. In addition
to comments about the work he dedicated to the memory
of Thomas Schippers, he also discusses the lack of
contemporary music in the programs of performers.
"'It's too bad that...artists think the only culture
that counts is the culture of the past.'"
    See: W239

B79.   Coe, Richard L. "Artists Put Fizz in White House Festi-
        val." Washington Post, June 20, 1965, sec. G, p. 1.

Brief mention of Ned Rorem as one of the participants
at the White House Festival of the Arts in June 1965.

B80.   Coelho, Miguel. "New Guitar Music & Books." Guitar Re-
        view (Fall 1982): 27.

        Review of the score of Suite for Guitar. "Rorem takes
        a neo-impressionist approach with emphasis on clarity
        of line and simplicity of structure."
        See: W220

B81.   Cohn, Arthur, Shirley Fleming, Russell Kerr, Igor Kip-
        nis, Ralph Lewando, and J. Roberton. "New York."
        Music Magazine 163 no. 12 (November 1961): 31-33.

        Mention of the New York premiere of Ned Rorem's Eleven
        Studies for Eleven Players in the October 12, 1961
        Concert of New American Music under the direction of
        Arnold Gamson.
        See: W206

B82.   Cohn, Arthur. Recorded Classical Music: a Critical
        Guide to Compositions and Performances. New York:
        Schirmer Books, 1981.

        Brief reviews of recordings listed by label number.
        Recordings of Ned Rorem's works include: Desto 6411/2,
        6443, 6462, 6480, 7101, 7147, 7174; CRI 202, 238, and
        362; Duke DWR 7306; Louisville LOU 57-5, 644, and 733;
        Serenus 12056; and Turnabout 34447.
        See: D6, D7, D8, D15, D16, D17, D18, D19, D20,
        D22, D23, D32, D33, D34, D46, D47

B83.   "Colleges of Mid-America to Premier Commissioned Choral
        Work in April." The School Musician Director and
        Teacher 45 (April 1974): 41.

        Announcement that Little Prayers was commissioned by
        Colleges of Mid-America, a ten college consortium.
        Dual premiers were scheduled for April 20, 1974 with
        the Sioux Falls Symphony, conducted by George Traut-
        wein; and April 21, 1974 with the Sioux City Symphony,
        conducted by Leo Kucinski.
        See: W141

B84.   "Composer, Poet to Visit Seton for Note-able Talk."
        Star-Ledger (Newark, NJ), November 9, 1976, p. 14.

        Preview of the 'Poetry in-the-Round' series at Seton
        Hall scheduled for November 10, 1976 when composer Ned
        Rorem and poet John Ashbery were scheduled to discuss
        'Setting Poetry to Music.'

B85.   "Composer Rorem Performs in NJFMC-MSC Concert." New
        Jersey Music & Arts (May 1969): 3.

        Written in anticipation of the all-Rorem concert given
        in the Recital Hall at Montclair State College, Upper
        Montclair, May 25, 1969. Included in the program: a
        selection of songs sung by Betty Allen, soprano, with
        the composer at the piano; From an Unknown Past, with
        Lois Winter, soprano, Helene Miles, contralto, Phillip

Olson, tenor, and Michael Stewart, bass; and Trio for Flute, Violoncello and Piano performed by the Trio de l'Academic.
See: W31, W222

B86.   "Composer Writes Song for KSU Choir." Manhattan Mercury (Manhattan, KS), March 3, 1974, sec. D, p. 4.

Written in anticipation of the March 3, 1974 premiere of In Time of Pestilence. The composer is interviewed and speaks of his dual role as composer and author. "Composing and writing can, at times, conflict. I have assumed that the two things express different sides of me but in actuality they don't."
See: W136

B87.   "Composers." Tempo 160 (March 1987): 61.

Brief announcement of the March 30, 1987 European premiere of End of Summer.
See: W207

B88.   _____. Tempo 164 (March 1988): 51.

Brief announcement of the January 28, 1988 premiere of The Death of Moses.
See: W125

B89.   "Composers Corner." Musical America 75 (July 1955): 29.

Brief announcement concerning the premiere of Design for Orchestra by the Louisville Orchestra, Robert Whitney, conductor.
See: W229

B90.   "Composers' Forum (Discussion between Morton Gould, Ned Rorem and Otto Luening)." Music & Artists 1 no. 2 (1968): 49-56.

Discussion covering a wide range of topics including modern trends in music, electronic music, computer music, and the audience reaction to these trends; collective composition; chance music; sentiment as an element in music; and the role critics play in the art of music.

B91.   "Composers' Symposium Set Next Week at UNM." Albuquerque Journal, April 5, 1973, sec. C, p. 3.

Written in anticipation of the University of New Mexico's Composers' Symposium in which Ned Rorem was a participant and the following works performed: Trio for Flute, Cello and Piano; Last Poems of Wallace Stevens; Night Music; and Poems of Love and the Rain.
See: W64, W108, W210, W222

B92.   Conarroe, Joel. "At His Best and Worst." Review of The Final Diary, by Ned Rorem. Philadelphia Evening Bulletin, December 29, 1974, sec. 2, p. 3.

"Like all personal journals, Rorem's shows man at his
finest and worst...the self-doubting and music-world
anecdotes can be informative, even liberating. This
is especially true if the book is read the way it was
written, a bit at a time--large chunks may induce psy-
chic indigestion."
See: W286

B93. Contemporary American Sacred Songs. New York: G. Schir-
      mer, 1985.

      Contains: A Song of David.
      See: W81

B94. "Contemporary Music: Observations from Those Who Create
      It." Music & Artists 5 no. 3 (1972): 11-23.

      Forum in which many individual composers give a brief
      opinion about the state of contemporary music. Ned
      Rorem says, "As things stand now, music appears in a
      state of redemption as 'an acceptable art.' The Wild
      has turned into Establishment."

B95. Cook, Bruce. "Literary Composer." Review of Pure Con-
      traption, by Ned Rorem. New Republic 170 (January 19,
      1974): 27-28.

      "What all this adds up to is that Ned Rorem is a
      writer who is worth reading simply on his own account
      ...He writes most often about music, but his subject
      is Ned Rorem...Given the variety of his mind, we can
      expect many more books as good as this from him."
      See: W295

B96. Cox, Ainslee, "Clarion Concerts." Music Journal 26 no.
      5 (May 1968) 58.

      Brief review of the Clarion Society's April 2, 1968
      concert featuring the New York premiere of Ned Rorem's
      Water Music. "...this listener found the piece one of
      the composer's most convincing works."
      See: W247

B97. _____. "The Journal Reviews." Review of Critical Af-
      fairs: A Composer's Journal, by Ned Rorem. Music
      Journal 28 no. 9 (October 1970): 58.

      Brief review of Critical Affairs: A Composer's Jour-
      nal, by Ned Rorem. "This reviewer would prefer to
      spend more time hearing Rorem and less time reading
      him."
      See: W285

B98. Croan, Robert J. "American Composer Named for Major
      Choral Work." Pittsburgh Post-Gazette, December 3,
      1982, p. 23.

      "American composer Ned Rorem has been commissioned to
      create a major choral work, to be premiered by the

Mendelssohn Choir of Pittsburgh with the Pittsburgh Symphony Orchestra in 1984." The work will be based on 19th-century American poems.
See: w118

B99. ____. "Pittsburgh Symphony: Rorem Premiere." High Fidelity/Musical America 21 no. 3. (March 1971): MA 26-27.

Review of the December 3, 1970 premiere of Ned Rorem's Concerto in Six Movements. Commissioned by the Aspen Music Foundation, "...the Rorem Concerto is an ingratiating work--eminently listenable, idiomatic for soloist and orchestra--a work that should find its niche in the repertory..."
See: W227

B100. Croyden, Margaret. "The Fashion of Peeping Toms." Review of The New York Diary, by Ned Rorem. The Nation 205 (November 27, 1967): 568-569.

A largely negative review of The New York Diary. "... it takes us into his narrow and sordid existence where instead of meeting the sophisticated composer and musician, we meet the narcissistic homosexual and alcoholic--the 'underground man,' living like a Baudelairean character in a kind of demimonde environment."
See: W291

B101. "Crozier Performs Definitive 'A Quaker Reader.'" The Daily News (Whittier, CA), December 8, 1981, p. 6.

Review of the performance of A Quaker Reader at Whittier College's Quaker Festival. "...a definitive performance of a superlative work..."
See: W189

B102. Crutchfield, Will. "Choir from Armenia at Avery Fisher Hall." New York Times, October 5, 1987, sec. C, p. 20.

Review of the October 3, 1987 concert by the State Choir of Armenia at Avery Fisher Hall. The Armenian Love Songs were included in the program.
See: W120

B103. Cumming, Robert. "Books." Review of The Final Diary, by Ned Rorem. Music Journal 33 no. 3 (March 1975): 22.

Brief review of The Final Diary. "...this major composer's unorthodox diary...is predictably naughty, controversial, perceptive and charming."
See: W286

B104. Cunningham, Carl. "Music: American Songs." Houston Post, July 31, 1982, sec. E, p. 2.

Review of the July 29, 1982 Santa Fe Chamber Music Festival concert of American songs by Ives, Foster, and Rorem. "A dozen songs by Rorem, garrulous to sensuous in mood and subject matter, offered the capacity audience a wonderful sampling of his compositional art. Though frequently dissonant and tonally vague, Rorem's vocal lines and keyboard accompaniments are often admirably adapted to the poetic images in his chosen texts."

B105. Davis, Deborah Louise Bodwin. "The Choral Works of Ned Rorem." Ph.D. diss., Michigan State University, 1978.

Analyses of Rorem's choral works to determine style periods.

B106. _____. "An Interview About Choral Music With Ned Rorem." Musical Quarterly 68 no. 3 (1982): 390-397.

Lengthy interview of Ned Rorem by Deborah Davis in which the general aspects of Ned Rorem's choral compositions are discussed. Topics include his choice of poetry; his views on analyzing his works; his choral style and tonality; and possible influences on his choral compositions.

B107. Davis, Peter G. "Golden Fleece in 3 Operas." New York Times, April 3, 1978, sec. C, p. 22.

Review of the April 1, 1978 Golden Fleece performance of Three Sisters Who Are Not Sisters. "Mr. Rorem's 35-minute opera...accomplishes precisely what it sets out to do with wit, economy and musical sophistication."
    See: W180

B108. _____. "In Tribute." New York 17 (March 12, 1984): 88-89.

Review of the memorial concert for Paul Jacobs at Symphony Space. "...it was coincidental, but very appropriate, that the few spoken remarks during the course of the evening came from three composers: Elliott Carter, Ned Rorem, and William Bolcom."

B109. _____. "Jersey Ensembles Offer Rorem Works." New York Times, March 22, 1971, p. 41.

Review of the March 21, 1971 choral concert of Ned Rorem's works. Included were Three Incantations From a Marionette Tale; From an Unknown Past; and Letters From Paris. Concerning the latter: "Both writer and composer entertain a great affection for Paris, and their combined nostalgia, gentle wit and elegantly lucid styles made a particularly winning marriage of words and music. It is certainly one of Mr. Rorem's most lovable efforts."
    See: W87, W130, W138

B110. _____. "'Miss Julie' by Ned Rorem Is Revived by Lyric Opera." New York Times, April 7, 1979, p. 14.

Review of the April 5, 1979 performance of the revised
Miss Julie by the New York Lyric Opera. "As sheer
music, the score is exceptionally well crafted and
often of unusual beauty."
See: W178

B111. _____. "N.Y. Philharmonic: Premieres." High Fidelity/
Musical America 17 no. 9 (September 1967): MA 7+.

Review of the July 1, 1967 premiere performance of Ned
Rorem's Sun. "...part of the work's seductive
strength lies in its rich poetical variety and Rorem's
very intense response to each poem...All in all a
blinding jewel---beautiful, fascinating, and totally
heartless."
See: W115

B112. _____. "Rorem's Song Forms Laurel for Stevens." New
York Times, November 15, 1972, p. 38.

Review of the November 13, 1972 premiere of The Last
Poems of Wallace Stevens. Mr. Rorem has achieved
"...a smooth blend of thematic unity and textural
variety by alternating, dovetailing and juxtaposing
the voice, piano and cello."
See: W108

B113. _____. "Shameless Romantics." New York 16 (November
21, 1983): 72-75.

Written on the occasion of Ned Rorem's birthday, the
author compares Rorem's method of composition with his
method of writing. "It seems to me that the ways in
which Rorem uses words and notes have many striking
parallels. The extended essays and compositions are
both usually built from related epigrammatic state-
ments or a sequence of pithy aperçus rather than a
methodically reasoned, step-by-step development of
ideas...Read any one of Rorem's recent articles in
Setting the Tone and you will find the same kind of
organizational focus and clarity, as well as the same
restless mental energy and impatience with smug or
easy solutions."
See: W296

B114. _____. "Short Operas: 2 by Golden Fleece." New York
Times, March 2, 1981, sec. C, p. 18.

Brief review of the New York premiere of Bertha, February 27, 1981 by the Golden Fleece Ltd. "Mr. Rorem's
elegant music flows along amiably enough, but it seems
to exist in an utter dramatic vacuum."
See: W172

B115. "Debuts & Reappearances." High Fidelity/Musical America
26 no. 4 (April 1976): 33.

Review of the December 11, 1975 premiere of Air Music.

"...Rorem molds every detail of pitch and rhythm into a coherent and durable musical structure, not a string of effects."
See: W224

B116. DeRhen, Andrew. "Fennimore: Hear America First." High Fidelity/Musical America 24 no. 1 (January 1974): MA 22-23.

Hear America First concert, October 3, 1973 celebrating Ned Rorem's fiftieth birthday, when a selection of his songs were performed. Specifically mentioned were: I Am Rose; Snake; Visits to Saint Elizabeths; and Hearing.
See: W33, W34, W75, W96

B117. _____. "Leonard Raver, Organ." High Fidelity/Musical America 27 no. 5 (May 1977): MA 25.

Review of the premiere of A Quaker Reader. "...the pervasive spirituality of the music imposes upon it a strong sense of stylistic unity."
See: W189

B118. _____. "Santa Fe Festival: Rorem's 'The Santa Fe Songs.'" High Fidelity/Musical America, 30 (December 1980): MA 17-18.

Review of the August 25, 1980 New York premiere of The Santa Fe Songs. "The music's most successful moments occur when Rorem exploits the rich potential of the unusual scoring."
See: W110

B119. de Schauensee, Max. "Philadelphians Cheer Rostropovich." Musical America 79 (December 1, 1959): 6-7.

Brief review of the October 23, 1959 premiere of Eagles. "Imperial in its feeling like the birds it depicted, Rorem's music was filled with dramatic turbulence and scored a solid success."
See: W230

B120. DeVine, George F. "Music Reviews." Notes (Music Library Association) 27 no. 1 (1970): 164.

Review of the score of Four Songs, for medium-high voice and piano. "To commend these songs as 'breather' material for a recital would be to speak slightingly of them, yet they do not make unreasonable demands upon the performer so long as he is a sensitive musician."
See: W29

B121. Diether, Jack. "A Language of the Subconscious?" American Record Guide 28 (September 1961): 12-13+.

"Is music really an abstract art, as Ned Rorem says,

or is it--A Language of the Subconscious?" A rebuttal
of "...Ned Rorem's stimulating essay, 'Pictures and
Pieces,' which appeared...in the July issue."
      See: B605

B122. Dirda, Michael. "Ned Rorem and the Music of Time." Re-
      view of The Nantucket Diary of Ned Rorem: 1973-1985,
      by Ned Rorem. Washington Post Book World (October 25,
      1987): 5.

      "In these later diaries Ned Rorem deservedly joins the
      great band of American introspectives, those obsessed
      observers of the soul...The reflections at times grow
      abstract and philosophical, but one expects wisdom
      from the old. For Ned Rorem is--in his sixties...
      Rorem now paints most feelingly a picture of domestic
      contentment in his Nantucket house, working, reading,
      visiting friends. This, it would seem, remains his
      final refuge. That and his music. And this diary."
      See: W290

B123. Ditsky. John. "Classical Hall of Fame." Fanfare (Sep-
      tember-October 1979): 164-165.

      Review of Vox Box SVBX 5354 recording of Missa brevis.
      "A pure clear curve in air is achieved in Ned Rorem's
      Missa brevis, where soloists lead the Singers in il-
      lustrating what may be referred to as Rorem's hark-
      ening back to his days in France; arguably, in fact,
      the influence of Poulenc may be felt."
      See: D48

B124.   _____. "Classical Hall of Fame."   Fanfare (January-
      February 1981): 216.

      Review of New World Records 305 recording of Mourning
      Scene. "The Rorem Scene is...well within the qualita-
      tive range of his early songs, and well worth attend-
      ing to."
      See: D38

B125.   _____. "Rejoice! Give Thanks and Sing--Music by Twenti-
      eth Century American Composers." Fanfare (September-
      October 1981): 223.

      Review of Gamut UT 7501 recording which includes Three
      Motets on Poems of Gerard Manley Hopkins.
      See: D25

B126. Dlugos, Tim. "Stopping Time." Review of The Nantucket
      Diary of Ned Rorem, 1973-1985, by Ned Rorem. Chris-
      topher Street 117 (November 1987): 60-61.

      "...in its sheer accumulation of things loved, things
      hated, and things lived through, The Nantucket Diary
      is a brilliant record of a remarkable sensibility pre-
      serving its creatures moment by moment."
      See: W290

B127. "Donald Gramm Sings." <u>New York Times</u>, January 28, 1956, p. 11.

Review of the January 27, 1956 Town Hall recital. <u>Another Sleep</u> was given its first United States premiere.
<u>See</u>: W5

B128. Dorian, Frederick. "Program Notes." <u>The Pittsburgh Symphony Orchestra Program Magazine</u> (December 3, 1970): 371-381.

Program notes from the December 3, 1970 premiere of <u>Concerto in Six Movements</u>.
<u>See</u>: W227

B129. Driver, Paul. "Gay Men's Chorus in 'Whitman Cantata.'" <u>Boston Globe</u>, May 2, 1984, p. 75.

Review of the April 29, 1984 concert of Rorem's <u>Whitman Cantata</u>. "The settings are striking without being instantaneously attractive."
<u>See</u>: W170

B130. _____. "Rorem's Works Heard at BU." <u>Boston Globe</u>, April 6, 1984, p. 63.

Review of the April 4, 1984 Encounters with Composers recital which featured Ned Rorem's <u>War Scenes</u>; <u>The Nantucket Songs</u>; <u>Last Poems of Wallace Stevens</u>; and <u>Trio for Flute, Cello and Piano</u>.
<u>See</u>: W52, W98, W108, W222

B131. Drobatschewsky, Dimitri. "Santa Fe Becomes Music Lovers' Mecca As Opera, Chamber Music Festivals Open." <u>The Arizona Republic</u> (Phoenix, AZ), June 30, 1985, sec. F, p. 1+.

Written in anticipation of the 1985 Santa Fe Opera and Chamber Music season. "Rorem will lead various discussions and rehearsals and present his latest work, <u>Scenes from Childhood</u>, commissioned for the occasion."
<u>See</u>: W214

B132. Dunning, William. "Chamber Festival to Unveil Composer's Childhood." <u>The New Mexican</u> (Santa Fe, NM), August 2, 1985, p. 4.

Written in anticipation of the August 11, 1985 premiere of <u>Septet: Scenes from Childhood</u>, during which the composer was present. "As we listen to Ned Rorem in Santa Fe, the composer and the performer united, we can form not only a standard for judging others' performances of his music, but of music in the modern world..." The <u>Santa Fe Songs</u> were also performed.
<u>See</u>: W110, W214

B133. _____. "Festival to Premiere Rorem Composition." <u>The</u>

New Mexican (Santa Fe, N.M.), August 11, 1985, sec. B, p. 3.

Review of the August 10, 1985 rehearsal for the world premiere of Ned Rorem's Scenes from Childhood at the Santa Fe Chamber Music Festival. "This entire piece is a sequel, the composer explained, to his...Winter Pages...This work similarly sketched images from his past."
See: W214

B134. Dyer, Richard. "Art and Artists on His Mind." Review of Setting the Tone: Essays and a Diary, by Ned Rorem. Boston Globe, June 21, 1983, p. 45.

"Rorem's new book is an addictive miscellany of gossip, memory, appreciation, put-down, and aperçu."
See: W296

B135. _____. "Dazzling Variety from King's Singers." Boston Globe, October 29, 1985, p. 39.

Review of the October 27, 1985 concert which included Pilgrim Strangers. "...it becomes apparent that there is Quaker strength in Rorem's work, rooted in the contours of folk song, and that he has caught the music in Whitman's words and the swell of feeling behind them."
See: W150

B136. _____. "How Rorem Composed for the King's Singers." Boston Globe, October 25, 1985, p. 64.

Rorem relates the circumstances surrounding the composition of Pilgrim Strangers and the first time it was sung for him by the King's Singers.
See: W150

B137. _____. "Ned Rorem Tells All." Boston Globe, September 30, 1984, magazine sec., p. 15-34+.

"At home on Nantucket, the composer and diarist reflects on music, writing, and an extraordinary life."

B138. _____. "A Rorem Premiere at Santa Fe Festival." Boston Globe, July 30, 1982, p. 25.

Review of the premiere of Winter Pages. "'Winter Pages' is a kind of diary, and, like Rorem's famous and notoriously candid prose diaries, it veers between serious thought and discussion and offhanded remark, between anecdotal reminiscence and cries from the heart."
See: W223

B139. _____. "Theater, Music and Other Arts Enhance Vistas of Santa Fe." Boston Globe, August 15, 1982, sec. A, p. 15.

A brief history of the performing arts in Santa Fe coupled with the program for 1982. At the National Symposium of Critics and Composers, Ned Rorem "...delivered an elegant and animated discourse entitled '13 Ways of Looking at a Critic,' most of them unflattering; the only real criticism of music, he argued, lies in the music itself."

B140. Emerson, Gordon. "On Razor's Edge with Ned Rorem." New Haven Register, October 23, 1983, sec. 3, p. 1.

Interview in anticipation of Ned Rorem's October 24-25, 1983 visit to the Yale campus and the performance of Lions by the New Haven Symphony, October 25. He says, "'I really feel fortunate that I have what a lot of people never have. I've won major prizes, I make a living as a composer--which is very unusual in America--and I'm appreciated pretty much for what I like best to do. I write exactly what I want to write with no compromises and it gets played. And my books get published.'" He comments on critics, "'I still don't know what a critic accomplishes or what critics themselves think they're accomplishing. My feeling is that a critic should tell exactly what he thinks, but if he feels a piece is bad he should say it with sadness rather than relish.'"
See: W233

B141. Epstein, Benjamin. "Pianist Reymond Berney at Caltech." Los Angeles Times, February 7, 1984, sec. 6, p. 2.

Review of the February 4, 1984 recital. Included were Eight Etudes for Piano, "...studies exploring a range from muted motionlessness to furious convulsive contrary motion."
See: W185

B142. Ericson, Raymond. "Concert: Disciplined North Carolina Symphony Comes to Town." New York Times, March 12, 1977, p. 14.

Review of the March 9, 1977 New York premiere of Assembly and Fall. "It is, like much of Mr. Rorem's music, romantic in conception, listenable, but so busy in its workmanship as to sound overdrawn."
See: W225

B143. _____. "Music: Utah Visitors." New York Times, June 4, 1971, p. 20.

Review of the June 2, 1971 Carnegie Hall concert by the Utah Symphony Orchestra. Included on the program was Rorem's Symphony No. 3.
See: W143

B144. _____. "Rorem, Rogers Works." Musical America 75 (June 1955): 13-14.

Review of the May 10, 1955 premiere of Ned Rorem's A

Childhood Miracle. "This wispy fantasy is clothed in a delicate, atmospheric score...Rorem writes effectively for voices, providing sensitive settings for English texts...Certainly, it is one of the best new operas to be heard in this area for some time."
See: W174

B145. Erwin, John W. "Book Reviews." Review of Critical Affairs: A Composer's Journal, by Ned Rorem. Notes (Music Library Association) 27 no. 3 (1971): 475-476.

"Although the fragmentary, aphoristic quality of each of Rorem's printed utterances may eventually prove tiresome, the urgency of his cry for attention to art in the contemporary wilderness of hysterical social consciousness is to be respected."
See: W285

B146. "Faculty Recital at UNO Focuses on Europe, America." Omaha World-Herald, January 12, 1986, Entertainment sec., p. 3.

Written in anticipation of the January 19, 1986 recital by Margaret Hemmen, mezzo-soprano, in Strauss Performing Arts Center on the University of Nebraska at Omaha campus. Included in the program were Early In the Morning; and O You Whom I Often and Silently Come.
See: W18, W57

B147. Farrell, Peter. "Music Reviews." Notes (Music Library Association) 42 no. 1 (1985): 155.

Brief review of the score of After Reading Shakespeare. "...this music springs directly from human experience or emotion. A kind of song cycle for solo cello, each song is perfectly conceived for the instruments."
See: W200

B148. "Featuring Ned Rorem in Composers' Concert." New Jersey Music & Arts (November 1969): 3.

Written in anticipation of the November 9, 1969 concert of the American Composers Series at the New Jersey State Museum, Trenton, N.J. Included in the program were Madrigals; Trio for Flute, Violoncello and Piano; and an unnamed cycle of songs.
See: W129, W222

B149. Feeney, Joan. "Books." Review of the Nantucket Diary of Ned Rorem: 1973-1985, by Ned Rorem. New York Times, November 1, 1987, sec. 7, p. 25.

"The intimacies recounted here are those of daily life, the entries often repeat themselves. The author's subjects are, for the most part, disarmingly benign: work, his sweet tooth, friends and his elderly

parents, about whom some of the most affecting passages in the book are written."
See: W290

B150. Felton, James. "'Andiamo, Ragazzi' vs. 'Let's Go, Fellows.'" <u>Philadelphia Evening Bulletin</u>, May 18, 1975, sec. 5, p. 2.

Discussion on the advantages of opera in English. Ned Rorem is quoted as saying, "We haven't printed the texts of the songs. I think you'll understand the singers. And it's ghastly to hear everyone turning mimeographed pages at the same time, trying to follow words when the singers are really presenting them with their personalities as well as their voices."

B151. _____. "Rorem Shows the Way." <u>Philadelphia Evening Bulletin</u>, May 13, 1975, p. 50.

Brief review of the May 11, 1975 Philadelphia concert of Rorem songs. "And if the piano parts are complex and independent in themselves--who can possibly play them with his own commanding touch? --the vocal parts let the language fall gracefully and clearly on the ear..."

B152. Finn, Robert. "Elegant Spite Is Rorem Theme Song." Review of <u>The Nantucket Diary of Ned Rorem, 1973-1985</u>, by Ned Rorem. <u>Cleveland Plain Dealer</u>, January 20, 1988.

"...the New York musical scene is thoroughly surveyed with Rorem's highly personal blend of jewel-like literary precision and elegant spite."
See: W290

B153. _____. "Orchestra Returns." <u>Cleveland Plain Dealer</u>, March 14, 1986, Magazine sec., p. 6.

Review of the March 13, 1986 concert which included <u>An American Oratorio</u>. "Anything Ned Rorem writes, especially if it has voices in it, is worth serious attention...he writes for the voice sometimes a little complexly, perhaps, but always with sympathy and a sense of flowing, lyric line..."
See: W118

B154. Fitzpatrick, Jim. "Rorem's Motive in Making Music? Money!" <u>Salt Lake Tribune</u> (Utah), March 23, 1967.

Interview in which Ned Rorem discusses the motivation and inspiration of composers and the methods they employ in subsidizing their work. "The artist...has an overweening ego so that, in society, he is in need of constant reassurance about himself and this comes, in our present day and age, in the form of money...The vast majority resort to...composing for television, movies or the theater; become a teacher or performer,

or obtaining fellowships from various foundations."
Brief biographical information is included.

B155. _____. "U.'s Ned Rorem Writes It All Down." Review of
Music From Inside Out, by Ned Rorem. Salt Lake Tribune (Utah), March 23, 1967.

"One of the most stimulating personalities on the Utah
musical scene for the past two years has been Ned
Rorem, the composer-in-residence at the University of
Utah...Last week, Mr. Rorem's second book, 'Music From
Inside Out,' was published...and it is trenchant, un-
derstanding and very well written."
See: W289

B156. _____. "Utah Orchestra, Dancers Impressive: Composer
Gives Views." Salt Lake Tribune (Utah), February 19,
1967.

Ned Rorem is quoted about his opinions concerning the
musical scene at the University of Utah and the Salt
Lake City environs.

B157. Flanagan, William. "Music Reviews." Notes (Music
Library Association) 8 (September 1951): 753.

Brief review of the score of Requiem. "...a poem of
Robert Louis Stevenson, has been given a setting with
the characteristic qualities of its composer, Ned
Rorem: the song is performable, musical, nostalgic and
rather facile."
See: W67

B158. _____. "Reviews of Records." Musical Quarterly 52 no.
4 (1966): 535-537.

Review of CRI-202 recording of Ned Rorem's Poems of
Love and the Rain with Regina Sarfaty, mezzo-soprano,
Ned Rorem, piano; and Second Piano Sonata with Julius
Katchen, piano. "The simplistic musicality of his
Piano Sonata (1949) shows no reflection whatever of
the 'progressive' neo-Classicism that was the dernier
cri of the period; and his Poems of Love and the Rain
(1963) were composed in evidently blissful disregard
of the current twelve-tone revival. But listen to
these two works chronologically and you will observe
that Rorem has carried his popularist Franco-American
stylistic sources to a point of considerable personal
refinement and sensibility."
See: D6

B159. Fleming, Shirley. "When This You See..." High Fideli-
ty/Musical America 21 no. 11 (November 1971): MA
10-11.

Review of the July 31, 1971 performance of Three Sisters Who Are Not Sisters. "The music by Ned Rorem
never lost its breath during a breathless child game

of multiple murders..."
See: W180

B160. Floyd, Jerry. "Reports: Vienna, VA." Opera News 49 no.
9 (January 19, 1985): 39-40.

Review of the October 13, 1984 performances of three
of Ned Rorem's short operas. Concerning Three Sisters
Who Are Not Sisters: "Soprano Elizabeth Kirkpatrick
compensated for her wide vibrato with a wicked under-
playing of the most murderous member of a group of
orphans." Concerning Fables: "...most of the singing
was unintelligible, the point of the various animal
tales remained largely unmade." Concerning Bertha:
"...the last proved the most successful, Thanks to Ann
Fox Conrad's combative Norwegian queen who gives away
her kingdom...Conrad's Valkyrie-sized physique and
deadpan comic timing were just right."
See: W172, W175, W180

B161. 4 Short Piano Pieces: by Ned Rorem, Joseph Maneri, Berge
Kalajian, Angelo Musolino. Plainview, NY; H. Branch
Publishing Co., 1976.

Contains: Slow Waltz.
See: W193

B162. Frankel, Melvin. "Diary of a Gay Guru." Review of An
Absolute Gift by Ned Rorem. Gay Community News, October 7, 1978, p. 14.

"Using the mask of Sophisticated Critic, Rorem discusses composers, gays, writers and movie makers, and
explores what he calls the 'perversity' of all art."
See: W284

B163. Frankenstein, Alfred. "Composer, Critic, and Racon-
teur--Ned Rorem Marks a Milestone." High Fidelity/
Musical America 18 no. 11 (November 1968): 88+.

Reviews of Ned Rorem's fourth book, Music and People
and two recordings: Odyssey 32 16 0274 and Desto DC
6462. Concerning Music and People, "...the best thing
in it is the long seventh interlude, a detailed,
high-spirited, and hair-raising account of what it's
like to compose and present an opera in America..."
The Odyssey recording is a reissue of a collection of
his songs originally issued by Columbia. Thirty-two
songs are sung by Gianna d'Angelo, Phyllis Curtin,
Regina Sarfaty, Charles Bressler, and Donald Gramm.
"Whatever the poem, Rorem's musical line fits it to
perfection...The poem is one thing; the musical setting is another; the third thing is not readily ana-
lyzed, but one is conscious of it at once when it is
manifested. Rorem's work on this record is one of its
richest manifestations of recent years. The Desto
recording contains Ideas for Easy Orchestra; Water
Music; and Trio for Flute, Cello, and Piano. Water
Music "...is rather thin and obvious." Ideas for Easy

Orchestra "...are wonderfully tuneful, bright and entertaining...regrettably only four have been recorded." Commenting on the <u>Trio</u>, "Here Rorem lets himself go a little and commits an innovation or two ...The work has profile, impact, a style of its own and it is here given a superb performance."
<u>See</u>: D17, D40; W288

B164. Franklin, Patrick. "Books." Review of <u>The Later Diaries of Ned Rorem, 1961-1972</u>, by Ned Rorem. <u>The Advocate</u> (August 21, 1984): 50-51.

"Cranky and charming, loving and biased, Rorem remains a real person. There are no coy masks to peer behind here, just a good writer writing honestly."
<u>See</u>: W287

B165. "'Fraulein Julie' Singt in New York Sopran." <u>Melos</u> 33 (February 1966): 62-63.

Review of the premiere of <u>Miss Julie</u>. "Rorems dritte Opernpartitur...kann sich nicht entscheiden, ob sie vorwiegend das pseudoskandinavische Kolorit widerspiegeln oder Hauptgewicht auf die langatmigen Dialoge..."
<u>See</u>: W178

B166. Fredrickson, Dolores. "The Composer As Pianist." <u>Clavier</u> 26 no. 5 (May-June 1987): 16-19.

While Ned Rorem is recognized as a very fine pianist, composition comes first in his priorities. "'Right from the beginning I've always been too busy composing. The difference between me and a concert pianist is that I don't have the endurance. I can't and won't take the time to practice my solo work.'" As a keyboard performer "...he exudes the joie de vivre of all great performers; his large, flexible hands show a relaxed easy technique free of mannerisms and bring forth a beautiful, velvety tone."

B167. _____. "Ned Rorem and Emanuel Ax." <u>Clavier</u> 26 no. 5 (May-June 1987): 14-23.

An interview with Ned Rorem and Emanuel Ax discussing the <u>Eight Etudes</u>. Includes scores for Etudes Nos. 5 and 7.
<u>See</u>: W185

B168. Freed, Richard. "American Songs for A Cappella Choir." <u>Stereo Review</u> 37 (July 1976): 113-114.

Review of Orion ORS 75205 recording by the King Chorale. The collection includes <u>Sing, My Soul</u>, by Ned Rorem and works by Barber, Hennagin, Pinkham, Stevens, Thompson, Berger, Adler, and Chorbajian. While there is no mention of any specific title, this "...is an interesting assortment of mostly recent material,

fetchingly sung and well recorded..."
        See: D43

B169. _____. "Ariel." Stereo Review 32 (February 1974): 120.

A review of Desto DC 7147 recording of Ariel and
Gloria. Ariel, "...is a pungent work and, not incidentally, one in which the demands on the singer are
formidable in terms of characterization as well as
vocal finesse." The Gloria is "...an imaginative setting of the liturgical text...This Gloria is more
exultant than serene, its chaste coolness warming at
intervals to brief glows of passion; it is a work that
will find a readier response than Ariel...The performances must be regarded as definitive..."
        See: D20

B170. _____. "Book of Hours." Stereo Review 39 (November
        1977): 141+.

Review of CRI SD 362 recording of Book of Hours.
"Dingfelder and Geliot have been playing Rorem's Book
of Hours all of its life: they commissioned the work,
introduced it in New York in February 1976, and recorded it three days after the première...Rorem refers
to the work as 'songs-without-words about memories of
the Roman Church which, having been taboo to my Prot-
estant childhood, always vaguely gave off a sense of
sin.' This performance must be regarded as uniquely
authoritative and is unquestionably committed."
Paired with Martinu's Trio for Flute, Cello, and
Piano.
        See: D8

B171. Freedman, Richard. "Palefaces and Redskins." Review of
        Music and People, by Ned Rorem. The Nation 207 (De-
        cember 9, 1968): 635-636.

Brief review of Music and People which is described as
"...a collection of modish reviews which hardly war-
ranted reprinting."
See: W288

B172. Freeman, John W. "New York." Opera News 32 no. 2 (Sep-
        tember 23, 1967): 21.

Review of three short contemporary works by Richard
Flusser's and Emmanuel Levinson's New School Opera
Workshop in May 1967. Included was Rorem's Last Day,
a ..."sonorous but conventional monologue to a text by
Jay Harrison about the thoughts of a condemned pris-
oner."
        See: W177

B173. _____. "Records: American Songs." Opera News 50 no. 1
        (July 1985): 44.

Review of CRI SD-485 recording of The Nantucket Songs

and Women's Voices.   Review of Leonarda LPI-116 recording of The Last Poems of Wallace Stevens which is
paired with Judith Lang Zaimont's The Magic World.
"...conservatism is alive and well, thanks to Ned
Rorem..."
See: D11, D30

B174. _____. "Rorem: Miss Julie (Excerpts)." Opera News 45
no. 18 (April 11, 1981): 52.

Review of Painted Smiles PS-1338 recording of Miss
Julie by the New York Lyric Opera. "Miss Julie, shorn
of some longueurs after a 1965 fizzle with the New
York City Opera, made a comeback in 1979 with the New
York Lyric Opera...Ned Rorem's songwriting gifts have
never been in question, and this sampling corroborates
his sensitivity as an orchestrator..."
See: D45

B175. Fremont-Smith, Eliot. "Books of the Times." Review of
The Paris Diary of Ned Rorem, by Ned Rorem. New York
Times, June 24, 1966, p. 35.

"It is a brash, rich, very readable, mildly annoying
book--a mixture of clever observations, tiny scandals,
fascinating comments about art and the artist's life,
coy boasts and jokes and real anguish, terror and
pain. It is probably an accurate mirror of what Ned
Rorem is..."
See: W293

B176. Friedberg, Ruth C. American Art Song and American
Poetry. Volume III: The Century Advances.   Metuchen,
N.J.: The Scarecrow Press, Inc., 1987.

A study of "...the interrelationships between the composer and the poet and the ways in which these have
influenced the completed song." A complete chapter is
devoted to the analyses of songs by Ned Rorem.

B177. "Frozen Interplay." Time 86 (November 12, 1965): 83.

Review of the New York City Opera's premiere of
Rorem's opera, Miss Julie. "Last week Rorem's opera,
based on Strindberg's Miss Julie, had its première.
The overall verdict: Rorem would have been better off
with the encyclopedia--and the U.S. is still looking
for its first major operatic composer...Not that Rorem
did not produce a singable and at times memorable
score. But the materials of the play resist trans-
mogrification into that elusive amalgam of drama and
music that is successful opera."
See: W178

B178. Frymire, Jack. "Reviews: Opera & Concert." Music &
Artists 2 no. 1 (February-March 1963): 37-38.

Review of the December 12, 1968 Town Hall concert of

"Musical Settings by Ned Rorem of American Poetry."
Poems of Love and the Rain are   "...a brilliant
achievement..." _Some Trees_, which was premiered, was
described as "...a kind of musical equivalent of Jack-
son Pollack's splatter-painting."
See: W64, W76

B179. Funke, Lewis. "Purdy's 'Color of Darkness' Throws Light
on Distressed World." _New York Times_, October 1,
1963, p. 34.

Review of the September 30, 1963 performance of James
Purdy's _Color of Darkness_ for which Ned Rorem wrote
the incidental music. "Ned Rorem's music underscores
the dark color of James Purdy's world..."
See: W266

B180. Galardi, Susan. "Premieres: The Composer Speaks." _High
Fidelity/Musical America_ 35 no. 1 (January 1985): MA
13.

Interview with the composer and brief review of the
January 4, 1985 premiere of _An American Oratorio_. It
"...is rife with Rorem's typically lyric--and sometimes haunting--melodies, coupled with lush sonorities
and strident chord cluster."
See: W118

B181. George, Earl. "Music Reviews." _Notes_ (Music Library
Association) 10 (June 1953): 497.

Review of the score of _Flight for Heaven_. "Perhaps
the most distinguished feature of his writing is its
spontaneous lyricism...If this same lyrical impulse
sometimes seems to lead him to sacrifice individual
phrases of the text to the requirements of the melodic
contour, the quality of the result makes it easy to
forgive him."
See: W24

B182. _____. "Music Reviews." _Notes_ (Music Library Association) 14 (March 1957): 205.

Review of the score of _Cycle of Holy Songs_. "Ned
Rorem's _Cycle of Holy Songs_ shows his talent at its
best. Throughout, the melodic lines follow their own
way without violating the needs of the text. The harmonic style is diatonic and perhaps over-mellifluous.
Everything is expressed lyrically, even the dramatic
qualities of the words. Yet within this narrow range,
Rorem manages to give the impression of variety and
musical resourcefulness."
See: W15

B183. "Gershwin Award Won by Ned Rorem." _Musical America_ 69
(January 1, 1949): 8.

"Ned Rorem's _Overture in C_ has been awarded the annual
George Gershwin Award..." Included with the brief

announcement is some biographical information.
See: W236

B184. Gold, Herbert.   "Books."   Review of Setting the Tone, by
Ned Rorem.   San Francisco 25 no. 8 (August 1983):
30-31.

"...just as outrageous and lively as his previous
volumes...His typical concerns--gay life, popular
culture, the state of music in America, all things
French--are still much in evidence."
See: W296

B185. Goldberger, R. N.   "Composer in Residence Finds 'Joy in
Writing.'"   Utah Chronicle (Salt Lake City, Utah),
January 12, 1967.

Ned Rorem "...spoke yesterday at the faculty luncheon
on an artists [sic] sensitivity and the arts." "'Artists,' said Rorem, 'being only people are no more
self-involved than others. They only show it more,'
sums up the creative involvement of an artist."

B186. Goldstein, Richard.   "Listen, Ned Rorem, for the Bang."
New York Times, November 2, 1969, sec. B, p. 19.

Richard Goldstein's rebuttal of an article by Ned
Rorem. "I believe a critic is obliged to impose his
own perceptions on a work so the reader (if he chooses
to apply those perceptions) can determine its value
for himself...objectivity isn't the totalitarian pur-
suit Ned Rorem makes it out to be."
See: B373, B497, B597

B187. Goth, Trudy.   "Stati Uniti: Balletti e Opere Nuove."
Musica d'Oggi 1 (July 1958): 447-449.

Review of the premiere performance of Ned Rorem's The
Robbers. "...difficile dire perché il compositore
abbia scelto questo tema orripilante, e perché non si
sia servito dell'opera di un librettista per la sua
musica."
See: W179

B188. Gotwals, Vernon.   "Books Reviewed."   Review of Critical
Affairs by Ned Rorem.   Music (AGO) 4 no. 11 (November
1970): 18-19.

"So we recommend this little quickie for pleasant entertainment but not for its philosophic content or its
critical acumen, though it has some of both."
See: W285

B189. Greco, Stephen.   "Ned Rorem: in Prose, in Music--a
Master of Composition."   The Advocate (October 4,
1979): 35.

Lengthy interview in which Ned Rorem discusses homosexuality and creativity, his early years in France,
music composition, his diaries and other publications.

B190. Griffiths, Richard Lyle. "Ned Rorem: Music for Chorus
      and Orchestra." D.M.A. diss., University of Washing-
      ton, 1979.

      Analyses of Ned Rorem's works for chorus and orches-
      tra.

B191. "Group to Honor 26 in Arts and Letters." New York
      Times, May 10, 1968, p. 53.

      Composer Ned Rorem is listed among the recipients of
      awards and grants by the American Academy of Arts and
      Letters and the National Institute of Arts and Let-
      ters.

B192. Groves, Bob. "'Adonis' Returns to New Mexico for Festi-
      val." Albuquerque Journal, June 30, 1985, sec. D,
      p. 1.

      Written in anticipation of the 13th Santa Fe Chamber
      Music Festival of 1985. In a telephone interview, Ned
      Rorem discusses Septet: Scenes from Childhood; com-
      posers John Eaton and Hans Werner Henze; music and
      politics; and his life after 50.
      See: W214

B193. _____. "Composer's New Work Takes Spotlight." Albu-
      querque Journal, August 13, 1985.

      Review of the August 11, 1985 premiere of Septet:
      Scenes from Childhood. "Even in the late 20th century
      it should not be considered decadent...for a serious
      composer to actually include consciously pleasurable
      melodies while striking out for new territory. With
      'Scenes,' Rorem has remained true to himself."
      See: W214

B194. Gruen, John."Ned Rorem." ASCAP Today 9 no. 1 (1978):
      14-16.

      John Gruen interviews Ned Rorem about winning the
      Pulitzer Prize; his works in progress and those re-
      cently completed; his diaries; his views on music
      critics; and his views about himself.

B195. _____. "Ned Rorem." In Close Up, p. 186-189. New
      York: The Viking Press, 1968.

      A profile of Ned Rorem written prior to the premiere
      of Miss Julie. Contains some biographical information
      about his years in France.
      See: W178

B196. _____. Ned Rorem Interview, April 27, 1975. Oral His-
      tory Project. Dance Collection of The New York Public
      Library.

      Ned Rorem is interviewed by John Gruen for the Dance

Collection of the New York Public Library. In addition to discussing his own works which have been choreographed, he describes his professional relationships with Martha Graham and other dance notables.

B197. _____. "'Now I Can Die Official,' Says Pulitzer-Winner Ned Rorem." New York Times, May 30, 1976, sec. 2, p. 12.

Interview with Ned Rorem on the occasion of being named Pulitzer Prize winner. "'I like glory and I like fame,' said composer Ned Rorem, this year's Pulitzer prize winner in music. 'To have won the Pulitzer has been totally satisfying. It's a once-in-a-decade refashioner, carrying the decree that bitterness is henceforth unbecoming. And if you die in shame and squalor, at least you die Official.'" Rorem also comments on performers, his seven major commissions during 1975-1976, and his literary output. Includes some biographical information.

B198. _____. The Party's Over Now: Reminiscences of the Fifties--New York's Artists, Writers, Musicians, and Their Friends. New York: The Viking Press, 1972, pp. 72-83.

Ned Rorem's reminiscences of the fifties, a period that shaped his life and career. "...the fifties made me what I am and I can't take it back...The fifties were a time of individual self-examination in every area. It doesn't seem to exist today."

B199. Grueninger, Walter F. "Recorded Music in Review." Consumers Research 67 (January 1984): 43.

Review of CRI 485 recording of The Nantucket Songs and Women's Voices.
        See: D11

B200. Grzesiak, Rich. "Ned Rorem: Settling the Musical Score." In Style for Men (Winter 1987): 35+.

"In a rare and exclusive interview with In Style, he discussed his views on death, religion, love, education, his friendship with writer Gore Vidal, his perspective on the subjects of opera, film music, rock and roll, and his highly individual thoughts about style..."

B201. Gussow, Mel. "Drama: A Rorem Double." New York Times, June 12, 1970, p. 28.

Review of two one-act plays by Ned Rorem given at The Extension, June 1970: The Pastry Shop and The Young Among Us. "Unfortunately the plays are written neither with the precision of his song cycles nor with the revelations of his memoirs. Instead, they are excessive and self-indulgent, the tone an odd reflection of the subject matter. The two plays seem mostly

about self-love."
See: W282, W283

B202. Gutekunst, Carl. "The American Concert Choir and Orchestra." <u>Musical Courier</u> 155 no. 5 (March 15, 1957): 14.

Review of the February 15, 1957 premiere of Ned Rorem's <u>The Poets' Requiem</u>. The texts "...concern themselves with death, and it is therefore surprising to find very little that is mournful in Rorem's engrossing music...striking melodic invention pervades the work...The orchestration is expert..."
See: W151

B203. Haines, Edmund. "A Week of New American Music." <u>High Fidelity/Musical America</u> 19 no. 8 (August 1969): MA 22.

Review of the May 8, 1969 May Festival of Contemporary American Music concert performed by the Eastman-Rochester Symphony conducted by Howard Hanson. "Ned Rorem's <u>Sun</u>, for soprano and orchestra, was effective for the voice and sensitively conceived in outline, but often inept in its orchestration, with repetitions of similar devices that made the work seem long and the orchestral sections almost unrelated to the overall conception."
See: W115

B204. Hall, David. "Catharine Crozier: Organ Recital." <u>Stereo Review</u> 44 (June 1980): 125-126.

Review of Gothic D-87904 recording of Rorem's <u>A Quaker Reader</u>. The recording includes works by J. <u>S</u>. Bach, Distler, Hindemith and Sokola. "...the only contemporary work here that comes within striking distance of the Hindemith in terms of effectiveness and craft is Ned Rorem's somewhat Messiaenic <u>A Quaker Reader</u>--in essence eleven meditations or ruminations on Quaker lore and texts from which Miss Crozier has chosen a half-dozen of the most striking."
See: D26

B205. Harmon, Carter. "Music by Kirchner Played at Forum; Final Composers Session Also Features Work by Rorem at McMillin Theatre." <u>New York Times</u>, May 20, 1949, p. 32.

Review of the May 19, 1949 Composers Forum Concert featuring works by Leon Kirchner and Ned Rorem. <u>Penny Arcade</u> sung by Nell Tangeman with Ned Rorem, piano, "...had moments of charm and cleverness..."; <u>A Mountain Song</u> was performed by Seymour Barab, cello with Byron Hardin, piano; and <u>Piano Sonata for Four Hands</u> played by Byron Hardin and Eugene Istomin, pianos.
See: W59, W187, W209

B206. "Harpsichordist Plays 4 Works of Unusual Interest." <u>Washington Post</u>, June 20, 1965, sec. G, p. 9.

Review of Decca 10108/710108 recording of <u>Lovers</u>, by
Ned Rorem.   While primarily consisting of comments
about Sylvia Marlowe's performance, it includes <u>Lovers</u>
among the three titles offering "...a strong sense of
style and great energy and line."
<u>See</u>: D14

B207. Harrison, Jay S.   "The Greatest."   <u>Musical America</u> 84
(May 1964): 53-54.

Review of Columbia ML-5961/MS-6561 recording featuring
32 songs by Ned Rorem.   The recording is described as
"...one of the most rewarding experiences currently to
be found on discs...With Mr. Rorem accompanying the
expert performers it provides a means to rejoice, for
it reflects an aspect of American culture that is too
often overlooked...Ned Rorem reminds us that it flour-
ishes with brilliance."
<u>See</u>: D4

B208. _____.   "Music Topics: American Composer at Home
Abroad." <u>New York Herald Tribune</u>, November 9, 1952.

Ned Rorem is interviewed during a short trip to New
York from Paris.   "Asked why he had chosen France as
his temporary home, Mr. Rorem indicated with all candor that his tastes and general orientation had always
leaned in directions abroad and centered specifically
in Paris itself...'And you know,' Mr. Rorem added,
'once you're a success in Paris there's a good chance
you'll remain a success for some time.'"

B209. Harrison, Max.   "Rorem: Symphony No. 3."   <u>Gramophone</u> 51
(July 1973): 201.

Review of Turnabout TV 34447S recording of Ned Rorem's
<u>Symphony no. 3</u> and William Schuman's <u>Symphony no. 7</u>.
Rorem's work "...begins seriously, almost impres-
sively, yet the composer seems never to have decided
on his aims."
<u>See</u>: D47

B210. Hartzell, Richard.   "Eye on Publishing."   <u>Wilson Library
Bulletin</u> 58 (March 1984): 496-497.

A report on the libel case of Edward Kantor vs. Random
House and the book <u>Poor Little Rich Girl</u>, by C. David
Heymann.   Ned Rorem brought factual errors and mis-
attribution to the attention of the publishers and
pointed out similarities of wording between his own
<u>Paris Diary</u> and some of Heymann's descriptions.
<u>See</u>: W293

B211. Hayden, Paul Murray.   "The Use of Tonality of Four
Concertos by American Composers."   D.M.A. diss.,
University of Illinois, 1982.

Includes a detailed analysis of Rorem's <u>Concerto in</u>

Six Movements.
See: W227

B212. Hazlett, Judi.   "Trio Dazzles with Musicianship."   The
Tribune-Star (Terre Haute, Indiana), November 21,
1986, sec. A, p. 3.

Review of the November 20, 1986 concert of the Verdehr
Trio at Indiana State University. Concerning Rorem's
End of Summer, "The piece evokes fall and the coming
of winter and is noticeably technically demanding on
all three members."
See: W207

B213. Henahan, Donal.   "Concert: 'Book of Hours.'"   New York
Times, March 1, 1976, p. 31.

Review of the February 29, 1976 premiere of Book of
Hours.   "Mr. Rorem's piece, conservatively tonal and
delicately scored, struck a sweetly contemplative pos-
ture and held it with too much determination."
See: W201

B214. _____ . "Is the Art Song Really Out of Date?" New York
Times, December 13, 1970, p. 28.

Review of Desto DC-7101 recording of War Scenes, Five
Songs to Poems of Walt Whitman and Four Dialogues.
Concerning War Songs: "It is easy to admire the sentiments, but easy too, to remain outside the music,
paying more attention to the elegant piano accompaniment than to the songs themselves." Concerning Five
Songs to Poems of Walt Whitman: "...there are long
moments of sustained grace and sensuality in these
1957 pieces. Still, the musical ideas often sound
commonplace, and carried out by instinct alone." Concerning Four Dialogues: "The O'Hara songs, in which
Anita Darian and John Stewart sing Poulenc-like dialogues in an intentionally shallow, cabaret style,
remind one of Bernstein's 'Trouble in Tahiti,' though
Rorem has the grace not to take too seriously what he
calls their 'comic-strip tightness' and flatness of
character."
See: D19

B215. _____ .   "Music: Flute and Guitar."   New York Times,
March 3, 1978, sec. C, p. 17.

Review of the March 1, 1978 premiere of Romeo and
Juliet.   "Mr. Rorem had done his homework. Most
composers who employ the guitar do not bother to in-
vestigate its basic resources, let alone master its
peculiarities, and so they consign it to unimaginative
strumming.   But this suite, prevailingly tonal and
traditionally melodic, gives both instruments enviable
opportunities to shine."
See: W213

B216. _____. "Music: Souzay Sings 'War Scenes.'" <u>New York Times</u>, November 6, 1969, p. 57.

Review of the November 5, 1969 New York premiere of <u>War Scenes</u>. There are few songs "...that set out to show wars as the stupid affairs they are, and succeed ...The five-part cycle, set to prose-poems drawn from Whitman's 'Specimen Days,' made an imaginative assault on the problem, however, even if it fell short of real success both as propaganda and as memorable music."
<u>See</u>: W98

B217. _____. "Recital: William Parker Sings Americana." <u>New York Times</u>, February 12, 1980, sec. C, p. 5.

Brief review of the February 10, 1980 concert of American music at Alice Tully Hall. Ned Rorem's <u>War Scenes</u> was included in the program.
<u>See</u>: W98

B218. _____. "2 Nights with Later-Day Rorem." <u>New York Times</u>, November 28, 1973, p. 38.

Review of two concerts of Ned Rorem's music on the occasion of his fiftieth birthday. The November 25-26, 1973 concerts at Alice Tully Hall included: <u>Day Music</u>; <u>Last Poems of Wallace Stevens</u>; <u>War Scenes</u>; <u>Gloria</u>; <u>Night Music</u>; <u>Ariel</u>; <u>Trio</u>; and <u>Bertha</u>. "...what these two programs of Mr. Rorem's recent music re-affirm are his continuing need to compose and his ability to find dedicated friends to present and perform his works."
<u>See</u>: W32, W98, W106, W108, W172, W205, W210, W222

B219. Henken, John. "Ketchum at Brand Library." <u>Los Angeles Times</u>, April 3, 1984, sec. 6, p. 2.

Brief review of the March 30, 1984 recital by Anne Marie Ketchum, soprano, with Adam Stern, piano. Rorem's <u>The Waking</u> and <u>Early in the Morning</u> were included in the program.
<u>See</u>: W18, W97

B220. _____. "State Choir of Armenia in Rorem Premiere." <u>Los Angeles Times</u>, September 13, 1987, sec. 6, p. 66.

Written in anticipation of the September 17, 1987 concert. The program included <u>Armenian Love Songs</u> by Ned Rorem, "...five short, unaccompanied choral love songs."
<u>See</u>: W120

B221. Henry, Derrick. "Ned Rorem Wins Awards for Writing His Words and Music." <u>The Atlanta Constitution</u>, October 27, 1985, sec. J, p. 5.

Interview in anticipation of the premiere of <u>String Symphony</u>. In addition to commenting about his new

work, Ned Rorem discusses his work both as a composer
and as a writer.
See: W241

B222. _____ . "Rorem's New Symphony Sparkles with Contrasts."
Atlanta Constitution (GA), November 2, 1985, Sec. A,
p. 2.

Review of the October 31, 1985 premiere of String Symphony. "Though there is nothing new about Rorem's
musical language, he employs traditional resources
with exquisite craftsmanship and imagination to create
something striking, personal, and immediately communicative."
See: W241

B223. "Here & There." Diapason 72 (April 1981): 19.

Announcement that Miracles at Christmas was performed
December 13-14, 1980 at Washington Cathedral under the
direction of Paul Callaway.
See: W146

B224. _____ . Diapason 78 (July 1987): 2.

Announcement that Ned Rorem accepted a commission from
All Saints Episcopal Church, Fort Lauderdale, FL, to
compose Seven Motets for the Church Year.
See: W158

B225. _____ . Diapason 78 (December 1987): 4.

Photo of Ned Rorem, Leonard Raver and Dino Anagnost
preparing for the October 21, 1987 New York premiere
of Organ Concerto.
See: W234

B226. Heymont, George. "Ned Rorem Lays It on the Line." Ova-
tion (October 1983): 23-26.

A lengthy interview in which Ned Rorem expresses his
views concerning a wide range of topics including in
part, critics who "...don't really know what they
think;" his 60th birthday which he considers "...a
milestone in terms of sheer survival;" composers and
how they are viewed; performers who use only music of
the past, ignoring contemporary works; and his own
success in making a living with his art.

B227. Hinson, Maurice. "Great Composers in Our Time: Ned
Rorem." Piano Quarterly 28 (1980): 6-7+.

Brief biography followed by an interview conducted via
correspondence. Ned Rorem replies to questions about
his style and methods of composition; his teachers and
other influences; and contemporary music. A large
portion of the interview concerns the development of
his piano compositions through the years.

B228. _____ . Guide to the Pianist's Repertoire. 2nd rev. ed.
Bloomington, IN: Indiana University Press, 1987.

Includes descriptive annotations for Piano Sonatas
1-3, Barcarolles, A Quiet Afternoon, and Eight Etudes.
See: W182, W185, W190, W191, W194, W195

B229. _____ . "The Keyboard Music of Ned Rorem." Piano Quarterly 28 (1980): 14-16.

Brief survey of Rorem compositions featuring piano,
both solo and in chamber works. Includes information
about premieres and comments made by the composer.
See: W27, W112, W182, W185, W189, W190, W191,
W192, W194, W195, W205, W208, W210, W222, W227,
W228

B230. _____ . Music for More Than One Piano: an Annotated
Guide. Bloomington, IN: Indiana University Press,
1983.

Includes descriptive annotations for Sicilienne and
Four Dialogues.
See: W27, W192

B231. _____ . Music for Piano and Orchestra: an Annotated
Guide. Bloomington, IN: Indiana University Press,
1981.

Includes descriptive annotations for Piano Concerto
No. 2 and Concerto in Six Movements.
See: W227, W228

B232. Holland, Bernard. "Cello Recital: Sharon Robinson."
New York Times, March 18, 1981, sec. 3, p. 22.

Brief review of the March 15, 1981 premiere of After
Reading Shakespeare. "His writing fit comfortably
into every soft curve of the cello's sonorous world
and offered Miss Robinson flattering opportunities to
appear at her best."
See: W200

B233. _____ . "Chamber: Schwarz Conducts Y Symphony." New
York Times, November 19, 1984, sec. C, p. 18.

Brief review of the November 17, 1984 premiere of
After Long Silence. The work is described as having
"...outgoing, wide-ranging, ecstatic qualities..."
See: W105

B234. _____ . "Concert: Musica Sacra Offers the Old and New."
New York Times, January 30, 1988, p. 14.

Review of the January 28, 1988 premiere of The Death
of Moses. "Mr. Rorem's brief, songful choral piece
appears to have been intended for church choirs of
middling capabilities...It is a modest piece, in other
words, meant not only to engage the relatively unso-
phisticated listener but to demand something of him as

well."
    See. W125

B235. _____. "King's Singers Perform at Avery Fisher Hall."
New York Times, November 20, 1984, sec. C, p. 19.

Review of the November 16, 1984 premiere of Pilgrim
Strangers. "Mr. Rorem has set Walt Whitman's candid
ruminations on the cruelty of war with a reticence
that seemed at times distant, almost impersonal."
See: W150

B236. _____. "Music: Debuts in Review." New York Times, May
1, 1983, sec 1, p. 67.

Review of the April 27, 1983 premiere of Three Calamus
Poems. "Mr. Rorem's songs had a very likable lyrical
grace about them. There is a calculated monotony in
his repetitions of short phrases; but along the way,
rhythmic and melodic alterations subtly enhance these
recurring ideas."
See: W86

B237. _____. "Music: Rorem 'Oratorio.'"   New York Times,
January 7, 1985, sec. 3, p. 11.

Review of the January 4, 1985 premiere of American
Oratorio. "Mr. Rorem's vocal music has always been
deeply shaped--some might say dominated--by its texts
...the earthbound simplicity of the words, both in
their moments of confidence and despair seem to have
tempered and smoothed the more acerbic tendencies in
his harmonic style."
See: W118

B238. _____. "Schubert Song Cycle on CD."   New York Times,
December 8, 1985, sec. 2, p. 28.

Review of GSS 104 recording of Ned Rorem's early
songs. "These items have a deftness, subtle dramatic
depiction and melodic charm which this busy and prolific composer may never have equaled since."
See: D29

B239. "Honors for Members." ASCAP Today 1 no. 3 (1967): 26.

Brief mention of the premiere of Hearing.
See: W33

B240. _____. ASCAP Today 2 no. 3 (1968): 39.

Brief mention of newly published Music and People; and
the premieres of Ideas for Easy Orchestra and He Shall
Rule from Sea to Sea.
    See: W133, W232, W288

B241. Horton, Charles. "Symphony Opens New Home."   Chapel
Hill Newspaper, October 13, 1975, sec. A, p. 5.

Review of the October 11, 1975 premiere of <u>Assembly</u> <u>and Fall</u>. Mr. Rorem "...has given us a piece of music that shows a command of new sound material that is woven together in a poetical context of convincing integrity."
<u>See</u>: W225

B242. "How New York Critics See New Works by Living Composers." <u>Music News</u> 41 (July 1949): 17.

Summaries of the reviews by Noel Straus (New York Times) and Francis D. Perkins (N.Y. Herald Tribune) for the May 7, 1949 premiere of <u>Overture in C</u>. Also summaries of the reviews by Arthur V. Berger (N.Y. Herald Tribune) and Carter Harmon (N.Y. Times) for the May 19, 1949 premiere of <u>Penny Arcade</u>.
<u>See</u>: B37, B205, B709; <u>W59, W236</u>

B243. "How New York Critics See New Works by Living Composers." <u>Music News</u> 41 (December 1949): 25.

Summaries of the reviews by Francis D. Perkins (N.Y. Herald Tribune) and Carter Harmon (N.Y. Times) for the October 6, 1949 premiere of <u>Piano Sonata No. 1</u>.
<u>See</u>: B460; W194

B244. Huff, Serge. "Abravanel Scores with Symphony Audience." <u>The Phoenix Gazette</u> (Phoenix, AZ), November 28, 1969, p. 62.

Review of the November 17, 1969 performance of <u>Lions</u>. "The program was headed by a work of many faces and moods by the modern American composer Ned Rorem." Lions "...seemed to be a study in variety of polytonality, orchestral color, harmonic dissonances and dramatic dynamic effects."
<u>See</u>: W233

B245. Hughes, Allen. "At Last, Enter 'Miss Julie.'" <u>New York Times</u>, October 31, 1965, sec. 2, p. 15.

Ned Rorem is interviewed in anticipation of the premiere of <u>Miss Julie</u> on November 4, 1965. He contrasts song composition with opera, "The fact that I may write graciously for the human voice does not necessarily mean that I can write an opera. The problem in opera is dramatic, not lyric." Further topics include: his reasons for choosing the Strindberg play; movies as an art form; and his reasons for dropping the project of an opera based on Heyward's <u>Mamba's</u> <u>Daughters</u>.
<u>See</u>: W178

B246. _____. "Composers Honor Frank O'Hara with Vocal Works." <u>New York Times</u>, April 28, 1972, p. 34.

Review of the April 26, 1972 Composers' Showcase Concert at the Whitney Museum, featuring premieres of

vocal works written to texts by Frank O'Hara. Two
Rorem songs: For Poulenc and I Will Always Love You
were performed, and about which was said, "Phyllis
Curtin sang these elegantly, and in the case of each
it was as though O'Hara had truly found a compatible
musician."
See: W25, W35

B247. _____. "Concert: Musical Elements Offers 5 Modern Composers." New York Times, January 11, 1986, p. 12.

Review of the January 8, 1986 Musical Elements Concert
during which Winter Pages was performed. "Best of all
was Mr. Rorem's 'Winter Pages,'...'Winter Pages' was
played last in the concert and, after one had heard
awkwardnesses of various kinds in earlier works, Mr.
Rorem's surety of calculation and skill came as a
special delight."
See: W223

B248. _____. "4 Leading American Composers Draw Full House to
the Whitney." New York Times, February 5, 1969,
p. 38.

Review of the February 4, 1969 Composers Showcase
Concert, featuring the works of Ned Rorem, Walter
Piston, Virgil Thomson, and Aaron Copland. Eight of
Ned Rorem's songs were performed by Betty Allen,
mezzo-soprano, accompanied by Ned Rorem. Concerning
Visits to St. Elizabeths: "Mr. Rorem's musicalization
is masterful in its evocation of madness."
See: W96

B249. _____. "Music in Review." New York Times, October 7,
1973, p. 78.

Review of the October 3, 1973 "Hear America First"
concert series at the New York Cultural Center. Included in the program was Rorem's Hearing and a group
of his songs. "The Rorem songs, pulsating always with
expressive vitality and at times, with impetuous
urgency to sum up complex poetic imagery in a single
musical phrase, demanded tonal and verbal adroitness,
which Miss Quivar provided in abundance."
See: W33

B250. _____. "Music: 'Quaker Reader,' Ned Rorem Organ Suite,
Has Premiere." New York Times, February 4, 1977, sec.
C, p. 18.

Review of the February 2, 1977 premiere of Quaker
Reader. "This music seemed on first hearing to have
its own logic, its own tensions and its own set of
proportions to follow...The result is a music-literary
work that one can listen to and read with pleasure,
and, despite its technical difficulties, it will
surely be welcomed by organists."
See: W189

B251. _____. "Ned Rorem's 'Sun' Is Given Premiere." New York
Times, July 3, 1967, p. 14.

Review of the July 1, 1967 premiere of Ned Rorem's
Sun. Sun was commissioned by the Lincoln Center Fund
for the Festival '67 program. "Since Mr. Rorem is
more conservative musically than he is literarily, the
score is not adventurous, but it is thoughtful, skill-
fully organized, colorful and expressive, and it has
something of the air of a major statement."
See: W115

B252. _____. "The Opera: Reminiscences of Gertrude Stein."
New York Times, October 6, 1972.

Brief mention that Ned Rorem's Three Sisters Who Are
Not Sisters was included in the October 4, 1972 per-
formance of a group of operas based on works by
Gertrude Stein.
See: W180

B253. Hume, Paul. "At the Pianists' Request." Washington
Post, February 19, 1975, sec. C, p. 6.

Announcement that the Edyth Bush Charitable Foundation
funded a $125,000 grant to permit twelve young Ameri-
can pianists to commission a major new work from a
composer of his or her choice for a series of concerts
during the Bicentennial Year. Ned Rorem was chosen by
Emanuel Ax.

B254. _____. "Choral Society." Washington Post, October 22,
1979, sec. B, p. 11.

A review of Paul Callaway's performance of A Quaker
Reader during the Washington Cathedral Choral Society
concert of October 21, 1979. "Paul Callaway opened
the program with the seeming paradox of Ned Rorem's 'A
Quaker Reader,' a suite of movements for organ inspired by writings of leading Quakers over three centuries...The music speaks to many conditions in many
moods, conveying what music along [sic] can convey
about many things words cannot describe. Callaway's
total command of the incredible complexities and haz-
ards in the score was flawless."
See: W189

B255. _____. "Founder's Day." Washington Post, October 30,
1978, sec. B, p. 11.

Review of the October 29, 1978 Founder's Day Concert
in which Letters From Paris was performed. "The
choral writing is a delight of textures and rhythms."
See: W138

B256. _____. "Music Reviews." Notes (Music Library Association) 11 (June 1954): 450.

Brief review of the scores for A Christmas Carol; Two Songs with XV Century Texts: The Call. Epitaph; Echo's Song; and Spring. "Rorem has steadily refined and sensitized his vocal line and its accompaniment. Though the emotional level of these five songs varies widely, he achieves in each a remarkable sense of mood and expressiveness, and always with the simplest means."
See: W9, W11, W19, W21, W83

B257. _____. "Ned Rorem." Washington Post, October 5, 1981, sec. D, p. 11.

Review of a concert of Rorem's works at Bradley Hills Presbyterian Church October 4, 1981. Featured works were War Scenes, The Nantucket Songs, and A Quaker Reader. The episodes from A Quaker Reader "...combine stunning technical acquaintance with the resources of the pipe organ and ideas of striking invention in using music to speak of silence and an inner spirit."
See: W52, W98, W189

B258. _____. "Ned Rorem's Cycles." Washington Post, October 31, 1979, sec. B, p. 3.

Review of the October 30, 1979 Founder's Day concert at the Library of Congress. Ned Rorem played and Phyllis Bryn-Julson sang two of his song cycles, Women's Voices and The Nantucket Songs, a world premiere for the latter. "Placing the two cycles on a single program demonstrated the many facets of Rorem's writing that have for three decades, kept his songs on the highest level." Concerning The Nantucket Songs: "It is likely that Rorem's new cycle will quickly be taken up by sopranos with the voices and the brains to handle it." Concerning Women's Voices: "There is shock and fear as well as bitter gloom and resignation in writings left by women over a period of 400 years."
See: W52, W103

B259. _____. "Ned Rorem's Visions in Songs." Washington Post, October 28, 1979, sec. G, p. 3.

Written in anticipation of the October 30, 1979 Founder's Day Concert at the Library of Congress during which The Nantucket Songs received its premiere. Rorem discusses his songs and gives his observations about good song writing. "Use only good poems--that is, convincing marvels in English of all periods. Write gracefully for the voice--that is, make the voice as seen on paper have the arched flow which singers like to interpret. Use no trick beyond the biggest trick--that is, since singing is already such artifice, never repeat words arbitrarily, much less ask the voice to groan, shriek, or rasp."
See: W52

B260. _____. "Tribute to Ned Rorem." Washington Post, September 24, 1981, sec. C, p. 3.

Review of the September 23, 1981 concert of Rorem's works. Concerning After Reading Shakespeare: "Sharon Robinson, who commissioned the Shakespeare scenes, played them with breathtaking mastery enhanced by an inner rapture in the quiet episodes." Toccata for piano, Etudes for piano and Barcarolles were performed by Jerome Lowenthal with "...the composer's own re-markable gifts as a pianist...clear in every piano phrase..." The Last Poems of Wallace Stevens "...represent the composer a decade ago with complexities of thought." Included among the songs sung by Ros-alind Rees and accompanied by the composer were Such Beauty As Hurts to Behold, Spring, and Visits to St. Elizabeths, "...songs from the 1950's glory in his gift of expressiveness in simplicity."
See: W83, W85, W96, W108, W182, W185, W198, W200

B261. _____. Boosey & Hawkes Newsletter 16 no. 3 (March 1987): 7.

A summary of the reviews of the End of Summer, per-formed by the Verdehr Trio during their 1986 tour.
See: W207

B262. "In Brief." Review of Music From Inside Out, by Ned Rorem. New York Times, March 19, 1967, sec. 7, p. 36.

Review of Music From Inside Out, "...a miscellany --seven lectures on music delivered at Buffalo Uni-versity in 1959 and 1960, a previously published arti-cle on Francis Poulenc, a review of a book by Arthur Honegger and some new excerpts from his diary. The result, though unambitious, is not unpleasant. ...The brief, final chapter of musical musings from that now-famous diary are engrossing enough to make the reader wish for more, and not doubt in time there will be more."
See: W289

B263. _____. Review of The New York Diary of Ned Rorem, by Ned Rorem. New York Times, October 22, 1967, sec. 7, p. 42.

"Like its predecessor, 'The New York Diary' affords the reader no middle ground. Mr. Rorem's continuing journal is likely to seem either a tediously vulgar contemporary Pepys-show or a sensitive and agonizingly honest portrait of the artist--in this case a talented and troubled young American composer--in search of himself."
See: W291

B264. Isacoff, Stuart. "Remembering Stravinsky." Key Clas-sics 1 no. 5 (1981): 12-15.

Review of the Stravinsky Festival held by the New York Chamber Music Society during September 1981. "...Ned Rorem...will give a lecture on Stravinsky as part of the Lincoln Center activities." Quoting Rorem, "'No one can avoid the fact that Stravinsky has been the biggest influence on everyone since 1910...So I thought it would be fun to talk about people Stravinsky himself had stolen from.'"

B265. Jacobson, Bernard. "New School Opera Workshop." High Fidelity/Musical America 17 no. 8 (August 1967): MA 8.

Review of the May 26, 1967 performances of several operas, during which Ned Rorem's one-act opera, Last Day, was premiered. "Jay Harrison's libretto is a positively embarrassing string of clichés, and it is matched by the stupefying banality of the music."
See: W177

B266. _____. "New Works." Music Journal 23 no. 5 (May 1965): 80.

Brief review of the April 9, 1965 premiere of Poems of Love and the Rain.
See: W64

B267. _____. "New Works." Music Journal 24 no. 1 (January 1966): 99.

Brief review of the October 28, 1965 New York premiere of Lions. "Ned Rorem has again shown that he is an able and interesting orchestrator."
See: W233

B268. Jacobson, Robert. "Books." Review of An Absolute Gift: a New Diary, by Ned Rorem. Opera News 43 no. 3 (September 1978): 78.

"...Ned Rorem will never be everyone's cup of tea, for he is a throwback to the essayists of past centuries people who not only thought and experienced but committed their innards to paper." In these essays, many of which appeared in papers, periodicals and talks "...he reveals not only a whirring, first class, discerning mind but depth, openness and sensitivity as well."
See: W284

B269. _____. "New York." Opera News 38 no. 11 (January 19, 1974): 25-26.

"Ned Rorem's 25-minute opera Bertha received its world premiere on the second of two all-Rorem evenings at Alice Tully Hall, November 25-26. The work, dating from 1968, proved to be slight diversion--both in music and text--and no more."
See: W172

B270. _____. "On the Occasion of His Fiftieth Birthday Ned Rorem Speaks to Robert Jacobson." Opera News 38 (December 8, 1973): 38-40.

Interview in which Ned Rorem discusses his opera
Bertha; opera composition and performance; and vocal
music in general.
See: W172

B271. Jeffers, Grant Lyle. "Non-narrative Music Drama: Settings by Virgil Thomson, Ned Rorem and Earl Kim of
Plays by Gertrude Stein and Samuel Beckett..." Ph.D.
diss., University of California, Los Angeles, 1983.

Includes an analysis of Three Sisters Who Are Not
Sisters.
See: W180

B272. Jellinek, George. "King Midas." Stereo Review 37 (July
1976): 106.

Review of King Midas on Desto DC-6443 recording.
Recording includes Argento's To Be Sung Upon the
Water. "These are provocative works by two American
composers...who know how to write for the singing
voice--a gift not shared by many of their contemporaries...More fluent, for musical purposes, are the
ten poems by Howard Moss which make up the Rorem cantata. The musical setting is done with the composer's
oft-praised skill and sensitivity. One of the songs
(The Princess' Speech) sounds exceptionally inspired
to me."
See: D16

B273. Jenkins, Speight. "Festive Evening with Rorem at Tully
Hall. New York Post, August 26, 1980, p. 30.

Review of the August 25, 1980 New York premiere of The
Santa Fe Songs during the Santa Fe Chamber Music
Festival. "The first seven songs...gave the more
impressive music to the accompaniment, not the singer
...the eighth song...and the twelfth song, were different: rich and flowing, lyrical and appealing, these
two should grace many a song program in days to come."
See: W110

B274. John, Evan. "Reviews of Music." Music & Letters 34 no.
4 (October 1953): 349-350.

Brief review of the score of Rorem's Flight for
Heaven. "Ned Rorem in his Herrick settings employs a
more heavy-handed harmonic technique and piano texture, without upsetting the logic of the music, which
cannot be complained of."
See: W24

B275. Johnson, Bret. "Still Sings the Voice: A Portrait of
Ned Rorem." Tempo 153 (June 1985): 7-12.

Survey on the development of Rorem's works in later
years, concentrating on the analyses of his orchestral
and concertante works and their characteristics. Beginning with the Third Piano Concerto (1969) "...a

landmark in his output," the author mentions all the
larger scale compositions of Rorem since then, concentrating more heavily on the analysis of Air Music,
Assembly and Fall, Remembering Tommy, Violin Concerto,
Organ Concerto, and American Oratorio.
    See: W118, W224, W225, W227, W234, W239, W246

B276. Johnson, Tom. "Spring Cleaning." Village Voice (New
    York, N.Y.), June 12, 1978, p. 64.

    Review of the April 28, 1978 "Meet the Moderns Series"
    concert. "The lyrics of Ned Rorem's Six Songs for
    High Voice and Orchestra were completely incompre-
    hensible...but it didn't really matter because the
    emotional qualities were defined so explicitly by the
    music. Of course, this is not expressionism. The
    emotions are never up front. They are always veiled
    in elegance, and often remind me of Britten. But they
    are quite believable all the same."
    See: W114

B277. "Joseph Brezniker Premieres Rorem." Soundboard 7 no. 4
    (1980): 150.

    Brief announcement of the July 25, 1980 premiere per-
    formance of Suite for Guitar.
    See: W220

B278. Kaufman, Wolfe. "Rorem's Paris Diary an Offbeat Mem-
    oir." Review of Paris Diary, by Ned Rorem. Variety
    243 (August 3, 1966): 59.

    Review of the first diary reflecting Ned Rorem's years
    in Paris during the 1950's. "This is an irritating
    and sometimes infuriating book. It is also, at the
    same time, a fascinating book...It doesn't teach any-
    thing, it doesn't explain anything, it doesn't help
    anyone. And yet--like the fellow said--it's full of
    names and gossip and, once having started to read it,
    it's a toughie to stop reading."
    See: W293

B279. Kendall, Elaine. "The Book Review." Review of Setting
    the Tone; and The Paris and New York Diaries of Ned
    Rorem, by Ned Rorem. Los Angeles Times, August 7,
    1983, sec. B, p. 1.

    "The diaries, first published in 1966 have been re-
    issued in conjunction with 'Setting the Tone,' a
    remarkable pairing inevitably suggesting the story of
    Dorian Gray in reverse as the gifted but wanton enfant
    terrible matures to generosity and responsibility,
    astounding admirers and detractors alike."
    See: W292, W296

B280. Kerner, Leighton. "Business Better Than Usual." Village
    Voice (New York), March 18, 1981, p. 70.

    Review of the February 5, 7, 10, 1981 concerts of

American music. Included was the New York premiere of
Sunday Morning. The work, "...commissioned by Eugene
Ormandy, the Philadelphia Orchestra, and the Saratoga
Performing Arts Center, and first performed by them in
1978, is an eight-movement suite whose wounds are
meant to reflect the moods of Wallace Steven's eight-
part 1915 poem of the same title...the movements sing
eloquently on their own with themes and motives that
are easy to perceive and enjoy and yet seem altogether
substantial and durable."
See: W242

B281. _____. "A Love That's Here to Stay."   Village Voice
(New York), March 13, 1984, p. 66.

Review of the February 24, 1984 concert in memory of
pianist Paul Jacobs. Included on the program was Ned
Rorem who accompanied William Parker and Susan Belling
in three Debussy song cycles. "Rorem played finely
tinted but always firm and clear-headed accompaniments..."

B282. _____. "Second Annual Obopies: Wait Till Next Year."
Village Voice (New York), July 9, 1979, p. 48-59.

Reviews of some of the better off-Broadway opera performances of the season, including a performance of
Rorem's Miss Julie by the New York Lyric Opera at New
York University Theatre (April 4, 1979). "In this
production the two-act original became a one-act music
-drama conforming to the shape of Strindberg's play.
But the opera works in either format. It works because Kenward Elmslie's libretto makes just the right
musical-stage readjustments to Strindberg's rises and
ebbs of tension and humor."
See: W178

B283. _____. "Songs, Serenades, and Sonatas."   Village Voice
(New York), September 27, 1980, p. 68.

A review of the touring version of the Santa Fe Chamber Music Festival at Tully Hall, August 25, 1980.
"...the highlight was easily the New York premiere of
Ned Rorem's The Santa Fe Songs, an approximately
half-hour cycle using 12 poems by a Santa Fe writer,
Witter Bynner. The Santa Fe Songs represent a heart-
ening shift in a different but not, for Rorem, new
direction. Rorem treated the violin, viola, and
cello--additional partners of the customary piano--as
mood-delineators nearly as expressive as the voice,
which had to do with the songs' impact."
See: W110

B284. _____. "With Celebration for Some." Village Voice (New
York), September 7, 1982, p. 64.

Review of the 10th Annual Santa Fe Chamber Music Festival which included the performance of Ned Rorem's
Winter Pages. "Rorem's Winter Pages, first performed

last season by the Chamber Music Society of Lincoln
Center, was played not quite so eloquently by a Santa
Fe quintet, yet well enough to project the cafe-
nostalgia of a Parisian waltz and the Coplandesque
sweetness (in the best sense of the word) of a page
entitled 'Dorchester Avenue.'"
See: W223

B285. Keys, Ivor. "Reviews of Music." Music & Letters 30 no.
1 (January 1949): 93.

Review of the score of Four Madrigals by Ned Rorem.
"The words are by Sappho, but she does not seem to
have kindled a lyrical flame in the music, which is
disappointingly stodgy and lacking in that flow which
is surely one of the prime ingredients of a madrigal."
See: W129

B286. ____. "Reviews of Music." Music & Letters 36 no. 1
(January 1955): 103-104.

Review of the scores of Spring and Echo's Song. "Ned
Rorem's marked tendency to disjunct motion means that
his songs, though not difficult, do not sing themselves. But being thus saved from superficial performance they should make a decidedly individual
effect..."
See: W19, W83

B287. Kinsey, Barbara. "Guest Book Review." Review of Music
and People, by Ned Rorem. NATS Bulletin 26 no. 1
(October 1969): 21+.

Review of Ned Rorem's book Music and People. "Mr.
Rorem raises some valid comments about today's society
and the composer's place in that society, particularly
the composer of songs...It is good to hear a composer
of Mr. Rorem's stature present cases for emotional
music, for appreciating performance and for conserva-
tives who as he wisely indicates, 'have taken time to
perfect their craft.' It is good to have a book that
draws attention even by what it does not say, to the
structure of today's music in society."
See: W288

B288. "KIOS to Broadcast Concerts, Interviews." Omaha World
Herald, August 2, 1986, p. 28.

Announcement that concerts and interviews of the Omaha
Symphony's Contemporary Music Festival, May 18-22,
1986, would be broadcast on five consecutive Sundays
beginning August 3, 1986. Interview with Ned Rorem
and tapes of his works are to be included.

B289. Kiraly, Philippa. "Rorem Oratorio Combines Nostalgia,
National Trauma." Akron Beacon Journal, March 14,
1986, sec. E, p. 7.

Review of the March 23, 1986 Cleveland premiere of An American Oratorio. "Rorem's settings are full of imagery in the orchestral parts against beautiful choral writing achieved without complications. While his harmonies and tonality are accessibly conventional, what he has done with them is arrestingly original."
See: W118

B290. Kirsch, Robert. "Rorem's 'Final Diary': Journey Toward Maturity." Review of The Final Diary: 1961-1972, by Ned Rorem, Los Angeles Times, November 12, 1974, sec. 4, p. 4.

"Rorem's journey from prodigy to a kind of maturity is recorded with candor and self-revelation, as incisive and unsparing to his own experience as he is to those around him...But if there is a central theme...it is finding in aging the desire for immortality as a musician, rather than as a character."
See: W286

B291. Kissel, Howard. "Ned Rorem: Only His Music is Conservative." Westsider (New York), October 10-17, 1980, p. 16.

Interview in which Ned Rorem gives his thoughts on such diverse topics as art song, popular song, singers and poets, particularly Witter Bynner, whose texts were set by Rorem in The Santa Fe Songs. "Setting a poem to music is a way of getting inside it...No artist wants to be 'understood.' If he's 'understood' he feel superficial. What an artist wants is not to be misunderstood."
See: W110

B292. Klein, Howard. "Concert Honors Adlai Stevenson." New York Times, October 29, 1965, p. 52.

Review of the October 28, 1965 premiere of Lions. "Mr. Rorem's 'Lions' was full of good ideas, but the most potent of them was the use of a jazz quartet... The program explained its use, but knowing the composer's purpose did not prevent the jazz interludes from upstaging the rest of the material."
See: W233

B293. Knight, Hans. "Music Can Be Pornography without the Dirty Words." Philadelphia Evening Bulletin, July 27, 1980, sec. G, p. 1+.

Interview with Ned Rorem at the time of his appointment to the faculty at Curtis Institute. He speaks about his teaching methods, "'I am not Socratic minded...The best way they can learn is by imitating me.'"

B294. Knisely, Richard. "Ned Rorem and His Art." Gay Community News, April 21, 1984, p. 17.

Written on the occasion of Ned Rorem's participation in Boston University's Encounter with Composers series, April 3-4, 1984, during which War Scenes was performed. It is a general article rather than a review of the performance, highlighting some of Rorem's views about his work and what is described as Rorem's "...reputation as a writer with an eloquently gay point of view."
See: W98

B295. _____. "Quintessential Narcissism." Review of The Paris and New York Diaries of Ned Rorem, by Ned Rorem. Gay Community News, April 14, 1984, p. 4.

Review of the 1983 reprint of The Paris Diary and The New York Diary. "These first two diaries, at least, deserve to be read by anyone interested in music, sex, culture, gay life, self-knowledge, cinema or fine writing."
See: W292

B296. Kolodin, Irving. "Carmelites and Quakers; Gilels, Pere et Fille." Saturday Review 4 (March 19, 1977): 47-48.

Review of the February 2, 1977 premiere of Quaker Reader. "Rorem, born a Quaker, had the difficult task of evoking sentiments expressed relative to that faith...since his gift is for sound and its commitment is to silence. This is a pretty paradox, which he resolved...in prevailingly pretty-sounding paraphrases of the texts, varied here and there by heavy rumbling in the bass, which Raver attacked as confidently with his feet as he did the responses on the keyboards with his hands."
See: W189

B297. _____. "Ned Rorem as Teacher." Saturday Review 7 (October 1980): 105-106.

Written at the time Ned Rorem was appointed to the faculty of Curtis Institute as instructor of composition. The former student of Rosario Scalero, Virgil Thomson, and Aaron Copland says, "Composition cannot be taught. But young composers can learn what to do and how to do it from those who have been through it themselves." Addressing his goals for his tenure at Curtis, Rorem says, "'What I would like to bring about in Curtis, which has so many skilled young performers, is a real liaison between the composition students and the performers...convey to those young performers how important it is for them to play the music being created in their own time...I would like the young composers who are working with me not merely to think about a work in the abstract, but to follow through on it, bring it to the point of being performed.'" There is a brief mention of The Santa Fe Songs, about which the author states, "...would in my view, serve as an

object lesson for Rorem's group somewhere in the first
semester--an object lesson in how to compose, not
merely write, music."
See: W110

B298. ____. "Second-Generation Bartok." Saturday Review 3
(February 7, 1976): 47-48.

Review of the December 5, 1975 premiere of Air Music.
"Air Music could have been subtitled 'Chamber Music
for Orchestra.'"
See: W224

B299. ____. "Two Cheers for the Met National Co.--Miss
Julie." Saturday Review 48 (November 20, 1965): 64+.

Review of the November 4, 1965 New York premiere of
Miss Julie. "Temperamentally, what the subject re-
quires is something on the order of Berg. What Rorem
provides is, for the most part, on the order of
Debussy. That is to say, he is more adept with long-
ing and fantasy than he is with fulfillment and bitterness...Thus it is more like a play with incidental
music and an occasional burst of song than a music
drama with an organic structure and a sure line of
procedure."
See: W178

B300. ____. "A Week of Song As Well As Singers." Saturday
Review 52 (November 22, 1969): 58.

Review of the November 5, 1969 New York premiere of
War Scenes. "In his own quietly distinctive way,
Rorem has trumped all the recent music of protest...in
his bitterly eloquent treatment of four selections
from Whitman"s Specimen Days...It is a sizable accom-
plishment for Rorem, and he deserved not only the
obeisance tendered by Souzay, but every bit of the
applause that the performers directed toward him."
See: W98

B301. Kostelanetz, Richard. "Modern Music Criticism and the
Literate Layman." Perspectives of New Music 6 no. 1
(1967): 119-133.

A discussion of the state of music criticism and music
critics. Concerning Ned Rorem: "As a writer, the
composer Ned Rorem places himself in the Thomsonian
tradition; and while his Paris Journal [sic] (1965) is
far more impolite and salacious as gossip than Thomson's disclosures, Rorem's Music from Inside Out
(Braziller, 1967), a collection of essays, lectures
and journal jottings, talks more substantially about
song, that genre for which he is most noted, than
about music in general, contemporary or otherwise."
See: W289, W293

B302. Kresh, Paul. "The Art Song in America, Volume II."
Stereo Review 34 (June 1975): 107.

Review of Duke University Press DWR 7306AX recording which includes: A Christmas Carol; Guilt; For Susan; Clouds; What Sparks and Wiry Cries, as well as songs by Persichetti, Duke, Cumming, Trimble, and Earls. Concerning the Rorem songs, "I was impressed and charmed by Rorem's medieval paraphrase of an ancient Christmas carol and this feel for prosody in the setting of Guilt with a text by Demetrios Capetanakis, which contains the devastating line, 'Murder means less than nothing to the dead' (too devastating, perhaps--it is lines like that which defeat our composers of art songs). Rorem's treatment of three poems by Paul Goodman also are clever and apt, and here there is a genuine fusion of text and tunes."
See: D23

B303. _____. "Miss Julie (Highlights)." Stereo Review 44 (June 1980): 120-121.

Review of Painted Smiles PS 1388 recording of Miss Julie. "One of the joys of Miss Julie is Kenward Elmslie's intelligent verse libretto...Rorem transformed the lyrics into splendid arias while supplying the turbulent orchestral atmosphere that precisely reflects the emotions boiling beneath the passage of dialogue..."
See: D45

B304. _____. "William Parker: An American Song Recital." Stereo Review 46 (June 1981): 128.

Review of New World NW 305 recording. In addition to Rorem's Mourning Scene, works by Griffes, Bacon and Niles are included on the recording. Concerning Mourning Scene: "Coached by the composer, Parker is perfected in Ned Rorem's early work for baritone and string quartet based on the Biblical passage about the death of Jonathan."
See: D38

B305. Kupferberg, Herbert. "CMS of Lincoln Center: Rorem 'Winter Pages.'" High Fidelity/Musical America 32 no. 6 (June 1982): MA 26.

Review of the February 14-16, 1982 premiere of Winter Pages, a work "...imbued with an overall lyric unity and is scored with exquisite taste."
See: W223

B306. Kyle, Marguerite K. "AmerAllegro." Pan Pipes 49 (1957): 67.

Information about 1956 premieres, performances, publications and recordings. Premieres and performances include: Symphony no. 2; Symphony no. 1; The Poets' Requiem; A Childhood Miracle; Another Sleep; Six Songs for High Voice.
See: W5, W114, W151, W174, W243, W244

B307. _____. "AmerAllegro." Pan Pipes 50 (1958): 70.

Information about 1957 premieres, performances, publications and recordings.   Premieres and performances
include: The Poets' Requiem; Sinfonia; Five Poems of
Walt Whitman; Design; and Symphony no. 1.
See: W23, W151, W229, W240, W243

B308. _____. "AmerAllegro." Pan Pipes 51 no. 2 (1959): 81.

Information about 1958 premieres, performances, publi-
cations and recordings.   Premieres and performances
include: The Robbers; incidental music for Garden
District (Suddenly Last Summer); Symphony no. 3; and
Sinfonia.
See: W179, W240, W245, W278

B309. _____. "AmerAllegro."   Pan Pipes 52 no. 2 (1960):
68-69.

Information about 1959 premieres, performances, publications and recordings.   Premieres and performances
include: Symphony no. 3; Eagles; Miracles of Christmas; Eight Poems of Theodore Roethke; ten songs;
Design for Orchestra; and Symphony no. 2.
See: W95, W146, W229, W230, W244, W245

B310. _____. "AmerAllegro." Pan Pipes 53 no. 2 (1961): 73.

Information about 1960 premieres, performances, publications and recordings.   Premieres and performances
include: Eleven Studies for Eleven Players; Trio for
Flute, Cello and Piano; Eagles; and Third Symphony.
See: W206, W222, W230, W245

B311. _____. "AmerAllegro." Pan Pipes 54 no. 2 (1962): 69.

Information about 1961 premieres, performances, publications and recordings.   Premieres and performances
include: Eleven Studies for Eleven Players; Trio for
Flute, Cello and Piano; Symphony no. 3; and Eagles.
See: W206, W222, W230, W245

B312. _____. "AmerAllegro." Pan Pipes 55 no. 2 (1963): 68.

Information about 1962 premieres, performances, publications and recordings.   Premieres and performances
include: King Midas; The Anniversary; Concertino for
Harpsichord and Seven Instruments; and Two Psalms and
a Proverb.
See: W40, W168, W171, W203

B313. _____. "AmerAllegro." Pan Pipes 56 no. 2 (1964): 78.

Information about 1963 premieres, performances, publications and recordings.   Premieres and performances
include: Two Psalms and a Proverb; Early Voyagers;
Eleven by Eleven; Lady of the Camellias; Color of

Darkness; and Eagles.
See: W168, W230, W254, W255, W266, W272

B314. _____. "AmerAllegro." Pan Pipes 58 no. 2 (1966): 82.

Information about 1965 premieres, performances, publications and recordings. Premieres and performances
include: Poems of Love and the Rain; Miss Julie;
Lions; and Sinfonia.
See: W64, W178, W233, W240

B315. _____. "AmerAllegro." Pan Pipes 61 no. 2 (1969): 73.'

Information about 1968 premieres, performances, publications, and recordings. Premieres and performances
include: Some Trees; Dancing Ground; and Water Music.
See: W76, W247, W251

B316. _____. "AmerAllegro." Pan Pipes 62 no. 2 (1970): 79.

Information about 1969 premieres, performances, publications and recordings. Premieres and performances
include: Sun; Letters From Paris; Lovers; and Eleven
Studies for Eleven Players.
See: W115, W138, W206, W258

B317. _____. "AmerAllegro." Pan Pipes 63 no. 2 (1971): 76.

Information about 1970 premieres, performances, publications and recordings. Premieres and performances
include: Third Piano Concerto and the Third Symphony.
See: W227, W245

B318. _____. "AmerAllegro." Pan Pipes 64 no. 2 (1972):
76-77.

Information about 1971 premieres, performances, publi-
cations and recordings. Premieres and performances
include: Ariel; Piano Concerto in Six Movements; Four
Fables of La Fontaine; Three Sisters Who Are Not
Sisters; music for the movie Panic In Needle Park;
incidental music for the play, The Nephew; and the
Third Symphony.
See: W106, W175, W180, W227, W245, W275, W276

B319. _____. "AmerAllegro." Pan Pipes 65 no. 2 (1973): 70.

Information about 1972 premieres, performances, publi-
cations and recordings. Premieres and performances
include: Day Music; Last Poems of Wallace Stevens;
Gloria; Seven Canticles; Night Music and the Third
Piano Concerto.
See: W32, W108, W122, W205, W210, W227

B320. _____. "AmerAllegro." Pan Pipes 66 no. 2 (1974):
69-70.

Information about 1973 premieres, performances, publications and recordings. Premieres and performances
include: Day Music; Night Music; Ariel; Bertha; Last

Poems; War Scenes; Gloria; and Trio.
See: W32, W98, W106, W108, W172, W205, W210, W222

B321. _____. "AmerAllegro." Pan Pipes 68 no. 2 (1976): 70.

Information about 1975 premieres, performances, publications and recordings. Premieres and performances
include: Assembly and Fall; Air Music; Book of Hours;
and Etudes for Piano.
See: W185, W201, W224, W225

B322. _____. "AmerAllegro." Pan Pipes 69 no. 2 (1977): 68.

Information about 1976 premieres, performances, publications and recordings. Premieres and performances
include: Air Music; Book of Hours; Etudes; Serenade;
Sky Music; and Eagles.
See: W112, W185, W201, W215, W224, W230

B323. _____. "AmerAllegro." Pan Pipes 70 no. 2 (1978): 60.

Information about 1977 premieres, performances, publications and recordings. Premieres and performances
include Romeo and Juliet; Pilgrims; and A Quaker
Reader.
See: W189, W213, W237

B324. _____. "AmerAllegro." Pan Pipes 71 no. 2 (1979): 44.

Information about 1978 premieres, performances, publications and recordings. Premieres and performances
include: Romeo and Juliet; and Sunday Morning.
See: W213, W242

B325. Laderman, Ezra. "Philharmonic Heard in NAACC Program."
Musical America 76 (March 1956): 16.

Review of the February 18, 1956 concert which included
Ned Rorem's Symphony No. 1. "The Rorem symphony is a
surprising work, for, after an aggressively brassy
opening, a calm placidity dominates the music. The
lyric lines evolve above marching rhythms and a bar-
carolle-jig, yet there are arid sections of little
pulsation."
See: W243

B326. LaFave, Kenneth. "Beauty and Evil Entwined." Tucson
Daily Citizen, August 19, 1985, sec. B, p. 1.

Review of the August 11, 1985 premiere of Ned Rorem's
Septet: Scenes from Childhood at the Santa Fe Chamber
Music Festival. The music suggests "...the inevita-
bility of evil as a companion to beauty...it is sen-
sual and immediate, intelligent and inviting..."
See: W214

B327. Lambert, Gavin. "Confessions of a Charmer." Review of
The Paris Diary of Ned Rorem, by Ned Rorem. New York

Times, July 10, 1966, sec. 8, p. 46.

"However private they may be, diaries are ultimately intended to be read...there are diaries—and Rorem's is one—that reflect an artist's need to express himself in a different medium, like the music of Paul Bowles or the paintings of Cocteau and Henry Miller ...He is not concerned to enlighten or improve, he wants to record and endure."
See: W293

B328. Lang, Paul Henry.   "American Vocal Music."   *New York Herald Tribune*, November 17, 1959, p. 22.

Review of the November 16, 1959 recital of songs by Virgil Thomson, William Flanagan and Ned Rorem. Concerning the Rorem songs: "Mr. Rorem knows the anatomy of art song inside out, in fact, the garland of songs heard last night presents a veritable textbook on song-writing."

B329. Lange, Art.   "Interview with Ned Rorem 6/18/77."   *Brilliant Corners* 7 (Fall 1977): 72-90.

Brief biographical sketch followed by lengthy interview in which Ned Rorem discusses song composition; the status of the art song; influences on music composition; his programmatic works; and comments about other composers.

B330. Lanier, Thomas P.   "New York."   *Opera News* 44 no. 1 (July 1979): 36.

Review of the April 7, 1979 performance of the revised version of *Miss Julie*. "The tonal score has sufficient lyricism and melodic appeal for the singers, and the often angular orchestral writing serves as a commentator, sometimes ironically, on the text."
See: W178

B331. Larson, Tom.   "Chamber Music Festival Plays Tribute to Memories of Rorem."   *The New Mexican* (Santa Fe, N.M.), July 27, 1982, sec. A, p. 3.

Review of the July 25-26, 1982 performance of *Winter Pages* at the Santa Fe Chamber Music Festival. "Basically what works in Rorem's opus is his lyricism, a melodic wholeness that dominates his music. This domination, regardless of how it is designed into the rhythm or the maniacal virtuosity of the players, makes many of the moments of this piece flex with power and expectation."
See: W223

B332. Lask, Thomas.   "Books of The Times."   Review of *Music and People*, by Ned Rorem.   *New York Times*, October 15, 1968, p. 45.

"Mr. Rorem writes in a conscious, careful, ornate language. He likes to employ an occasional frill, a circumlocution or two, a mandarin phrase. The language is frequently painfully languid, reflecting honestly Mr. Rorem's feelings at that moment."
See: W288

B333.   _____. "Books: Rorem's Diary." Review of An Absolute Gift, by Ned Rorem. New York Times, July 26, 1978, sec. 3, p. 22.

"Easily the best pieces in the book--and his best is very good--are to be found in the third section, one that includes assessments of the music of Britten, Ravel and Poulenc. His comments in these essays are of the kind that turn a listener back to the music. They convey the strengths and characteristic qualities of these musicians."
See: W284

B334. Lawrence, Arthur.   "ICO Philadelphia/Washington: a Review of the Third International Congress of Organists." Diapason 68 (September 1977): 1.

Review of the August 1, 1977 performance of A Quaker Reader at the International Congress of Organists. A Quaker Reader, an eleven-movement work, with each movement "...a little piece of its own and altogether they comprise fascinating contrasts of texture; individual moments which ranged from quietness to excitement..."
See: W189

B335.   _____. "New Organ Music." Diapason 69 (March 1978): 3+.

Review of the score for A Quaker Reader. "...this will be judged one of the significant new solo organ works of our time..."
See: W189

B336.   _____. "Reviews...Music & Books." Review of An Absolute Gift: a New Diary by Ned Rorem. Diapason 69 (October 1978): 5.

Review of An Absolute Gift: a New Diary. "I would not be surprised to discover many readers judging Rorem's literary compositions more interesting than his musical ones."
See: W284

B337. Lemco, Gary. "Sounding Out a Radical: A Chat with Ned Rorem." Southline, February 26, 1986.

Ned Rorem is interviewed at the time of the world premiere of String Symphony. Rorem reiterates his concern about the lack of recognition for composers, describing a contemporary composer as "'...something or someone negligible, not even attaining the status

of pariah, since a pariah must be recognized before he can be despised.'" Rorem discusses such topics as the works of David Diamond, Elliot Carter, William Flanagan, Orson Welles; the craft of composition; his commission by the Atlanta Symphony Orchestra; and AIDS.
See: W241

B338. Levinger, Henry W.   "League of Composers in Premieres." Musical Courier 142 no. 8 (December 1, 1950): 22.

Brief review of the November 19, 1950 premiere of Ned Rorem's song cycle Flight for Heaven.   "The songs confirm the talent of Mr. Rorem in expressing the emotional content of the poem. His musical language gives the voice the necessary preponderance, but using the accompaniment as an equally important atmospheric element."
See: W24

B339. Levinson, David.   "Composer Ned Rorem's Wish-It-Wasn't-So List." Press-Telegram (Long Beach, CA.), March 22, 1987, sec. F, p. 1.

Written in anticipation of the March 26, 1987 performance of Ned Rorem's Lions. The interview centers "...on a fairly long list of Rorem discontents..." in the world of music.
See: W233

B340. Lewando, Ralph.   "New Works."   Music Journal 23 no. 6 (September 1965): 89.

Brief review of the premiere of Ned Rorem's Four Dialogues. "Here is a composition which blends strikingly with Frank O'Hara's amusing and sometimes funny lyrics."
See: W27

B341. Leyland, Winston.   "Ned Rorem: an Interview."   Gay Sunshine 22 (Summer 1974): 6-12.

Ned Rorem discusses, in part: the effects of homosexuality on work and art; loneliness; aging and death; and his views of Lou Harrison, Paul Goodman, Frank O'Hara, Jean Cocteau, Paul Bowles and Gore Vidal. Includes some excerpts from The Final Diary.
See: W286

B342. Libbey, Theodore W., Jr.   "Chamber: a New Cycle by Rorem." New York Times, February 20, 1982, p. 47.

Review of the February 14, 1982 premiere of Winter Pages. "The writing for the instruments was idiomatic but lacked the expressive intensity that the composer can bring to his writing for the human voice; there were even times when the treatment did not seem especially imaginative, unusual for Mr. Rorem. The piece

was well received..."
See: W223

B343. _____. "Music: Ned Rorem is Pianist in Program of His
Songs at Y." New York Times, February 1, 1982, sec.
3, p. 11.

Review of January 30, 1982 concert of Ned Rorem works.
Included in the concert were Women's Voices, Gloria
and a group of unnamed early songs. "...the songs of
Ned Rorem deal with familiar images in a distinctive
and sometimes disturbing way, combining intensity and
accessibility in a way that can leave a vivid imprint
on the imagination."
See: W32, W103

B344. Lowens, Irving. "Book Reviews." Review of Music and
People, by Ned Rorem. Notes (Music Library Association) 26 no. 2 (1969): 280-281.

"With the publication in recent years of his Paris and
New York Diaries...Ned Rorem won for himself a rather
racy literary reputation. Those looking for his
favorite combination of name-dropping and homosexual
chatter will not find it in this book. Rather, they
will discover clean, trenchant prose and incisive commentary on things and persons musical--and a much more
thoughtful and analytical musician."
See: W288

B345. _____. "King Chorale: American Songs." High Fidelity/
Musical America 26 no. 11 (November 1976): 126-127.

Brief review of Orion ORS 75205 recording which includes Sing, My Soul, "...a very simply and naturally
harmonized work."
See: D43

B346. _____. "The Seventh Inter-American Music Festival."
High Fidelity/Musical America 26 no. 9 (September
1976): MA 34+.

Review of the Seventh Inter-American Music Festival,
Washington, D.C., May 17-24, 1976. The May 20, 1976
concert featured Ned Rorem's Eagles, "...pleasant
enough, but not of Pulitzer Prize quality."
See: W230

B347. Lowenthal, Jerome. "Pianist's Diary: Birth of a Concerto." Music Journal 29 no. 1 (January 1971): 23+.

Mr. Lowenthal documents the evolution of the Concerto
in Six Movements through to its premiere, December 3,
1970.
See: W227

B348. Lowry, David. "A.G.O. National Convention, Washington,
D.C., 1982. Organ Recitals." Diapason 73 (September

1982): 6.

Reviews of two recitals featuring Rorem compositions.
A Quaker Reader "...exhibits a certain improvisatory
nature in all its movements...the effect was that of
an impressive work embodying an astounding array of
ideas, cast in a style that is unusual, yet still
organistic." Views from the Oldest House is "...a
welcome addition to organ repertory."
See: W189, W199

B349. Luten, C. J. "Gossip, Grace, and Sex: Ned Rorem." Review of The Paris Diary of Ned Rorem, by Ned Rorem.
American Record Guide 33 (November 1966): 264-267.

"With the gossip one gets worthwhile bonuses: the
discovery of a personality believably alive with a
good deal on his mind about a generous variety of
subjects--music being merely one..."
See: W293

B350. McCardell, Charles. "Colanders & Cowbells."   The
Washington Post, November 1, 1983, sec. B, p. 6.

Review of the Washington Music Ensemble's Festival
Americana October 27-30, 1983. The opening symposium
featured influential 20th century composers including
Ned Rorem. The second concert featured the pairing of
works by Virgil Thomson and Ned Rorem. "...Thomson's
Serenade...seemed world's apart from Rorem's Ariel,
five poems of Sylvia Plath given an electric reading
by soprano Elizabeth Kirkpatrick."
See: W106

B351. McCray, James. "Ned Rorem's Music for Chorus & Organ."
Diapason 71 (February 1980): 16-18.

Lengthy survey of Rorem's choral music with organ.
Each work is "...discussed briefly with commentary on
the writing for chorus and organ; some observations on
performance considerations..."   Includes: The Corinthians; Miracles of Christmas; Lift Up Your Heads;
Proper for the Votive Mass of the Holy Spirit; Truth
in the Night Season; He Shall Rule from Sea to Sea;
Praises for the Nativity; Three Motets; and Surge,
illuminare.
     See: W119, W124, W133, W139, W146, W153, W156,
     W163, W166

B352. Mac Farland, D. "Martha Graham." Music Journal 25 no.
4 (April 1967): 61.

Review of the February 24, 1967 performance of Dancing
Ground, with music by Ned Rorem. "It is enchanting."
See: W251

B353. McInerney, John. "David Leisner, Guitar." High Fidel-
ity/Musical America 32 no. 9 (September 1982): MA 22.

Brief review of the May 4, 1982 performance of Suite for Guitar.
See: W220

B354. McKenzie, Don. "Music Reviews." Notes (Music Library Association) 37 no. 3 (1981): 688.

Review of the score of Romeo and Juliet: Nine Pieces For Flute and Guitar. "I believe this is an important new work which illuminates many of the expressive possibilities available to contemporary composers...It is demanding for the performers, especially the guitarist who must negotiate several near-impossible reaches along with difficult passage work and high tessitura. Yet the rewards for both players and listeners will be substantial."
See: W213

B355. Mackinnon, Douglas A. "The New York Area." Opera News 23 no. 7 (November 10, 1958): 12.

Review of the April 14, 1958 premiere of the one-act opera The Robbers. "...the composer, who has a way with melody, has harmonized his music harshly enough to underline the drama's grisly element without alienating the listener once in the course of thirty-five minutes."
See: W179

B356. McLellan, Joseph. "And Yet Another Rorem Diary: More on the Man." Review of An Absolute Gift, by Ned Rorem. Washington Post, May 27, 1978, sec. B, p. 2.

Rorem "...writes about music, his own and others, with a grace and precision matched by few writers who use our language...If 'An Absolute Gift' is read as it deserves to be, it will do more service to the art of music than most technical treatises addressed to specialized readerships."
See: W284

B357. _____. "Competing with Beethoven." Washington Post, June 16, 1973, sec. B, p. 7.

A report of the 1973 American Symphony Orchestra League National Conference. Composer-conductor dialogue at one session questioned "...why orchestras don't perform more contemporary music..." Ned Rorem was quoted, "Conductors, as far as I'm concerned, should play exclusively contemporary music, but garnish it occasionally with Beethoven."

B358. _____. "Rorem's 'Eagles.'" Washington Post, May 21, 1976, sec. B, p. 9.

Review of the May 20, 1976 performance of Rorem's Eagles. "Ned Rorem has become better known as a writer than as a composer in recent years, and he was

never particularly renowned as an orchestral composer. But his credentials in this field were upheld last night in the Kennedy Center Concert Hall by no less an advocate than the Philadelphia Orchestra under Eugene Ormandy...Rorem's orchestration is superbly controlled in its flashes and stabs of color to depict its soaring, graceful but also savage subject, managing to include big melodic lines along with all the to-do in the brass and percussion. It is a perfect showpiece for an orchestra like the Philadelphia and they did it to a turn."
See: W230

B359. _____. "Song of a 'Shy' Man." Washington Post, October 31, 1979, sec. B, p. 3.

An interview with Ned Rorem on the occasion of the premiere of The Nantucket Songs. He discusses his time in France during the 1950's, singers, and his early introduction to contemporary music.
See: W52

B360. _____. "Songs in the Classical Tradition." Washington Post, February 26, 1984, sec. K, p. 9.

Review of "Vocal Music by Ned Rorem," on Composers Recordings CRI 485 featuring The Nantucket Songs and Women's Voices. The Nantucket Songs, "...beautiful not only in its melodies and harmonies, but in the exquisite choice and arrangements of texts. Rorem is particularly valuable for his sensitivity to words, his knack for discovering poems and giving them new life through music." Women's Voices, "...powerful music, tightly and lucidly integrated in its themes and superbly interpreted."
See: D11

B361. _____. "A Treacherous Decade." Review of The Final Diary, 1961-1972, by Ned Rorem. Washington Post, January 3, 1975, sec. B, p. 6.

Review of the book which records Rorem's life during his 40's. "This is one of those rare books that can be opened at random with the assurance that something worth reading will be found within the page, readily detachable from all the pages before and after. It is held together by the author's personality...but its strongest attraction lies in its disembodied perceptions, paradoxes, aphorisms, not in the personal notes which abound..."
See: W286

B362. McQuilkin, Terry. "Rorem's 'Quaker Reader' in Whittier." Los Angeles Times, December 8, 1981, sec. 6, p. 3.

Review of the December 5, 1981 organ concert during the Whittier College Quaker Festival. Concerning A Quaker Reader: "...well constructed musical pictures, acquired even more poignancy with Richman's eloquent

reading.   But as a complete cycle...needs far greater variety."
<u>See</u>: W189

B363. Maldonado, Charles.   "Rorem Work Highlights Memorable Concert." <u>Albuquerque Journal</u>, July 28, 1982, sec. B, p. 8.

Review of the July 25, 1982 performance of <u>Winter Pages</u> during the Santa Fe Chamber Music Festival. "Rorem has given us a work of profound beauty, strength, and sensitivity."
<u>See</u>: W223

B364. Malitz, Nancy.   "Rorem's New Double Concerto Is a Hit." <u>Cincinnati Enquirer</u>, November 14, 1981, sec. B, p. 6.

Review of the November 13, 1981 premiere of <u>Remembering Tommy</u>. "The piece is everything you might expect from Rorem..."
<u>See</u>: W239

B365. Manchester, P. W.   "The Season in Review."   <u>Dance News</u> (April 1967): 9.

Review of the February 24, 1967 premiere of <u>Dancing-Ground</u>. "...'Dancing-Ground' shows the infinite variety of moods of which dance is capable...Ned Rorem's Eleven Pieces for Eleven Players is especially apt here."
<u>See</u>: W251

B366. Marcus, Wendy.   "Festival Audience Hears Local Debut of Rorem's Songs." <u>Seattle Times</u>, August 20, 1980, sec. D, p. 7.

Review of the August 19, 1980 Seattle premiere of <u>The Santa Fe Songs</u>. "At times, the songs sound abstract, dissonant and lost. At other times, they gave me the feeling of glimpsing genius...Those who grumbled about his songs not being easy to listen to and thus dismissed them, missed an auditory challenge...The songs were perplexing and wonderful...in time they will take their rightful place in the classical music literature."
<u>See</u>" W110

B367. _____. "Ned Rorem Bitter About Lack of Support for Composers." <u>Seattle Times</u>, August 20, 1980, sec. D, p. 1.

Interview on the occasion of the Santa Fe Chamber Music Festival Concerts in Seattle, August 1980. The article deals with Mr. Rorem's opinions on compensation for composers. "Contemporary composers generally earn less than artists in other fields...a star soprano...will receive more money for a single performance of his work than he has earned for those same songs in the 25 years since he wrote them." Mr. Rorem contends that "...contemporary classical music is the only art form in America in which such a large discrepancy occurs between recognition and financial success."

B368. Mardirosian, Haig.   "Catharine Crozier in Recital." Fanfare (July-August 1980): 168-169.

Review of Gothic D-87904 recording which includes six selections from A Quaker Reader. "Rorem's work is a recondite succession of programmatic fragments on pieces of Jessamyn West's Quaker Reader. With it ...Miss Crozier ascends to the highest level of her skill and musical simpatico."
See: D26

B369. Margrave, Wendell.   "Music Reviews."   Notes (Music Library Association) 9 (December 1951): 168.

Brief review of the score of Mountain Song, for flute and piano. "...it is a skillful job, and pleasant to play and hear."
See: W209

B370. Mark, Michael. "Alice Tully Hall."   Music Journal 29 no. 5 (May 1971): 71.

Review of the March 21, 1971 performance of Letters from Paris. "It impressed with its simple but witty thematic content and by its highly successful combination of various styles."
See: W138

B371. _____. "Collections." American Record Guide 43 (November 1979): 55-56.

Review of Vox Box SVBX 5354 recording which includes Ned Rorem's Missa brevis. "The melodic content is beautiful, but especially striking are the contrasts Rorem has set up in this five-movement work."
See: D48

B372. _____. "Guide to Records." American Record Guide 43 (October 1980): 35-36.

Review of Painted Smiles PS 1338 recording of Miss Julie. The music is "...very well put together, containing beautiful, expressive vocal lines."
See: D45

B373. Marks, J. "How About No Critics at All?" New York Times, November 9, 1969, sec. B, p. 19.

Written in support of Richard Goldstein in the Rorem/ Goldstein controversy on pop music and critics. "...I am inclined to side with Goldstein if I have to side with one breed of critic rather than another. At least intuitional criticism admits to a fallible private opinion whereas elite critics are always talking

about 'one's' opinion as if critical words possess
pontifical arrogance."
See: B186, B497, B597

B374. Marlboro Music School. <u>Marlboro Music: Programs 1951–
1984</u>. Marlboro, VT: Marlboro Music School and Festival, n.d.

Programs of concerts held at Marlboro between 1951 and
1984. Includes: <u>Day Music</u>; <u>Ariel</u>; <u>Such Beauty as
Hurts to Behold</u>; <u>Visits to Saint Elizabeths</u>; <u>Alleluia</u>;
<u>I Am Rose</u>; <u>Last Poems of Wallace Stevens</u>; and <u>Mourning
Scene</u>.
See: W2, W34, W85, W96, W106, W108, W109, W205

B375. Mérimée, Prosper. <u>Mateo Falcone</u>. Translated from the
French by Ned Rorem. <u>Antaeus 2</u> (Winter 1975): 55–65.

Translation of a short story by Prosper Mérimée, author of <u>Carmen</u>.

B376. Merkling, Frank. "New York: Miss Julie." <u>Opera News</u> 30
no. 7 (December 18, 1965): 29.

Review of the November 4, 1965 premiere of <u>Miss Julie</u>.
"Strindberg's taut story demands a stronger hand than
Rorem has learned to wield in his first full-length
opera. The musical texture, essentially homophonic,
is short on tension...As a result, <u>Miss Julie</u> joins
the well-populated limbo of works that are no longer
plays and not quite operas.
See: W178

B377. Middaugh, Bennie. "The Songs of Ned Rorem: Aspects of
Musical Style." <u>NATS Bulletin</u> 24 no. 4 (May 1968):

An analytical study of Ned Rorem songs (1946–1963).

B378. Millard, Max. "Westsider Ned Rorem." <u>Westsider</u> (New
York), June 17, 1978, p. 28.

A general article giving Rorem's reaction to such
diverse topics as a negative review of his book, <u>An
Absolute Gift</u>; his definition of art song, "...a song
sung by a trained singer in concert halls...;" a guid-
ing principle of his life, "I've never done what I
didn't want to do...I've never been guided by other
than my heart. And certainly not by money." Information on Rorem's Pulitzer Prize winning <u>Air Music</u> and
the premiere of <u>Sunday Morning</u> is also given.
See: W224, W242, W284

B379. Miller, Kenneth E. <u>Principles of Singing; a Textbook
for First-Year Singers</u>. Englewood Cliffs, N.J.:
Prentice-Hall, Inc., 1983.

Contains <u>A Christmas Carol</u>.

See: W11

B380. Miller, Philip L.   "The Best in American Song: Ned Rorem." _American Record Guide_ 30 (May 1964): 864-865.

Review of Columbia ML-5961 recording.   "...a major contribution to the propagation of the best in American song."
See: D4

B381. ____. "Guide to Records." _American Record Guide_ 47 (March 1984): 47-48.

Review of CRI-SD-485 recording of The Nantucket Songs and Women's Voices. The Nantucket Songs are "...emotional rather than intellectual, and need not be understood to be enjoyed."
See: D11

B382. ____. "Guide to Records." _American Record Guide_ 47 (September 1984): 35-36.

Review of Leonarda LPI-116 recording of Last Poems of Wallace Stevens. "Rorem is an acknowledged master of word setting, but his vocal lines at this stage do not aim to follow the verbal inflection as faithfully as in his early songs; the melodies are more angular, varied by stretches of monotone."
See: D30

B383. ____. "Guide to Records." _American Record Guide_ 48 (May/June 1985): 32-33.

Review of GSS 104 recording of a collection of 27 songs by Ned Rorem.
See: D29

B384. ____. "A New and Novel Song Cycle by Ned Rorem." _American Record Guide_ 32 (October 1965): 158.

Review of CRI-202 recording of Poems of Love and the Rain and Second Piano Sonata. Concerning Poems of Love and the Rain: "His melodic lines are smooth in effect, but do not avoid wide intervals. His piano parts are transparent and economical..." Concerning the Second Piano Sonata: "...bright and attractive work."
See: D6

B385. ____. "On Desto, Music by Rorem Not for Singing." _American Record Guide_ 35 (January 1969): 416.

Review of Desto DC-6462 recording of Water Music, Ideas for Orchestra, and Trio. Concerning Water Music: "It is music of sophistication, well calculated to develop the abilities and understanding not only of the two star performers but also of the other young players." Concerning Ideas for Orchestra: "...Rorem best sums up their spirit...in the word 'whimsy.'"

Concerning <u>Trio</u>: "...everyone is kept busy exploring sonorities and harmonic and rhythmic effects. And all emerge with flying colors."
<u>See</u>: D17

B386. _____. "Recordings from CRI, Odyssey, Westminster, and Desto: the Music of Ned Rorem." <u>American Record Guide</u> 36 (December 1969): 252-254.

Review of Odyssey 32-16-0274 (reissue of Columbia MS-6561; <u>32 Ned Rorem Songs</u>); Desto DC-6480 (<u>Poems of Love and the Rain</u>; <u>Four Madrigals</u>; <u>From an Unknown Past</u>); CRI-238 (<u>Some Trees</u>; <u>Little Elegy</u>; <u>Night Crow</u>; <u>The Tulip Tree</u>; <u>Look Down, Fair Moon</u>; <u>What Sparks and Wiry Cries</u>; <u>For Poulenc</u>); Westminster WST-17147 (<u>Trio</u>).
<u>See</u>: D4, D7, D18, D40, D50

B387. _____. "The Songs of Ned Rorem." <u>Tempo</u> 127 (December 1978): 25-31.

An examination of Rorem's song compositions, his choice of poets, and his style of writing. "To be America's leading song writer at a time when practically nobody is writing songs may seem on the surface like no great distinction. But to have over a hundred songs in print, many of them sung and recorded by leading artists is a real achievement." While some songs and cycles are mentioned, the analysis really concerns Rorem's song writing style rather than a detailed analysis of specific titles.

B388. _____. "Two Very Different Sides of Ned Rorem." <u>American Record Guide</u> 37 (June 1971): 730-731.

Review of Desto 7101 recording of <u>War Scenes</u>; five songs to poems by Walt Whitman (<u>As Adam, Early in the Morning</u>; <u>O You Whom I Often and Silently Come</u>; <u>To You</u>; <u>Look Down, Fair Moon</u>; <u>Gliding o'er All</u>); and <u>Four Dialogues</u>. "The two sides of this disc show two very different sides of Ned Rorem, neither, perhaps, exactly what we have come to think of as characteristic."
<u>See</u>: D19

B389. Mimaroglu, Ilhan K.   "Gamson Conducts New American Music." <u>Musical America</u> 81 (December 1961): 44+.

Review of the October 12, 1961 New York premiere of Ned Rorem's <u>Eleven Studies for Eleven Instruments</u>. "The writing is tuneful, the texture highly coloristic. It is evocative and a little sentimental, yet never banal. The work has much of the elegance and grace usually described as Gallic."
<u>See</u>: W206

B390. "Moderns at Work." <u>Time</u> 69 (February 25, 1957): 60-61.

Review of the February 15, 1957 premiere of <u>The Poet's Requiem</u>. "The <u>Requiem</u>, a dissertation on death, uses

lines from such as Kafka, Rilke, Cocteau, Freud and Gide, weaving them into a melodic, bright-textured, intermittently impressionistic and generally success-ful score."
See: W151

B391. Monaco, Richard A.   "Secular Choral Octavos."   Notes (Music Library Association) 26 no. 1 (1969): 150.

Brief review of the score of Three Incantations from a Marionette Tale.   "These songs, dating from 1948, are suitable for a children's chorus. The vocal range is limited, and the rhythm is simple."
See: W87

B392. Moore, David W.   "Guide to Records."   American Record Guide 40 (July 1977): 30-31.

Review of CRI SD 362 recording of Book of Hours.   "It is meditative in mood but sufficiently colorful in texture to maintain its attractiveness to the lis-tener's ear."   Paired with Trio for Flute, Cello, and Piano, by Bohuslav Martinu.
See: D8

B393. _____.   "Guide to Records."   American Record Guide 43 (March 1980): 36.

Review of Grenadilla 1031 recording of Serenade on Five English Poems.   "...the tone of the work is som-bre and lonely, with extended passages of meditative monologue for each instrumentalist between songs." Paired with Robert Starer's Piano Quartet.
See: D27

B394. Moore, J. S.   "Rorem: Serenade on (5) English Poems." The New Records 47 no. 11 (January 1980): 6.

Review of Grenadilla GS-1031 recording of Serenade on (5) English Poems.   "Rorem has created a virtuosic piece for the instrumentalists and the vocalist. Opening with an extended solo string cadenza, the work proceeds with fierce intensity through all five poem fragments...Rorem is one of the most intelligent and innovative composers of our time...he has produced with this Serenade one of the rare contemporary works which will certainly stand the test of time..." Paired with Quartet for Piano and Strings, by Robert Starer.
See: D27

B395. Morrison, Bill.   "Maestro Prepares New Symphonic Star." The News and Observer (Raleigh, N.C.), October 5, 1975, sec. 5, p. 3.

Written in anticipation of the October 11, 1975 pre-miere of Ned Rorem's Assembly and Fall.   The interview with John Gosling, conductor of the North Carolina Symphony, includes information on the history and a

description of the work commissioned by the Symphony;
plans for future performances of the work; and notes
that the composer would be present for the premiere.
See: W225

B396. "Music Festival Honors Composer-in-Residence." Utah
Chronicle (Salt Lake City, Utah), January 28, 1966.

Introduction of Ned Rorem as the new composer-in-
residence at the University of Utah on the occasion of
the 18th Annual Chamber Music Festival. The announced
program for the first concert included: Mourning
Scene; Trio for Flute, Piano and Cello; and Four Dialogues.
See: W27, W109, W222

B397. "Music Notes from the Southeast Area." Pan Pipes 63 no.
4 (1971): 11-13.

Brief announcement that Four Fables by Ned Rorem was
premiered May 21-22, 1971 by the University of Tennessee (Martin) Opera Workshop under the direction of
Marilyn Jewett.
See: W175

B398. "Music: Rorem Work by Atlanta Symphony." New York
Times, April 12, 1986, p. 11.

Review of the April 6, 1986 New York premiere of
String Symphony. "...it is an attractive work, de-
spite--or perhaps because of--its long series of
well-worn expressive devices...even the most casual of
concertgoers could greet them all as old friends."
See: W241

B399. "Music: Three Premiers." New York Times, February 19,
1956, p. 79.

Review of the February 18, 1956 Carnegie Hall concert
presented by the National Association for American
Composers and Conductors during the seventeenth annual
American Music Festival. Among the three premieres
was Ned Rorem's First Symphony, "...a work of unusu-
ally sound craftsmanship showing richness of musical
invention...The composer shows an impressive grasp of
symphonic form and the ability to fill it with mean-
ingful music."
See: W243

B400. "Music Whys, Hows Fill Rorem Book." Salt Lake Tribune
(Utah), December 28, 1966.

Announcement of the publication of Music from Inside
Out, with liberal quotes from the text of the book.
See: W289

B401. "Names." Music Journal 39 no. 2 (March-April 1981): 6.

Brief mention of the premiere of Back to Life by Ned

Rorem in Hartford, Connecticut, March 28, 1981.
See: W107

B402. "Names to Remember." Vogue 127 (May 1, 1956): 117.
"Ned Rorem, an American composer with grave seraphic
charm..." is included among seven young, outstanding
artists of 1956.

B403. Nazzaro, William J.   "Intelligent and Exasperating."
Review of An Absolute Gift, by Ned Rorem. Philadelphia Evening Bulletin, July 30, 1978, sec. 5, p. 7.

"Reading a book by Ned Rorem is something like having
a handsome, cultured, intelligent, but exasperating
friend over for dinner...This is a book to dip into
rather than read straight through. Open to almost any
page, and you start right in with an intellectual
argument.   The verdict here is: sometimes incoherent,
often annoying, always provocative."
See: W284

B404. "Ned Rorem." Composers of the Americas 12 (1966): 136-
145.

Biographical information and a list of Rorem's works
through 1966. Written in English and Spanish.

B405. _____ . Pan Pipes 43 (1950): 128.

Announcement of the premiere of the Sonata for Violin
and Piano in Four Scenes in Washington, D.C.
See: W217

B406. "Ned Rorem, a Note on the Composer of This Month's
Supplement." Musical Times 106 (June 1965): 429.

Virelai was included as a supplement in this issue of
the periodical. Short biographical sketch about the
composer was also included.
See: W169

B407. "Ned Rorem 1976 Pulitzer Prize Winner for 'Air Music.'"
Woodwind World Brass & Percussion 15 (July 1976): 31.

Air Music is announced as the 1976 Pulitzer Prize winner for music.   Includes information about the December 4, 1975 premiere performance and the subsequent
performances the same month in Washington, D.C., New
York City and Pittsburgh.   "The 30-minute work has
been described as a 'genuine showpiece for a virtuoso
orchestra.'"
See: W224

B408. "Ned Rorem: October 23 (65th)." Boosey & Hawkes Newsletter 17 no. 2 (March 1988): 7.

Announcement of premieres, performances and publications of Ned Rorem's works during his 65th year.
Premieres include: The Death of Moses, January 28,

1988; Three Poems of Baudelaire, March 23, 1988; The Schuyler Songs, April 23, 1988; the orchestral version of A Quaker Reader, June 21, 1988; and Bright Music, summer 1988. Performances of his works include: Winter Pages, June 21, 1988; and String Symphony, March 4 and April 15-18, 1988. Also announced: the publication of The Nantucket Diary.
> See: W111, W125, W164, W202, W223, W238, W241, W290

B409. "Ned Rorem, of Many Talents." Boosey & Hawkes Newsletter 3 no. 1 (Fall/Winter 1968): 4.

A summary of 1968-69 premieres, performances, publications and new recordings of Ned Rorem's works. Mentioned are the premieres of Some Trees and Letters from Paris; performances of Lions, and the Third Symphony; recordings of Water Music, Ideas, Third Symphony; and his book, Music and People.
> See: D17, D47; W76, W138, W233, W245, W288

B410. "Ned Rorem on Chamber Music." American Ensemble 3 no. 4 (1980): 10-11.

Ned Rorem speaks to the 1980 Chamber Music America Conference. "I'd like to point out...that the song recital is chamber music par excellence. The human voice and piano is a chamber music entity."

B411. "New Music Corner: Ned Rorem." Key Classics 3 no. 5 (1983): 32-33.

Includes a short biography of Ned Rorem and the score for "Etude No. 2" from Eight Etudes for Piano. Ned Rorem describes the work as "...a study in silence. In context with the other Etudes, it acts as an island...appearing and disappearing through a silken fog fifty miles away...But do not think of it as 'impressionistic,' for the tune--the top voice--is not allusive and vague but must be evident and vocal.'"
> See: W185

B412. "New Publications." Musical Courier 139 (January 15, 1949): 24.

Announcement that Ned Rorem was the recipient of the George Gershwin Award, winning $1,000 for his composition Overture in C.
> See: W236

B413. "New Publications in Review." Musical Courier 142 no. 10 (December 15, 1950): 26.

Review of the score for The Silver Swan. "Rorem treats it in a quiet manner with a touch of modal harmonies and a bit of imitative melisma...Altogether a very well-done, expertly constructed song..."
> See: W74

B414. _____ . Musical Courier 143 no. 8 (April 15, 1951): 30.

Review of the score of Mountain Song. "...the quiet
melody has strong folk characteristics, and is highly
lyrical and modal...Flutists will find his an attractive work, well suited for concert."
See: W209

B415. _____ . Musical Courier 146 no. 7 (November 15, 1952):
31.

Review of the score of Flight For Heaven. "These
range from a rather heavy chromatic style in the accompaniment to songs that are charmingly simple and
transparent in texture. The texts are exquisite and
sensuous love poetry...An original and worthwhile
cycle for a gifted interpreter."
See: W24

B416. Newlin, Dika. "Books." Review of Setting the Tone:
Essays and a Diary, by Ned Rorem. Pan Pipes 77 no. 2
(Summer 1985): 13.

"As usual, this gifted composer/writer is original,
quirky and sometimes controversial. In 'Women and
Music'...he poses the rhetorical query, 'could a case
be made that even the greatest women have never given
way to the same vast flights of fancy as men?' I
could make a case that he and others (both women and
men) who think this way are part of the problem which
women composers have long faced...Read Rorem for entertainment, information, stimulation, titillation and
indignation!"
See: W296

B417. "News Notes." Inter-American Music Bulletin (English
Edition) 84 (July-October 1972): 9-11.

"Ned Rorem's 'Piano Concerto in Six Movements,' was
commissioned by the Aspen Music Foundation for the
pianist Jerome Lowenthal and premiered by him with the
Pittsburgh Symphony under William Steinberg in Pittsburgh in December, 1970."
See: W227

B418. "News Section: Composers." Tempo 126 (September 1978):
57.

Three-part announcement about Ned Rorem: the August
24, 1978 premiere of Sunday Morning; a commission from
the Cincinnati Symphony Orchestra; a commission by the
Elizabeth Sprague Coolidge Foundation for a new song
cycle to be premiered at the 1980 Coolidge Chamber
Music Festival.
See: W242

B419. _____ . Tempo 131 (December 1979): 37.

Brief announcement of the October 30, 1979 premiere of

The Nantucket Songs.
    See: W52

B420. _____ . Tempo 133-134 (September 1980): 96.

Brief announcement of the July 27, 1980 premiere of
Santa Fe Songs at the Santa Fe Chamber Music Festival.
    See: W110

B421. _____ . Tempo 136 (March 1981): 54.

Brief announcement of the March 15, 1981 premiere of
After Reading Shakespeare.
    See. W200

B422. _____ . Tempo 147 (December 1983): 49.

Brief announcement of the September 11, 1983 premiere
of Whitman Cantata, and the February 14, 1984 premiere
of Picnic On the Marne.
    See: W170, W211

B423. _____ . Tempo 149 (June 1984): 54.

Brief announcement of the May 6, 1984 premiere of
Dances, and the European premiere of After Long Silence, June 4, 1984.
    See: W105, W204

B424. _____ . Tempo 150 (September 1984): 59.

Brief announcement of the November 16, 1984 premiere
of Pilgrim Strangers.
    See: W150

B425. _____ . Tempo 151 (December 1984): 55.

Brief announcement in anticipation of the premiere of
An American Oratorio, January 1985. There is also a
note that Rorem is completing a Violin Concerto and an
Organ Concerto.
    See: W118, W234, W246

B426. _____ . Tempo 152 (March 1985): 49.

Brief announcement of the January 22, 1985 United
Kingdom premiere of Pilgrim Strangers and the March
19, 1985 premiere of Organ Concerto.
    See: W150, W234

B427. _____ . Tempo 153 (June 1985): 54.

Brief announcement that Scenes of Childhood would be
premiered in Santa Fe, NM by the Santa Fe Chamber
Ensemble, August 11, 1985.
    See: W214

B428. _____ . Tempo 157 (June 1986): 51-52.

Brief announcement of the April 12, 1986 premiere of
Frolic.
See: W231

B429. Nicholas, Louis.   "UTM Group Delightful at Belmont."
The Nashville Tennessean, November 21, 1971, sec. D,
P. 19.

Review of the November 20, 1971 performance of Fables.
"The modest requirements and the many possibilities
offered by 'Fables' should recommend it to many groups
for performance."
See: W175

B430. _____ .   "Diarist."   New York Times, July 24, 1966, sec.
7, p. 8.

Profile of Ned Rorem as a diarist.   From age 11, Mr.
Rorem kept a diary.   "He does not set down the entries
day by day but when the mood strikes him, and he re-
gards 'the diary as the disorderly side of myself, the
music the orderly side.'"

B431. "1984-85 Season Premieres."   Symphony Magazine 35 no. 5
(1984): 38.

Brief announcement that An American Oratorio would be
premiered January 4, 1985.
See: W118

B432. North, William Sills Wright.   "Ned Rorem as a Twentieth
Century Song Composer."   D.M.A. diss., University of
Illinois, 1965.

A study comparing "...thirty-two of the songs of Ned
Rorem to selected songs of twelve acknowledged leaders
in the field of contemporary song."

B433. Noss, Luther.   "Music Reviews."   Notes (Music Library
Association) 10 (September 1953): 686.

Review of the score of Pastorale for organ.   "The
Andantino from Symphony No. 1, written by Rorem in
1949, has been arranged for organ by the composer and
appears now under the title Pastorale.   Lacking the
color of the orchestra...the musical ideas of the
piece, however attractive, wear thin before the end."
See: W188

B434. "Notes on the Arts."   Philadelphia Inquirer, July 15,
1986, sec. F, p. 5.

Ned Rorem is included among seven composers commissioned to write works for the New York International
Festival of the Arts.

B435. Oberlin, Russell.   "Music Reviews."   Notes (Music
Library Association) 26 no. 4 (1970): 850.

Review of the score of <u>Three Poems of Paul Goodman</u>, for voice and piano. "These early songs show a young, derivative, sophisticated, and talented American in Paris already exercising his customary deftness for selected exquisite poetry. Prosody, always a strong point in Rorem's vocal writing, keeps eloquent hold on the reins of Goodman's poetic flights."
<u>See</u>: W12, W26, W100

B436. Ogasaplan, John. "Catharine Crozier in Recital." <u>American Organist</u>, 14 no. 9 (September 1980): 12.

Review of Gothic D-87904 recording of selections from <u>A Quaker Reader</u>. "...the music stands on its own as a <u>distinguished</u> contribution, not only to the literature for the organ but to twentieth-century musical literature as a whole."
<u>See</u>: D26

B437. Oliver, Michael. "American Songs for a Capella Choir." <u>Gramophone</u> 59 (August 1981): 307.

Review of Orion ORS 75205 recording of American choral music. Brief mention is given to Ned Rorem's <u>Sing My Soul</u>, "...a sentimentally chromatic hymn-tune..."
<u>See</u>: D43

B438. _____. "20th-Century American Choral Works." <u>Gramophone</u> 59 (March 1981): 1224.

Review of Gamut UT 7501 recording of American choral music including Ned Rorem's <u>Three Motets on Poems of Gerard Manley Hopkins</u>. These are "...simple and melodious, at times rather ploddingly syllabic, but with a touch of charming pictorialism..."
<u>See</u>: D25

B439. "On a Sad Note." <u>Hartford Courant</u> (Connecticut), December 1, 1986. (Located in Newsbank, Review of the Arts [Microform]. Review of Performing Arts, February 1987, 96:F14-G1.

Written in anticipation of the December 2-3, 1986 performance of <u>Concerto for Violin and Orchestra</u>. Includes an interview with Ned Rorem discussing topics in contemporary music.
<u>See</u>: W246

B440. "Opera Boom." <u>Time</u> 65 (May 23, 1955): 62-63.

Review of the premiere of <u>A Childhood Miracle</u>. The work "...was a fragile piece of Hawthorne about two little girls whose snowman comes to life and entertains them until grownups drag him indoors and he melts to a puddle by the firelight of reality. Composer Rorem...wields his Ravelian style with an almost too delicate hand. But he is, at 32, a master writer

for the human voice."
See: W174

B441. "Opera Review." Variety 240 (November 10, 1965): 81.

Review of the November 4, 1965 premiere performance of
Miss Julie. It "...must be recorded as workmanlike
modern score, hard-working if not inspired cast,
faithful libretto and busy staging--all adding up to
less than hit total."
See: W178

B442. Oppens, Kurt. "Program Notes." Aspen Music Festival,
August 23, 1968.

Program notes for the August 23, 1968 performance of
Trio for Flute, Cello, and Piano.
See: W222

B443. Osborne, Conrad L. "'Miss Julie' at City Center." High
Fidelity/Musical America 16 no. 1 (January 1966):
126-127+.

Lengthy review of the November 4, 1965 premiere of
Miss Julie. "...if one is going to use this play as
basic material at all, one is going to have to come to
grips, musically, with the two characters. This is
what has not been done in Rorem's work...It is impos-
sible not to like Rorem's melodic and rhythmic invention, the gifts that have served him so well as a song
writer."
See: W178

B444. _____. "Regina Sarfaty." High Fidelity/Musical America
15 no. 7 (July 1965): 106.

Review of the April 9, 1965 concert which included Ned
Rorem's Poems of Love and the Rain. "...at least one
of the more ambitious settings, e.e. cummings' Song
for Lying in Bed During a Night Rain, struck me as
really sustained lyric writing of a very high order."
See: W64

B445. _____. "Rorem: Songs." High Fidelity 14 no. 6 (June
1964): 78.

Review of Columbia ML 5961/6561 recording of thirty-
two Rorem songs. Mentioned specifically in the review
are: Upon Julia's Clothes; Early in the Morning; Song
for a Girl; The Nightingale; Sally's Smile; Visits to
St. Elizabeths; Root Cellar; and My Papa's Waltz.
Other songs include: To the Willow Tree; Echo's Song;
The Silver Swan; Three Psalms (Nos. 134, 148, 150);
The Lordly Hudson; Snake; Rain in Spring; Such Beauty
as Hurts to Behold; I Am Rose; See How They Love Me; A
Christmas Carol; The Call; Spring and Fall; Spring; To
You; Youth, Old Age, and Night; O You Whom I Often and
Silently Come; Pippa's Song; Lullaby of the Woman of

the Mountain; What If Some Little Pain; In a Gondola;
Requiem.
See: D4

B446. Page, Tim. "Books: 4-Part Harmony." Review of Setting
the Tone: Essays and a Diary, by Ned Rorem. New York
Times, December 28, 1983, sec. C, p. 24.

This book "...may well be his finest literary achievement to date...The tone Mr. Rorem has chosen in this
book is markedly less lachrymose than in some earlier
volumes and, despite a philosophic commitment to artifice, his insights have grown steadily more cohesive
and convincing."
See: W296

B447. _____. "Golden Fleece Ltd. Offers New Triple Bill."
New York Times, March 24, 1986, sec. C, p. 15.

Brief review of the March 22, 1986 performance of
Fables, "...elegant brittle settings of poems by Jean
de La Fontaine, staged without props or scenery."
See: W175

B448. _____. "Gregg Smith Singers at St. Peter's Church."
New York Times, January 17, 1984, sec. C, p. 13.

Brief review of the January 14, 1984 concert. Included in the program was Mercy and Truth Are Met,
described as "...deeply affecting, a brief, direct
expression of devotion."
See: W144

B449. _____. "Mini-Opera: Rorem-Stein Collaboration." New
York Times, November 24, 1985, p. 82.

Review of the November 21, 1985 performance of Three
Sisters Who Are Not Sisters. "It was staged with wit
and concision, and decently sung..."
See: W180

B450. _____. "Music: Debuts in Review." New York Times,
February 19, 1984, sec. 1, p. 89.

Review of the February 14, 1984 premiere of Picnic On
the Marne. "Achingly nostalgic, murky and raucous by
turn, this set of seven waltzes for saxophone and
piano is one of Mr. Rorem's finest instrumental compositions and deserves a place in the chamber-music
repertory."
See: W211

B451. _____. "Music: Debuts in Review." New York Times,
October 14, 1984, sec. 1, p. 63.

Review of the October 9, 1984 concert. Included in
the program was Ned Rorem's Suite for Guitar, "...a
succession of attractive vignettes, expertly crafted

for the instrument..."
<u>See</u>: W220

B452. Palatsky, Gene.   "Recitals.:   <u>Musical America</u> 83 (April 1963): 37-38.

Review of the February 9, 1963 premiere of <u>Sonata No. 3</u>, for piano. The sonata "...contained effective mood coloring in the Andante, buoyancy in the Scherzando, and some brilliant invention in the opening and closing Allegros."
<u>See</u>: W195

B453. Parmenter, Ross.   "Opera: New 1-Act Works."   <u>New York Times</u>, April 16, 1958, p. 40.

Review of the April 14, 1958 premiere of <u>The Robbers</u>. "His music, which had some attractively lyric moments and a good male trio, was not gripping or graphic enough to convey much atmosphere and it was hard to believe in his characters."
<u>See</u>: W179

B454. Pasles, Chris.   "A Musical Gentleman of a Certain Age." Review of <u>Nantucket Diary of Ned Rorem, 1973-1985</u>, by Ned Rorem.   <u>Los Angeles Times</u>, September 20, 1987, sec. B, p. 2.

Comparing this new volume with the previous diaries, the reviewer states, "In this new volume, the composer's record is even more sprawling and burdened with excessive, trivial details." But there are rewards "...for readers willing to slog through a mass of details."
<u>See</u>: W290

B455. Paton, John Glenn.   "Music Reviews."   <u>Notes</u> (Music Library Association) 37 no. 3 (1981): 698.

Brief review of the score of <u>Serenade on Five English Poems</u>. "Ostinatos lend a sense of control to several passages, and the final song summons up harmonic energy for a strong climax."
<u>See</u>: W112

B456. _____. "Music Reviews."   <u>Notes</u> (Music Library Association) 39 no. 4 (1983): 953-954.

Review of the score of <u>The Nantucket Songs</u>. "Too much that came between the earliest and the latest works has struck me as marred by harmonic indirection, by casual accompaniments in the manner of a clever improviser, even sometimes by careless handling of poetic rhythms. Reluctantly, I note these same flaws in an uneven new collection, <u>The Nantucket Songs</u>. Rorem uses the word 'cycle' for these songs written on Nantucket Island, but they have nothing in common as

to music or text."
See: W52

B457. Pearson, Allan.   "Rorem Caps Santa Fe Visit Tonight."
Albuquerque Journal, July 27, 1980, sec. D, p. 2.

Written in anticipation of the premiere of The Santa
Fe Songs, Mr. Rorem discusses the circumstances surrounding the commissioning of the work, and his choice
of a poet.   "Witter Bynner spoke to my condition, as
we Quakers say..."
See: W110

B458. _____. "Rorem-Parker Music Team Recalls Its Birth in a
Storm."   Albuquerque Journal, July 25, 1980, sec. H,
p. 30.

Written in anticipation of the premiere of The Santa
Fe Songs and a performance of War Scenes during the
Santa Fe Chamber Music Festival.   William Parker
describes the circumstances surrounding his first
meeting with Ned Rorem.
See: W98, W110

B459. "People." Symphony News 27 no. 3 (1976): 53.

Brief announcement that Ned Rorem was awarded the 1976
Pulitzer Prize in Music for Air Music which was pre-
miered December 5, 1975.
See: W224

B460. Perkins, Francis D.   "Stimer at Town Hall."   New York
Herald Tribune, October 7, 1949, p. 17.

Review of the October 6, 1949 premiere of Ned Rorem's
Piano Sonata I.   It reveals "...some individual and
cogent musical ideas and also expressive communica-
tiveness, although the style and idiom has its contemporary and earlier influences.   Frequent contrast of
moods, stormy and meditative, marked much of the well
received new work."
See: W194

B461. Peyser, Joan.   "New Rorem Delivers a Solo on the State
of Music."   New York Times, May 3, 1987, sec. H,
p. 21.

Lengthy interview in which Ned Rorem discusses his
work both as a writer and a composer, and in which he
openly criticizes the state of contemporary music and
contemporary composers.   Some biographical information
is included.

B462. Pfunke, Peter C.   "Collections."   American Record Guide
46 (July 1983): 63-64.

Review of Opus One 73 recording of Sonata No. 1.   "...
beautiful lyric writing..."   The record includes Sona-

tina, by Samuel Adler, and Spirals by Roger Briggs.
See: D41

B463. Phillips, Harvey E.   "New York."   Opera News 37 no. 6
(December 9, 1972): 35-37.

Review of the October 4, 1972 performance of Three
Sisters Who Are Not Sisters.   "Ned Rorem's Three Sisters Who Are Not Sisters went on twice as long as
necessary, its slippery musical idiom at odds with the
repetitive but quaintly mesmerizing text."
See: W180

B464. Picano, Felice.   "Revelatory Rorem."   Review of Setting
the Tone; The Paris and New York Diaries; and The
Later Diaries, by Ned Rorem.   Christopher Street 7 no.
12 (January 1984): 51-53.

Review of three of Ned Rorem's books, one newly
published and two reprinted.   "Especially in the
diaries, but also in the collected essays, the portrait gallery he presents is bustling, choice, sharply
observed, intuitive, with the just right amount of
offhandedness...to be utterly convincing and worth a
shelfload of definitive biographies."
See: W287, W292, W296

B465. Pilar, Lilian Nobleza.   "The Vocal Style of Ned Rorem in
the Song Cycle Poems of Love and the Rain."   Ph.D.
diss., Indiana University, 1972.

Analyses of the 17 songs of the cycle.
See: W64

B466. Plum, Nancy.   "A Conversation with Composer Ned Rorem."
Voice (November/December 1985): 1+.

Interview, with Ned Rorem giving his opinions on contemporary music, composers, his compositional style,
and audiences.   He gives details about some of his
choral music, the people and circumstances surrounding
the composition and premieres of The 70th Psalm, Four
Madrigals, String Symphony, The Poets' Requiem, Missa
brevis, American Oratorio, and Whitman Cantata.
See: W118, W129, W147, W151, W159, W170, W241

B467. Pochkanawalla, Jimmy F.   "Inspired Concert."   Indian
Express (Bombay, India), April 10, 1986.

Review of the March 31, 1986 world premiere of Ned
Rorem's End of Summer.   "There is a bit of descriptive
programming involved in the work which, on the whole
is quite enjoyable."
See: W207

B468. Porter, Andrew."Ducal Splendor."   New Yorker 58
(November 15, 1982): 199-201.

Review of the November 2, 1982 recital which included Ned Rorem's Ariel. "...Rorem caught the poet's tone of disciplined desperation, of high emotion forced into controlled imagery."
See: W106

B469. _____. "Musical Events." New Yorker 56 (September 15, 1960): 161-164.

Review of the Santa Fe Chamber Music Festival concerts in New York during August 1980. Concerning Santa Fe Songs: "...a lyrical and beautiful work...music of eloquence, unself-conscious charm, and fine, inventive workmanship." Includes an analysis of the work.
See: W110

B470. _____. "Musical Events."   New Yorker 63 (July 20, 1987): 72.

Review of the Houston Symphony Orchestra's Fanfare Project honoring the Texas Sesquicentennial. Twenty-one fanfares were commissioned and performed, among them Frolic by Ned Rorem. It "...is a catchy, tuneful charmer; some moments bring Bernstein to mind, others early Stravinsky, and all is buoyant, playful, and sure."
See: W231

B471. "Premieres." American Organist 22 (January 1988): 52.

Announcement of the October 21, 1987 New York premiere of Organ concerto.
See" W234

B472. _____. Music Educators Journal 60 no. 8 (April 1974): 125.

Brief mention of the March 3, 1974 premiere of In Time of Pestilence.
See: W136

B473. _____. Music Educators Journal 63 no. 8 (April 1977): 11.

Brief mention of the November 4, 1976 premiere of Women's Voices.
See: W103

B474. _____. Music Journal 29 no. 2 (February 1971): 63.

Brief mention of the December 3, 1971 premiere of the Concerto in Six Movements.
See: W227

B475. _____. Music Journal 30 no. 10 (December 1972): 4+.

Brief mention of the premieres of Day Music, October 15, 1972; Last Poems of Wallace Stevens, November 13, 1972; Canticles and Gloria, November 26, 1972; and

Night Music, January 13, 1973.
See: W32, W108, W122, W205, W210

B476. _____ . Music Journal 31 no. 2 (February 1973): 8-11.

Brief mention of the November 13, 1972 concert which
featured the premiere of Last Poems of Wallace
Stevens.
See: W108

B477. _____ . "Premieres." Music Journal 32 no. 7 (September
1974): 18.

Brief mention of the premiere of Little Prayers. The
work "...consists of a setting of 15 brief invocations
to the Creator Spirit written by the composer's late
friend, Paul Goodman."
See: W141

B478. _____ . Music Journal 35 no. 5 (May 1977): 47.

Brief mention of the premiere of Ned Rorem's chamber
opera Hearing during the Festival of Contemporary
Vocal Chamber Music, March 15, 17, and 22, 1977.
See: W176

B479. _____ . Symphony News 26 no. 6 (1975): 34.

Brief announcement of the premiere of Assembly and
Fall.
See: W225

B480. _____ . Symphony News 27 no. 2 (1976): 29.

Brief announcement of the December 5, 1975 premiere of
Air Music.
See: W224

B481. _____ . Symphony News 29 no. 5 (1978): 41.

Brief announcement of the August 25, 1978 premiere of
Sunday Morning.
See: W242

B482. "Present Ned Rorem in Unique Program." New Jersey Music
& Arts (January 1969): 3.

Written in anticipation of the February 2, 1969 all-
Rorem concert at Montclair (N.J.) State College.
Included in the program were a selection of songs and
the Trio for Flute, Cello and Piano.
See: W222

B483. "Program Notes." Aspen Music Festival, July 11, 1982.

Program notes for the July 11, 1982 performance of
Lions (a Dream).
See: W233

B484. _____ . Aspen Music Festival, August 1, 1982.

Program notes for the August 1, 1982 performance of Remembering Tommy. Contains information on the evolution of the title of the work.
See: W239

B485. _____ . Aspen Music Festival, August 3, 1982.

Program notes for the August 3, 1982 performance of The Santa Fe Songs.
See: W110

B486. _____ . Aspen Music Festival, August 10, 1982.

Program notes for the August 10, 1982 performance of Sun.
See: W115

B487. "Pulitzer Won by Post's Dance Critic." Washington Post, May 4, 1976, sec. A, p. 1.

Winners of the Pulitzer Prizes are announced, among them, Ned Rorem for Air Music.
See: W224

B488. "PW Forecasts." Review of Setting the Tone: Essays and a Diary, by Ned Rorem. Publishers Weekly 223 no. 18 (May 6, 1983): 89.

"Now almost 60, Ned Rorem...brings together 35 new essays and diary entries and 12 earlier pieces in which he contemplates himself and his contemporaries. Here are fresh but also repetitious musings on vanity, being alone, lovers and friends..."
See: W296

B489. Raether, Keith. "Chamber Music Festival Defies Money Woes, Forges on." Albuquerque Journal, June 28, 1985, sec. F, P. 3.

General article about the Santa Fe Chamber Music Festival, including information about Ned Rorem as composer-in-residence; the August 11, 1985 premiere of Septet: Scenes from Childhood; and the August 18-19, 1985 performance of Santa Fe Songs.
See: W110, W214

B490. Ramey, Phillip. "Ned Rorem: Not Just a Song Composer." Keynote 4 no. 3 (1980): 12-15.

Lengthy interview during which Ned Rorem discusses the effect of the Pulitzer prize on his work; the economics of music; his methods of music composition; the works of other composers; teaching composition; and self-criticism.

B491. _____ . "Songs of Ned Rorem." Liner notes on New World

Records 229, <u>Songs of Samuel Barber and Ned Rorem</u>.

Program notes and interview in which Ned Rorem discusses his songs.
<u>See</u>: D37

B492. Raney, Carolyn. "Rorem at Intercession." <u>Music (AGO)</u> 7
no. 2 (February 1973): 52-52.

Review of the November 26, 1972 concert which featured
works by Ned Rorem. The <u>Gloria</u> "...expresses the composer at his best, fashioning his arched vocal lines
from a few interlocking motives and building climaxes
into each section." The <u>Canticles</u> were "...less impressive than the <u>Gloria</u>." <u>The Proper for the Votive</u>
<u>Mass of the Holy Spirit</u> "...proved to be a pleasant
work...with a dramatic section for communion as the
emotional climax." <u>Poèmes pour la paix</u> are "...most
vocal and moving."
<u>See</u>: W32, W63, W121, W122, W156

B493. Raver, Leonard. "Music Reviews." <u>Notes</u> (Music Library
Association) 35 no. 3 (1979): 726-727.

Review of the score of <u>A Quaker Reader</u>; 11 pieces for
organ. "Ned Rorem's first major organ work is a most
impressive suite...the music has great power, variety
and lyric charm so characteristic of Rorem's music...
Without question, Ned Rorem has added a major work of
impressive proportions to contemporary organ repertoire and there is already evidence that it will grow
in stature and be widely played."
<u>See</u>: W189

B494. _____. "The Solo Organ Music of Ned Rorem." <u>American</u>
<u>Organist</u> 17 (October 1983): 67-71.

Survey of Ned Rorem's organ compositions with analysis
of <u>A Quaker Reader</u> and <u>Views from the Oldest House</u>.
<u>See</u>: W189, W199

B495. "Raver, Seven Composers in Residence at UNO Festival."
<u>Omaha World Herald</u>, May 18, 1986, Entertainment sec-
tion, p. 13.

Brief biographical sketches of Leonard Raver and seven
composers, including Ned Rorem, who were in residence
during the Contemporary Music Festival at the University of Nebraska at Omaha, May, 1986.

B496. Read, Gardner. "Music Review." <u>Notes</u> (Music Library
Association) 25 no. 3 (1969): 591-593.

Review of the score of <u>Lions</u>. "This is a highly romantic work, the temperament of its composer evident
on every page. Also in constant evidence is Rorem's
skill as an orchestrator and his ability to make a

musical point without equivocation."
See: W233

B497. "Readers React to Rorem vs. Goldstein." <u>New York Times</u>,
November 16, 1969, sec. B, p. 36.

Letters to the editor concerning the Goldstein/Rorem
controversy over pop music and critics.
See: B186, B597

B498. "Renowned Composer Comes to University." <u>Utah Chronicle</u>
(Salt Lake City, UT), May 17, 1965.

Announcement by the University of Utah that "Ned
Rorem, a distinguished composer...is joining the
University Music Department faculty as lecturer in
music and composer-in-residence."

B499. Rice, Joe D. "Symphony Opens Season at New Home." <u>The
News and Observer</u> (Raleigh, N.C.), October 13, 1975,
p. 19.

Review of the October 11, 1975 premiere of <u>Assembly
and Fall</u>. "The piece began interestingly enough with
the strings providing a flat, but not colorless, back-
ground for a variety of tonal colors from winds and
percussion...Unfortunately the composition never quite
got off the ground in terms of fresh new ideas. With
the exception of a luscious viola solo it had little
to say."
See: W225

B500. Rich, Alan. "'I Have No Chez Moi Here.'" Review of <u>The
Nantucket Diary of Ned Rorem,1973-1985</u>, by Ned Rorem.
<u>Newsweek</u> 110 (October 12, 1987): 86.

"Early in the glory days of his 'Paris Diaries,' Ned
Rorem had asked whether the beauty of youth--un-
ashamedly self-celebrated with elegant bitchcraft in
those pages--could coexist with the wisdom of age.
Thirty-five years later comes his ringing affirmative
answer...the author of these intense if effulgent
diary lines <u>is</u> someone who matters, a composer reck-
oned among this country's best, a concerned observer
of contemporary culture."
See: W290

B501. _____. "Maximum Literate." <u>New York</u> 6 (December 17,
1973): 108.

Review of the November 25-26, 1973 concerts at Tully
Hall, featuring all-Rorem programs. "If the two concerts of Rorem's music produced at Tully Hall late
last month accomplished nothing else, they at least
served to convince the doubters that Rorem is one of
the most gifted, versatile, and important composers
this country has produced."

B502.   _____. "NAACC Honors Hadley in Concert." Musical Amer-
        ica 81 (February 1961): 51.

        Review of the December 19, 1960 concert in honor of
        Henry Hadley. Ned Rorem's Trio for Flute, Cello and
        Piano received its New York premiere performance.
        "The Rorem Trio...teemed with interesting experiments
        in sonority, bristling rhythmic quirks and harmonic
        surprises, but vacillated uneasily among the more
        fashionable of today's compositional techniques."
        See: W222

B503.   Rickert, Lawrence Gould. "Selected American Song Cycles
        for Baritone Composed Since 1945--Part 3."   NATS
        Bulletin 23 no. 3 (1967): 13-15.

        Includes three cycles by Ned Rorem, historical infor-
        mation and analysis of each, and some biographical
        information about the composer. Another Sleep has
        "...an interesting use of the same thematic material
        in the first and last song of this cycle. This cyclic
        treatment helps to make Another Sleep a cycle in the
        Beethoven tradition." Flight for Heaven "...demands
        an accomplished pianist and singer, it lies within the
        possibility of successful performance with careful
        preparation. This is the type of music which grows on
        the performer with repeated work and study." From an
        Unknown Past, a "...cycle of songs with a madrigal
        character is simple and effective enough to be suit-
        able for most singers."
        See: W5, W24, W31

B504.   Ringo, James. "Acts of Faith with the Past." Review of
        Music and People, by Ned Rorem. American Record Guide
        36 (May 1970): 760-762.

        "Ned Rorem's thought-provoking Music and People is not
        wholly a memory volume; in addition to soundings of
        the past there are reviews, a 'sermon,' a letter to
        the press, a puff about a fellow composer...and hap-
        pily--as always in Rorem's books...more of his diary
        entries..."
        See: W288

B505.   _____. "Contemporary Music: Whence, and Whither?" Re-
        view of Critical Affairs: a Composer's Journal, by Ned
        Rorem. American Record Guide 38 (May 1972): 442-444.

        "Critical Affairs, offers random thoughts, an assort-
        ment of considerations, and a crotchet or two--whim-
        sical conceits of an inquiring mind and a lively
        intelligence."
        See: W285

B506.   _____. "Rorem: Some Trees, Songs." Opera News 36 no.
        11 (February 5, 1972): 34.

        Review of CRI 238-USD recording with "...secure,

flavorful performances by Phyllis Curtin, Beverly
Wolff and Donald Gramm..." and Ned Rorem, piano. The
recording also includes works by William Flanagan,
Ezra Laderman, and David Ward Steinman.
See: D7

B507. _____. "Rorem: War Scenes, Song." Opera News 36 no. 11
(February 5, 1972): 34.

Review of Desto DC-7101 recording of War Scenes, songs
to poems by Walt Whitman; and Four Dialogues. Concerning War Scenes: "The vocal lines are simple and
declamatory, wedded to accompaniments of an austerity
greater than usual for this composer." Concerning the
Whitman songs: "...a welcome contrast." Concerning
Four Dialogues: "...a tough comedy of love's cross-
currents."
See: D19

B508. _____. "Scanning the Geography of the Heart." Review
of The New York Diary of Ned Rorem, by Ned Rorem.
American Record Guide 34 (May 1968): 863-864.

Review of The New York Diary. "Rorem's diaries remain
the seismograph of a human heart, recording tremors,
subterranean explosions, upheavals, and also perilous
periods of treacherous calm."
See: W291

B509. Rivers, Earl G., Jr. "The Significance of Melodic
Procedure in the Choral Works of Ned Rorem." D.M.A.
diss., University of Cincinnati, 1976.

Analyses of Ned Rorem's choral works published prior
to 1974.

B510. Rizzo, Eugene R. "Strindberg in Song." Opera News 30
no. 7 (November 6, 1965): 20.

Written in anticipation of the November 4, 1965 premiere of Miss Julie. Information is given about the
cast, the history of the composition, and plot innova-
tions which deviate from Strindberg's original play.
See: W178

B511. Robb, Anne. "Ned Rorem Offers a Bounty of Songs, a Gift
of Words, the Stuff of Art." Hartford Courant (Connecticut), March 27, 1981. (Located in Newsbank,
Review of the Arts [Microform]. Review of Performing
Arts, July 1980-June 1981, 118: F14-G1, fiche).

Written in anticipation of the March 28, 1981 per-
formance of Ned Rorem's works at Trinity Episcopal
Church, Hartford, CT, during which Back to Life was
premiered. Other works on the program were The Last
Poems of Wallace Stevens and Flight for Heaven.
See: W24, W107, W108

B512. Rockwell, John.   "Cantilena Players Honor Rorem."   New York Times, November 22, 1977, p. 49.

Review of the first of three 'Helena Rubinstein Concerts' on November 20, 1977.   Included was Rorem's Serenade on Five English Poems.   "It's a most effective score, one of the most moving and passionate of Mr. Rorem's that this listener has heard."
See: W112

B513. _____.   "Chamber: 'Santa Fe Songs' Given New York Premiere."   New York Times, August 27, 1980, sec. 3, p. 23.

Review of the Santa Fe Chamber Music Festival Concert at Alice Tully Hall, August 25, 1980.   Included was the New York premiere of The Santa Fe Songs.   "Mr. Rorem has long been noted as perhaps America's foremost contemporary composer of art songs, and this latest piece counts among his masterpieces...the whole work would seem to count as a milestone of recent American composition."
See: W110

B514. _____.   "Concert: Rorem Premieree at Juilliard."   New York Times, February 4, 1982, sec. 3, p. 13.

Review of the January 29, 1982 New York premiere of Remembering Tommy.   "Characteristically conservative in idiom...it seemed atypical of the composer's work in other respects.   It is long; even a bit rambling, and bereft of vocal parts...There are many gripping moments, but the overall coherence was difficult to discern on a first hearing."
See: W239

B515. _____.   "Music: Composers Showcase."   New York Times, March 4, 1983, sec. C, p. 32.

Review of the March 2, 1983 Composers Showcase Concert.   Included were Ned Rorem's Women's Voices, War Scenes, Gloria and Early In the Morning.
See: W18, W32, W98, W103

B516. _____.   "Music: Verdehr Trio in Five Recent Works."   New York Times, December 13, 1986, p. 13.

Review of the December 10, 1986 performance of The End of Summer.   The work "...had a sad quality that was really very moving, an elegant mourning for something lost that never stooped to bathos.   The gentle quotations of the second movement seemed especially affecting."
See: W207

B517. Rogeri, Alfredo.   "New Works."   Music Journal 23 no. 2 (February 1965): 106-107.

Review of the December 15, 1964 premiere of <u>Lovers</u>.
<u>See</u>: W208

B518. Roos, James. "Ned Rorem: Musical Question Man." <u>Miami</u>
<u>Herald</u>, October 18, 1978, sec. B, p. 6.

Written in anticipation of the October 18, 1978 concert of Rorem compositions at the University of Miami
Concert Hall. Rorem addresses the state of women composers, composers in general and says, "...he feels
'dangerously lucky to be a composer...Because I live
off my music and there's no assurance where the next
commission will come from.'"

B519. _____. "New World Festival of the Arts." High Fidel-
ity/Musical America 32 no. 11 (November 1982): MA 27+.

Review of performances at the New World Festival of
the Arts in Miami, June 1982. Included were <u>Winter</u>
<u>Pages</u> and the premiere of <u>After Long Silence</u>. <u>After</u>
<u>Long Silence</u> is "...a major statement..."
<u>See</u>: W105, W223

B520. Rorem, Ned. "After-thoughts on Francis." <u>American</u>
<u>Record Guide</u> 35 (September 1968): 11-14.

Commentary on Francis Poulenc and his works. Rorem
describes his last meeting with Poulenc, who told him,
"No, song is not your real nature, instruments are.'"

B521. Rorem, Ned. "All's in a Name." <u>Perspectives of New Mu-</u>
<u>sic</u> 19 nos. 1-2 (1981-1982): 51.

A tribute "For Aaron Copland at 80," for which Ned
Rorem contributed a theme derived from both their
names.

B522. _____. "The American Art Song from 1930 to 1960: a Personal Survey." Liner notes on New World Records NW
243, <u>But Yesterday Is Not Today</u>.

Brief history and discussion of American art song.

B523. _____. "...and Another Perspective." Review of <u>The</u>
<u>Toscanini Musicians Knew</u>, by B. H. Haggin. <u>American</u>
<u>Record Guide</u> 34 (January 1968): 421+.

"The tone of such a book naturally would depend largely on who was interviewed...And the content, because
it is redundant and one-sided, is boring."

B524. _____. "...and His Music." <u>Bulletin of the American</u>
<u>Composers Alliance</u> 9 no. 4 (1961): 13-17.

A comprehensive discussion of the works of William
Flanagan.

B525. _____. "Approaching a Centenary: a Note on Stravinsky."

London Magazine 21 no. 11 (February 1982): 58-68.
(Also published as "Happy Birthday, Dear Igor." Opera
News 46 (January 2, 1982): 10-13+)

Ned Rorem comments on the works of Stravinsky, which
"...come less through a reappraisal of his career than
through a reassessment of my response to that career
..."

B526. Rorem, Ned. "An Auden."   Review of W. H. Auden, a
Biography, by Humphrey Carpenter. Christopher Street
5 no. 9 (September/October 1981): 40-45.   (Also in
Christopher Street Reader, edited by Michael Denneny,
Charles Ortleb, Thomas Steel, 281-289.   New York:
Perigee Books, 1983)

"Humphrey Carpenter's survey is a model of scholarship.   It is virtually without editorializing, and
almost willfully without style, a wise choice...since
to write with style about style is to becloud the
issue."

B527. _____ . "Being Alone."   The Ontario Review 13 (1980-
1981): 5-26.

Miscellany of diary, ideas, and observations written
between 1977 and 1979.

B528. _____ . "Being Ready: From the Diary of a Composer."
Washington Post Book World (August 12, 1979): 17-24.
(Also published in Christopher Street 5 no. 5 (May/
April 1981): 58-59)

Observations on a wide variety of topics including:
language, charm, and learning; and being artistic.

B529. _____ . "Bernard Shaw on Music: a Clear-Minded Muck-
raker."   Review of The Great Composers: Reviews and
Bombardments, by Bernard Shaw, edited by Louis Crompton.   Chicago Tribune, September 10, 1978, sec. 7,
p. 1+.

"...Louis Crompton...has expertly assembled a huge
wreath of Shavian musicana curving around a central
theme, Shaw's view of greatness, and held together by
choices that focus more on what is played than on who
plays it."

B530. _____ . "Beyond Playing."   In The Lives of the Piano,
edited by James R. Gaines, 115-141.   New York: Holt,
Rinehart and Winston, 1981.

Contains biographical information about Ned Rorem; his
recollections and early experiences with the piano;
his teachers and training through the years.   He includes observations about many pianists and composers
as performers.
    See: B68

B531. Rorem, Ned. "Books on Music." Reviews of Stravinsky: The Chronicle of a Friendship, Robert Craft; Walt Whitman & Opera, by Robert D. Faner; and Music Primer, by Lou Harrison. New Republic 166 (June 3, 1972): 23-25. (The second title also published in part under the title "Pure Contraption" in West Hills Review: A Walt Whitman Journal 2 (Fall 1980): 73-78)

Concerning Stravinsky: The Chronicle of a Friendship: "The book is a diary in the real sense of depicting Stravinsky's days of finicky order in his own work and unflagging interest in other people's." Concerning Walt Whitman and Opera: It "...is sometimes inadvertently funny, but from the standpoint of an American composer or historian it is often beneath contempt." Concerning Music Primer: "There are pages of crystalline maxims, earthy advice and charts of exercises geared to start off a pupil immediately on the creation of music rather than theory."

B532. _____. "Boulez. Christopher Street 5 no. 1 (October 1980): 50-53.

Discussion of the works of Pierre Boulez and his influence on contemporary music.

B533. _____. "Britten's Venice." New Republic 172 (February 8, 1975): 31-32.

Review of a performance of Benjamin Britten's Death in Venice. "In his opera, Britten, by telling what we've always heard without listening, rejuvenated our ears."

B534. _____. "Can't Eat Politics...Can't Eat Art." Vogue 154 (December 1969): 92+.

A commentary on the lack of recognition received by the Arts.

B535. _____. "Cocteau." London Magazine 22 nos. 1-2 (April/May 1982): 38-59. (Abridged version published in Christopher Street 6 no. 2 (February 1982): 56-59)

Discussion of Cocteau's influence on music, composers, and the arts. "Yet if he had neither an ear nor an eye for music, he did have a nose for it, and that nose was infallible for how music could decorate his own art."

B536. _____. "Come Back Paul Bowles." New Republic 166 April 23, 1972): 24+. (also published under the title "Paul Bowles: The Composer as Author" in London Magazine 12 no. 3 (August/September 1972): 124-127)

Review of Paul Bowles' autobiography. "...the final crabbed product comes to less than the sum of its parts...his prose in this book seems momentarily exhausted."

B537. Rorem, Ned. "Complete Songs of Fauré." <u>Stereo Review</u> 39
no. 2 (August 1977): 120-121.

Review of Connoisseur Society CS-2127/8 and Musical
Heritage Society 3438/3448 recordings of the songs of
Fauré.

B538. _____. "Composer and Performer." <u>American Record Guide</u>
29 (January 1962): 348-350+.

Description of the compositional process and the joys
and disappointments on hearing one's work performed.
"The composer will never hear his music in reality as
he heard it in spirit. Small wonder that his interest
sometimes wanes when notation or even formation, is
accomplished."

B539. _____. "The Composer and the Music Teacher." Review of
<u>Nadia Boulanger: a Life in Music</u>, by Leonie Rosen-
stiel. <u>New York Times Book Review</u> (May 23, 1982): 1+.
(Also published in <u>London Magazine</u> 22 (December 1982/
January 1983): 112-117)

"Information, as a documentary mass, is the book's
main and irreplaceable asset."

B540. _____. "A Composer Offers Some Candid Thoughts on His
Art." <u>New York Times</u>, May 1, 1983, sec. 2, p. 21.

"Looking about, seeing death everywhere, I realize
that my gaudy past is past. Anyone can be drunk, anyone can be in love, anyone can waste time and weep,
but only I can pen my songs in the few remaining years
or minutes."

B541. _____. "Considering Carmen." <u>Opera News</u> 43 no. 7
(December 9, 1978): 8-11+ (Reprinted in <u>San Francisco</u>
<u>Opera Magazine</u> 4 (Summer 1983): 24+)

Ned Rorem gives his personal recollections and impressions of Bizet's <u>Carmen</u>.

B542. _____. "The Copy of Music." <u>Confrontation</u> 33 (1986):
236 (Previously published in <u>Confrontation</u> 9 (1974):
129)

A protest concerning the practice of church choirs
using photocopied music. "A living composer...re-
ceives neither money nor the token consolation of
published praise."

B543. _____. "Courageous Coward." Review of <u>The Noel Coward</u>
<u>Diaries</u>, edited by Graham Payn and Sheridan Morley.
<u>Christopher Street</u> 6 no. 7 (August 1982): 56-71.

"Uneasy as I was made by the superficiality of his
book, I, who am morbidity incarnate and who also keep
a diary, was nonetheless elated by his ability ever to
rise above adversity, mainly by sheer conceit. Courageous Coward!"

B544. Rorem, Ned. "Critics Criticized." Harper's Magazine 241 (August 1970): 90-92.

Commentary on critics and musical criticism.

B545. _____. "Cruising from Coast to Coast." Review of States of Desire: Travels in Gay America, by Edmund White. Washington Post Book World (January 27, 1980): 3.

"The prose of Edmund White...as he recounts his travels in gay America, glimmers and surges into channels far wider than his stated theme, and in a mode that could make even bee-raising a hit course at West Point."

B546. _____. "Decors of Sound." House Beautiful 111 no. 4 (April 1969): 102-103+.

"Musical thoughts on emotion and environment."

B547. _____. "Diary." "Centerpoint 2 no. 3 (1977): 32-40.

Undated entries of Ned Rorem's diaries from the years 1973-75. "The hero of my diary is a fictional man upon whom I've worked hard but who has little to do with me--including the me penning this sentence, who is also the hero of my diary."

B548. _____. "Diary of a Composer." Music Journal 23 no. 7 (October 1965): 26-27+.

Random thoughts extracted from his diary.

B549. _____. "A Diary: Paris, Piaf, Picasso--and Rorem." New York Times, June 12, 1966, p. 15+.

Selections from The Paris Diary of Ned Rorem.
See: W293

B550. _____. "A Dissonant Elegy by a Soviet Composer." Review of Testimony: the Memoirs of Dmitri Shostakovich, edited by Solomon Volkov. Chicago Tribune, November 18, sec. 7, p. 1+.

"The editor...has not seen how to tread that fine line between the literal and the literary. Despite his attested organization the result is a mess--albeit a thrilling mess..."

B551. _____. "Elliott Carter." Review of Flawed Words and Stubborn Sounds, by Allen Edwards. New Republic 166 (February 26, 1972): 22+.

Ned Rorem reviews a book about Elliott Carter. "On closing this book we ache from structure talk and long for living notes - for what...Wallace Stevens called not ideas about the thing but the thing itself."

B552. Rorem, Ned. "'Everything Comes Out Berlioz!'" New York
Times, August 2, 1970, sec. 2, p. 11.

An adaptation of a chapter from Ned Rorem's Critical
Affairs. "An artist may see deeper than others, but
only into himself...Never ask his advice about a
neighboring art. How can he know about that? Never
listen to him on politics. Don't listen to me."
See: W285

B553. _____. "Ezra Pound as Musician." American Record Guide
34 (May 1968): 708-710+. (Also published as "Introduction." In Antheil and the Treatise on Harmony, by
Ezra Pound. New York: Da Capo Press, 1964; and London
Magazine 7 (January 1968): 27-41)

General discussion of Ezra Pound's Antheil and the
Treatise on Harmony in which Pound attempted to revo-
lutionize musical and literary art.

B554. _____. "Five Portraits from 'An Absolute Gift.'" Gays-
week 53 (February 20, 1978): 45.

Brief vignettes of Proust, Antonioni, Wilson, Barber,
and Ailey.

B555. _____. "Four Questions Answered." Music Journal 24 no.
5 (May 1966): 41-42+.

Rorem answers four questions most frequently asked of
him: "Do you write popular or classical?...Do you compose at the piano"...How do you make a living?...Where
do you get inspiration?"

B556. _____. "Francis Poulenc (1899-1963)." Village Voice,
February 21, 1963, p. 7. (Also published in Tempo 64
(spring 1963): 28-29)

Eulogy by "...his friend and colleague...Ned Rorem."

B557. _____. "From a Composer's Journal." Commentary 42
(November 1966): 82.

Selection from Music from Inside Out.
See: W289

B558. _____. "From a (New) Diary." Music Journal 35 (March
1977): 16-18+.

Diary excerpts; includes John Gruen/Ned Rorem interview.

B559. _____. "'Gay America.'" New York Times Book Review
(March 9, 1980): 27.

Letter to the editor in which Ned Rorem responds to a
review of Edmund White's States of Desire: Travels in
Gay America. "The New York Times...should think

twice...before assigning such an author to a hetero-
sexual who mistakes a work of literature for a guide-
book."

B560. Rorem, Ned. "Good Listener."   Review of Twentieth
Century Music: Its Evolution from the End of the
Harmonic Era into the Present Era of Sound, by Peter
Yates. New York Times Book Review (February 5, 1967):
10+.

"The volume represents years of realistic and deep
examination. But what Yates has gained in depth he
has lost in breadth: his book is too long and by the
same token too short. He reiterates aspects of fa-
vored trends while almost ignoring others."

B561. _____. "'He Is Like a Song-Filled Rock of Gibraltar.'"
New York Times, November 10, 1985, sec. 2, p. 1.

A tribute to Aaron Copland on his 85th birthday. "And
Aaron is again loved by the young, though less as
model than as a fact of sonic geology, like a throb-
bing song-filled rock of Gibraltar."

B562. _____. "Historic Houses: Maurice Ravel at Le Belvédère." Architectural Digest (September 1986): 182
-188+.

Description of Le Belvédère at Montfort-L'Amaury,
Ravel's home where "...the composer felt the need to
withdraw from...distractions into the inner realm of
his fancy."

B563. _____. "I'd Take the Fire (A Souvenir of Jean)." Village Voice, October 17, 1963, p. 5. (Also published
as the introduction in The Difficulty of Being, by
Jean Cocteau. New York: Coward-McCann, Inc., 1967)

Eulogy for Jean Cocteau.

B564. _____. "Introduction." In Past Tense: Diaries, by Jean
Cocteau. San Diego, CA: Harcourt Brace Jovanovich,
1987.

Ned Rorem traces the influence of Cocteau in all forms
of the arts. "...I love the work of this wildly controlled, snobbish, adorable...genius, I want to share
it with America. And because I love his work, I want
to keep it to myself."

B565. _____. "Is It Too Late for an Artists' Lib?" New York
Times, August 29, 1971, sec. 2, p. 11.

Commentary on a variety of topics. "...anyone can
write opinions...while only I can write my music, and
there's just so much time left. These notes signal my
permanent withdrawal from the critical scene."

B566. _____. "Is New Music New?" London Magazine 1 no. 5

(August 1961): 66-71.

Discussion of the dominant trends in modern composition: jazz, experimental and conservative.

B567. Rorem, Ned. "Jesus Christ Superstar." Harper's Magazine 242 (June 1971): 22-24. (Also published with revised initial paragraph in London Magazine 11 (October/November 1971): 122-127)

Review of Decca DL 71503 recording of Jesus Christ Superstar. The rock opera "...contains two ingredients necessary to most lasting religious works: frenzy and clarity...The combination results in eighty-eight minutes of a theatricality which, though uneven, is never boring."

B568. _____. "Julius Katchen (1926-1969)." High Fidelity/Musical America 19 (September 1969): 61.

Eulogy for Julius Katchen.

B569. _____. "Letter to Claude." In Men Without Masks: Writings from the Journal of Modern Men, by Michael Rubin, 108-116. Reading, MA: Addison-Wesley Publishing Company, 1980.

Unsent letter to a former lover. Originally printed in the New York Diary.
See: W291

B570. _____. "Letters to the Editor." Utah Chronicle (Salt Lake City), November 18, 1965.

Letter to the editor stating that he was misquoted in Time (November 12, 1965) when he allegedly described Utah as a boring place.

B571. _____. "Life's Deaths." Confrontation 9 (Fall 1974): 15-21.

Diary excerpts dated December 1968 through September 1969.

B572. _____. "Listening and Hearing." Music Journal 21 no. 9 (December 1963): 28+.

An exploration of the differences between listening to music and hearing it.

B573. _____. "Living with Gershwin." Opera News 49 no. 13 (March 16, 1985): 10-14+.

"Composer-essayist Ned Rorem airs a lifetime of thoughts on the melodist who has become part of America's consciousness."

B574. _____. "Lord Byron in Kansas City." New Republic 166

(May 6, 1972): 23-24.

Review of the premiere of Lord Byron by Virgil Thomson. "...Lord Byron would not appear to possess the
spontaneous combustion of Thomson's previous operas."

B575. Rorem, Ned. "Lou Harrison." Vol. 8, The New Grove Dic-
tionary of Music and Musicians, edited by Stanley
Sadie. Washington, DC: Grove's Dictionaries of Music
Inc., 1980.

Short biography and list of the works of Lou Harrison.

B576. _____. "Lukas' Latest." Musical America 81 (December
1961): 53.

Review of Victor LM/LSC 2558 recording of Studies in
Improvisation, by Lukas Foss. "The listener is addressed by Babel, not by an artist with well-wrought
ideas."

B577. _____. "Masterpieces." Christopher Street 5 no. 6 (May
1981): 54-57.

Discussion of the components of masterpieces in music.
"Now a perfect piece, which any well-schooled hack can
learn to make, cannot be guaranteed to bleed and
breathe, and even God just hopes for the best."

B578. _____. "Matters of Music." Review of The Classical
Style, by Charles Rosen. Modern Occasions 1 (Fall
1971): 637-641.

"...insofar as this book is involved, Rosen and I face
opposite directions, the past and the future, so I'm
incapable of having an attitude toward his work. I
cannot, so to speak, face it."

B579. _____. "A Melisande Notebook." Opera News 42 no. 16
(March 4, 1978): 12-14+.

"These random notes have sought briefly to set forth a
few facts and opinions not generally bandied about in
the now vast wastes of Debussiana."

B580. _____. "Messiaen and Carter on Their Birthdays." Tempo
127 (December 1978): 22-24. (Also published in Christopher Street 5 (January 1981): 55-56; and Listener
100 (December 14, 1978): 806-807)

A tribute to Olivier Messiaen and Elliott Carter on
their 70th birthdays. "...Oliver Messiaen has regiven
a good name to inspiration, and Elliott Carter has
regiven a good name to mastery."

B581. _____. "Mistress of the Arts." Review of Misia: The
Life of Misia Sert, by Arthur Gold and Robert Fizdale.
Washington Post Book World (February 3, 1980): 1.

"The strength of any book about Misia Sert lies in showing how she openly responded to the principle... that artists are finally less in need of understanding than they are of ready cash."

B582. Rorem, Ned. "Monologues and Dialogues." Opera News 41 no. 13 (February 5, 1977): 10-16. (Also published in San Francisco Opera Magazine 6 (Fall 1982): 31-36+)

Ned Rorem "...recalls Francis Poulenc, the man and his music."

B583. _____. "The More Things Change, the More They Stay the Same." Mademoiselle 68 (November 1968): 156-157+.

Discussion of French popular music and musicians. Rorem concludes that "...the tone of France's '40s remains inviolable."

B584. _____. "Most Likely to Survive?" Review of I Am a Composer, by Arthur Honegger. New York Times Book Review (August 28, 1966): 6.

"...personal and poignant, bold and witty, a trifle old-fashioned."

B585. _____. "The Music of the Beatles." In The Age of Rock: Sounds of the American Cultural Revolution, edited by Jonathan Eisen, 149-159. New York: Vintage books, 1969. (Previously published in New York Times Book Review (January 18, 1968): 23-27; Music Educators Journal 55 no. 4 (December 1968): 33+; and under the title, "America and the Beatles." London Magazine 7 (February 1968): 54-64)

Commentary on the Beatles as they relate to the musical culture of society.

B586. _____. "A Nantucket Diary." Geo 6 (October 1984): 26-27+.

Ned Rorem's description of life on Nantucket. "I wrote Air Music, made pies, felt no competition, was content."

B587. _____. "Nantucket Diary." Triquarterly 40 (Fall 1977): 184-207.

Excerpts from Ned Rorem's Nantucket Diary, June through September 1974. The major work completed during this time was Air Music, details of which are mentioned throughout.
    See: W224

B588. _____. "'No, No.' Says Ned to Nudity." New York Times, July 6, 1969, sec. 2, p. 1+.

Letter to the editor in which Ned Rorem says he had

been asked by <u>Esquire</u> to pose nude "'in a group pho-
tograph of notable people from many fields of endeavor.'" He quotes from his reply to the magazine,
"Through my musical composition and published prose, I
have already, like any artist worthy of the name, publicly stripped. I feel no further need to bare my
literal flesh."

B589. Rorem, Ned. "Notes from Last Year." <u>Modern Occasions</u>
(Spring 1971): 403-416.

Diary excerpts, aphorisms, and notes.

B590. _____. "Notes on a French Bias." <u>Christopher Street</u> 5
no. 11 (1981): 52-54. (Previously published in <u>Stage-
bill Magazine</u> (Winter 1980): 9+)

Ned Rorem discusses his preference for French music,
specifically in the works of Debussy, Ravel, and
Poulenc.

B591. _____. "Notes on Death." <u>Christopher Street</u> 2 no. 6
(December 1977): 20-27.

Miscellaney of observations, ideas, and diary on the
topic of death. "With each friend that dies, some of
me dies. I am bereft, not because that part of me
which he embodied is lost, but because that part of
him which I embodied is lost."

B592. _____. "Notes on Parade." <u>Opera News</u> 45 no. 13 (February 28, 1981): 8-18.

"Ned Rorem shares his impressions of the theater
pieces of Ravel, Poulenc and Satie."

B593. _____. "Notes on Ravel." <u>Commentary</u> 59 (May 1975):
64-67.

Tribute to Ravel. "Nobody dislikes Ravel, and nobody
disapproves. Can that be said of any other musician?"

B594. _____. "Notes on Sacred Music." <u>Music (AGO)</u> 7 no. 1
(January 1973): 43-46.

"I do not believe in God. I do believe in poetry...
When I write music on so-called sacred texts it is for
the same reason I write on profane texts: not to make
people believe in God but to make them believe in
music. Music is not a short cut to heaven, it is an
end in itself."

B595. _____. "Notes on Song." <u>Christopher Street</u> 5 no. 2
(December 1980): 51-53.

Ned Rorem discusses song composition. "...anyone can
be taught to write a perfect song, but no one...knows
how to lend that song a living pulse and inject it

with flowing blood."

B596. Rorem, Ned. "Of Vanity."   Christopher Street 3 no. 8
      (March 1979): 45-52.

      Excerpts from his diaries 1975-1978. "Vanity is the
      paper-thin placenta of civilization that protects us
      awful humans, with a delicate transience, against the
      mad logic of the sky beyond the sun."

B597. _____. "Oh, Richard Goldstein, Don't You Groove for
      Me." New York Times, October 26, 1969, sec. B, p. 19.

      Essay on what Ned Rorem considers good and bad in rock
      music, and good and bad criticism as well. He is
      especially critical of critic Richard Goldstein "...
      because he imparts no appropriate information: he does
      not illuminate the music, but offers only his reaction
      to it."
      See: B186, B373, B497

B598. _____. "On Being Artistic." Christopher Street 5 no. 8
      (August 1981): 45-46.

      Ned Rorem gives his opinion about the creative pro-
      cess. "What such romantic laymen refuse to grasp is
      that the 'creative process' (if that's the term for
      the action of making so-called art) is no more and no
      less than hard work."

B599. _____. "Only the Non-Poets Look Like Poets." Vogue 152
      (September 15, 1968): 134-135.

      Excerpt from Music and People.
      See: W288

B600. _____. "Ordinary Genius." Review of Richard Strauss:
      The Life of a Non-Hero, by George R. Marek. New York
      Times Book Review (April 23, 1967): 5+.

      "George Marek...does not...unreservedly admire one
      single work of Strauss. And yet he did write the
      book. That he wrote it, I repeat, must be because he
      loved something in the music. What he has given in
      honor of that love is a fairly valuable biographical
      study, though he has come no closer than anyone else
      to demonstrating what makes a composer a composer."

B601. _____. "Our Music Now." New Republic 171 (November
      30, 1974): 31-34.

      Diary excerpts on a variety of topics.

B602. _____. "Paul Bowles." Vol, 3, The New Grove Dictionary
      of Music and Musicians, edited by Stanley Sadie.
      Washington, DC: Grove's Dictionaries of Music Inc.,
      1980.

Short biography and list of the works of Paul Bowles.

B603. Rorem, Ned. "Paul Goodman, 1911-72: Remembering a Poet."
Village Voice (New York, NY), August 10, 1972, p. 17.

Eulogy for Paul Goodman. Rorem recounts his acquaintance with the poet from the late 1930's. "My first
songs date from then, all of them settings of Paul
Goodman's verse. I may have written other kinds of
song since, but none better. That I have never in the
following decades wearied of putting his words to
music is the highest praise I can show him; since I
put faith in my own work, I had first to put faith in
Paul's...He was my Goethe, my Blake, and my Apolli-
naire."

B604.   . "Péleas et Mélisande." American Record Guide 37
(March 1971) 405-407.

Review of Columbia M3-30119 recording of Debussy's
Péleas et Mélisande. "We hear it as a symphonic piece
with human voices superimposed...Boulez's tempos are
as supple as a vast canvas on which his singers are
allowed to draw their little lines of tune."

B605.   . "Pictures and Pieces." American Record Guide 27
(July 1961): 844-847+.   (Also published in London
Magazine 1 no. 8 (November 1961): 64-68)

A comparison of art and music in which Ned Rorem pro-
poses "...that music and painting are less resemblant
than generally supposed...After all, if the arts could
express each other we wouldn't need more than one."
See: B121

B606.   . "Pictures from the Fifties."   Paris Review 10
no. 37 (spring 1966): 144-155.

Excerpts from The Paris Diary.
See: W293

B607.   . "Poulenc and Bernac--French Song, with Pure
Pleasure the Aim." High Fidelity/Musical America 17
(November 1967): 85-86.

Review of Pathe FALP 50036 and Odyssey 32 26 0009 recordings Pierre Bernac and Francis Poulenc performing
French songs.

B608.   . "Program Notes." Aspen Music Festival, July 27,
1982.

Program notes for the July 27, 1982 performance of Day
Music.
See: W205

B609.   . "Program Notes." Aspen Music Festival, July 29,
1982.

Program notes for the July 29, 1982 performance of <u>A</u>
<u>Quaker Reader</u>.
<u>See</u>: W189

B610. Rorem, Ned. "The Promoter and the Composer." Review of
<u>Bagazh: Memoirs of a Russian Cosmopolitan</u>, by Nicolas
Nabokov.   <u>New York Times Book Review</u> (December 28,
1975): 6.

Review of the memoirs of Nicolas Nabokov who "...has
done as much as any Russian since Koussevitzky toward
putting American music on the map."

B611. _____. "Random Notes." <u>Music Journal</u> 31 no. 8 (October
1973) 22-23+.

Excerpts from <u>Pure Contraption</u>.
<u>See</u>: W295

B612. _____. "The Real Music of Morocco." <u>Musical America</u> 70
no. 2 (January 15, 1950): 8+.

Commentary on the ethnic music of Morocco.

B613. _____. "Recalling Martha." <u>After Dark</u> (October 1968):
42-45.

Recollections about Martha Graham for whom Ned Rorem
once served as dance accompanist. Includes comments
about Rorem works choreographed by Martha Graham.

B614. _____. "Return to Paris." <u>Antaeus</u> 29 (1978): 41-50.

Excerpt from his diary concerning a return trip to
Paris in 1973.   Subsequently included in <u>Nantucket</u>
<u>Diary</u>, May 23-June 10, 1973.
<u>See</u>: W290

B615. _____. "Rorem on Barbirolli." <u>Musical America</u> 84 no. 8
(October 1964): 4.

Letter to the editor in which Ned Rorem takes issue
with Sir John Barbirolli's comments about performing
contemporary music. In Rorem's opinion, "...it is
only laziness which allows us to prefer museum
pieces."

B616. _____. "A Rose Journal." <u>Opera News</u> 47 (March 12,
1983): 16-18+.

"Composer Ned Rorem jots down some highly personal
impressions of Richard Strauss and <u>Der Rosenkavalier</u>."

B617. _____. "Setting the Tone." <u>Christopher Street</u> 4 no. 12
(September 1980): 45-48.

Miscellany of ideas, diaries, and observations.
"Seemingly random, the foregoing notes actually con-

tain in microcosm all that has ever concerned me."

B618. Rorem, Ned. "Smoke Without Fire." New Republic 166
      (April 8, 1972): 19.

      Review of the New York City Opera premiere of Lee
      Hoiby's Summer and Smoke. "Lee Hoiby's devices reso-
      lutely failed to alter the emphasis of any character's
      motion or word."

B619. _____. "Some Last Thoughts on the Beatles." Village
      Voice, December 21, 1967, p. 26+.

      "We've become so hung up on what they mean, we can no
      longer hear what they're performing."

B620. _____. "Some Notes (Mostly Sour) On Singing Songs."
      New York Times, April 20, 1975, sec. 2, p. 1.

      An expression of disapproval for American singers who
      exclude contemporary American song literature from
      their programs.

B621. _____. "Some Notes on Debussy." American Record Guide
      37 (March 1971): 404+.

      Reprint of program notes originally written to accom-
      pany a Desto recording of Debussy's complete piano
      music performed by Beveridge Webster.

B622. _____. "Song and the Singer." American Record Guide 30
      (February 1964): 468-470+.

      Commentary on the relationship of song and singer.
      "The history of music is the history of song since all
      music evolves from vocal expression...the recitalist
      has forgotten traditions--not of singing, but of
      song."

B623. _____. "The State of Contemporary 'Classical' Music."
      ASCAP (Fall 1984): 28-29.

      Ned Rorem discusses some of the problems faced by
      contemporary music today.

B624. _____. Stravinsky at 100. Tapes of a lecture given by
      Ned Rorem, August 3, 1982, Aspen Music Festival. 2
      tape cassettes.

      Ned Rorem speaks about his early introduction to the
      music of Igor Stravinsky and its influence on his own
      career. Includes an interview and question and answer
      session on many topics.

B625. _____. "Stravinsky on a Grand Scale." Review of
      Stravinsky in Pictures and Documents, by Vera
      Stravinsky and Robert Craft. Washington Post Book
      World (January 14, 1979): 1-2.

Referring to the book as a "gorgeous scrapbook," Rorem says, "My irritation clothes admiration, seeing how much of this book's strength lies in Craft's weakness --an inability to cope with certain viewpoints not his own.   But all biographers are biased.   Robert Craft, more skilled with words and more educated than most, is better suited than anyone in the world to present that world with a case for Stravinsky the Man."

B626. Rorem, Ned. "Sun." <u>Philharmonic Symphony Society of New York Program Notes</u> (July 1, 1967): D.

Program notes for the July 1, 1967 premiere performance of <u>Sun</u>.   Includes a history of the composition and the text of each poem used.   "...I chose words, not as I understood, but as I felt them."
<u>See</u>: W115

B627. _____. "Survivors Outside the Echo Chamber." Review of <u>Great Songs of the Sixties</u>, edited by Milton Okun. <u>New York Times</u>, November 15, 1970, sec. 7, p. 59.

This collection "...should appeal primarily to an older generation that both reads a little piano and likes some of the tunes, yet found the sixties sound mostly unpalatable."

B628. _____. "Tennessee Now and Then." Review of <u>Eight Mortal Ladies Possessed</u>, by Tennessee Williams. <u>London Magazine</u> 15 no. 2 (June-July 1975): 68-74. (Previously published in <u>Saturday Review</u> (September 21, 1974): 24-26)

"The new stories are so fragile that when absorbed into their creator's <u>oeuvre</u> they won't disturb the surface, nor will they pollute the depths as do the later plays."

B629. _____. "Thinking of Ben." <u>Christopher Street</u> 5 no. 4 (February 1981): 49-52.

Eulogy for composer, Ben Weber.   "These few hundred words have briefly served...to call back a lost friend and introduce him to you."

B630. _____. "Truth and Lies About a Composer's Craft." <u>New York Times</u>, June 5, 1977, sec. 2, p. 17.

Commentary on the emotional and intellectual processes of composing.

B631. _____. "Variations on Mussorgsky." <u>Opera News</u> 50 no. 10 (February 1, 1986): 11-14+.

"Composer-essayist Ned Rorem explores the Russian master."

B632. _____. "Vocabulary." <u>Christopher Street</u> 1 no. 11

(May 1977): 7-16.

"Originally these paragraphs were sprinkled through a
diary-in-progress, nesting incongruously among other
concerns...The general vocabulary (by which I mean the
inescapable validity of every sexuality) is now part
of the general consciousness and needs no pleas.   But
the personal vocabulary which is mine--ours--answers
to more fragile desires, some of which are uttered in
the present paper..."

B633. Rorem, Ned. "A Wagnerian Opus: Musings of a 'Monster
Goddess.'" Review of Cosima Wagner's Diaries, volume
1, 1869-1877, edited by Martin Gregor-Dellin and
Dietrich Mack.   Chicago Tribune, November 26, 1978,
sec. 7, p. 1.

"The best of Cosima's often intelligent and sometimes
piercing commentary on literature and on music (though
not on painting) arises from quotes of R. W. which are
seldom relieved by levity and never by humor."

B634. _____. "Weill, Lenya and Marie-Laure." London Magazine
24 nos. 1-2 (April-May 1984): 60-74. (Previously published as "Notes on Weill" in Opera News 48 (January
21, 1984): 12-16+)

Commentary on the works of Kurt Weill and his influence on contemporary music.

B635. _____. "What Future for American Opera? New York
Times, September 3, 1972, sec. 2, p. 9.

"But a new species of American opera is appearing,
equally unexperimental as to musical speech, but adventurous as to libretto, which is dadaist rather than
poetistic, situational rather than narrative."

B636. _____. "What Truman Capote Means to Me." Christopher
Street 8 no. 9 (October 1984): 50-59.

Ned Rorem comments on the works of Truman Capote and
gives details of their friendship and subsequent feud.

B637. _____. "When Paul Jacobs Plays Debussy." Christopher
Street 6 no. 4 (May 1982): 57-59.

Review of Nonesuch H-71322, HB-73031, and H-71365 recordings of Debussy piano works played by Paul Jacobs.
"One hears Debussy, not Jacobs."

B638. _____. "Why I Write as I Do." Tempe 109 (June 1974):
38-40. (Also published under the title "Why I Compose
as I Do" in High Fidelity/Musical America 24 (September 1974): MA 16-17)

"...I compose for my own necessity, because no one

else makes quite the sound I wish to hear."

B639. Rorem, Ned. "William Flanagan."   Vol. 6, The New Grove
       Dictionary of Music and Musicians, edited by Stanley
       Sadie. Washington, DC: Groves's Dictionaries of Music
       Inc., 1980.

       Short biography and list of the works of William
       Flanagan.

B640. _____ . "Women and the Arts: Variations on a Theme."
       Pan Pipes 72 no. 2 (Winter 1980): 5-6.

       Excerpt from a lecture about women and the arts given
       by Mr. Rorem at Rutgers University. "Finally, there
       is no Women's Art, but only art by a woman."

B641. _____ . "Woman: Artist or Artist-ess?" Vogue 155 (April
       1, 1970): 172-173+.

       Rorem poses the question, "Why can women write, paint,
       dance, perform--but not compose music?" His conclu-
       sion, "...because writing and drawing are languages
       integral to everyone's everyday life, musical compo-
       sition...is not a language for dabblers. A minimum of
       professionality and a maximum of time are required to
       produce a communicable score...it is hard to picture a
       woman achieving this proficiency in her art while
       raising a family with the comparatively unneurotic
       ease of her sisters 'in poetry.'"

B642. _____ . "Words Without Song." In The Artistic Legacy of
       Walt Whitman, edited by Edwin Haviland Miller. (Also
       published in American Record Guide 36 (March 1970)
       468-469 ; West Hills Review 2 (Fall 1980): 70-72; and
       under the title "Poetry of Music" in London Magazine 9
       no. 11 (February 1970): 26-36)

       Rorem discusses the artistic strength of Walt Whitman
       which has drawn so many composers, including himself
       "...to set their music to the poems of Whitman!" He
       gives further insights into Whitman poems which served
       as inspiration for his own compositions.

B643. _____ . "The World's Most Influential Music Teacher,
       Other Women in the Art." Vogue 169 (September 1979):
       324.

       "Thoughts from a prizewinning composer on what women
       add to serious music." Ned Rorem discusses the con-
       tribution of teachers, composers, performers, and
       patrons of the arts who happen to be unique, indi-
       vidual women.

B644. _____ . "Writing Songs." Part 1, 2. American Record
       Guide 26 (November 1959, February 1960): 164-166+,
       406-409+. (Also published in Parnassus 10 no. 2
       (1982): 210-224)

"In emphasizing songs I will present some general principles which underlie all composition, as well as some practical problems which face the individual composer."

B645. Rorem, Ned. "A Zip of My Own." New York 13 (October 20, 1980): 37-38.

Ned Rorem describes his neighborhood which "...houses more first-rate creative artists than any one place since Paris in the 1920s."

B646. "Rorem at Buffalo U." Musical Courier 160 no. 4 (October 1959): 29.

Brief announcement that "Ned Rorem, composer, has been appointed Slee Professor at the University of Buffalo for the 1959-60 season."

B647. "Rorem Symphony Premiere." Tempo: 41 (Autumn 1956): 4.

"Ned Rorem's second symphony, commissioned by the La Jolla Musical Arts Society, was given its premiere at the final concert of the season, early in August. It is a spirited work and was well received by press and public alike. Mr. Rorem is now writing an opera."
See: W244

B648. "Rorem, Then and Now." Saturday Review 54 (April 24, 1971): 52.

Review of Desto DC-7101 recording of Rorem's War Scenes; Five Songs to Poems of Walt Whitman; Four Dialogues. Concerning War Scenes and the Five Songs to Poems of Walt Whitman: "Gramm sings both sequences of Whitman material with the richness of sound and the aptness of articulation one has grown to expect of him; and Isotomin transcends anything previously heard in Rorem's keyboard writing with the impact as well as the precision of his piano playing." concerning Four Dialogues: "Anita Darian and John Stewart make a likable pair of interpreters...the former sounding especially well in the last of the sequence, while Cumming and the composer chat happily at the two pianos."
See: D19

B649. "Rorem to Speak." Utah Chronicle (Salt Lake City, Utah), January 10, 1967.

Brief announcement that Ned Rorem would be the speaker at the American Association of University Professors' Faculty Discussion Series on January 11, 1967. The topic: "Self Portrait of the Artist as a Middle-Aged Man."

B650. "Rorem Tone Poem, 'Lions,' to Premiere Tuesday." Salt Lake Tribune (Utah), January 22, 1967.

Announcement of the January 24, 1967 Utah premiere of

Lions.   The occasion was the University of Utah's
Eighth Annual Festival of Contemporary Music.
See: W233

B651. "Rorem Wins Pulitzer."   Clavier 15 no. 6 (September
1976): 62.

Announcement that Ned Rorem "...best known for his
songs, won the Pulitzer prize...for an orchestral work
entitled Air Music..."
See: W224

B652. "Rorem's New String Symphony Enters Atlanta Repertoire."
Boosey & Hawkes Newsletter 15 no. 3 (February 1986):
1-2.

Brief article concerning the October 31, 1985 premiere
of String Symphony, with quotes from reviewers. Also
mentioned were the performances of An American Oratorio March 13-15, 23, 1986 and April 24-26, 1986;
Dances, December 1985.
See: W118, W204, W241

B653. Rothstein, Edward. "Clarinet: Jean Kopperud." New York
Times, November 5, 1982, sec. C, p. 15.

Brief mention that Ned Rorem's Ariel was included in a
Nov. 2, 1982 program.
See: W106

B654. _____. "Concert: 'First Gay Choral Festival.'" New
York Times, September 13, 1983, sec. C, p. 12.

Brief review of the September 11, 1983 premiere of the
Whitman Cantata. The work, performed at Avery Fisher
Hall, was commissioned for the National Gay Choral
Festival.
See: W170

B655. _____. "Music: Rorem's 'Nantucket.'" New York Times,
December 3, 1981, sec. 3, p. 14.

Review of the December 1, 1981 concert which included
Ned Rorem's Nantucket Songs. "The settings created a
straightforward catalogue of sensations, tersely
etched, accumulating to evoke the mysterious simplicity at the heart of the intimately familiar."
See: W52

B656. Rowes, Barbara.   "Composer, Author, Critic, Matter-
Of-Fact Gay, Ned Rorem Is an American Phenomenon."
People 10 (August 21, 1978): 38-43.

Article which includes some biographical information,
but is mostly popular treatment of "a day in the life
of Ned Rorem" on Nantucket.

B657. Sabin, Robert. "American Song Program." Musical America 79 (December 15, 1959): 23.

Review of the November 16, 1959 concert featuring the
works of Ned Rorem, William Flanagan, and Virgil
Thomson. Rorem's Jack l'Eventreur was given its New
York premiere. Other Rorem songs included were:
Spring and Fall; Bedlam (Visits to St. Elizabeths); To
You; The Midnight Sun; and I Am a Rose. Concerning To
You: "The music has precisely the right casualness,
yet, like the verse, it says much more than it seems
to." Concerning Visits to St. Elizabeths: "...the
composer gets away from his bland modulatory accompaniments and writes with a stinging rhythmic drive and
direction that he should employ oftener."
See: W34, W37, W48, W84, W91, W96

B658.   ____. "American Songs Reveal Wide Variety of Styles."
Musical America 71 (July 1951): 30.

Review of the score of Requiem. "...like almost all
of the settings of Stevenson's poem I have encoun-
tered, founders in the attempt to evade the sing-song
quality of the lyric. Nor is Rorem's rather misty and
French harmonic palette suited to the bold, crude colors of his subject."
See: W67

B659.   ____. "Mannes College Gives New Operas." Musical
America 78 (May 1958): 38-39.

Review of the April 14, 1958 premiere of The Robbers.
"Mr. Rorem has based his libretto on 'The Pardoner's
Tale,' from Chaucer's 'Canterbury Tales'...But Mr.
Rorem has spoiled it with wishy-washy music that lacks
dramatic bite and by writing a long, reflective, inert
trio at the climax of the action."
See: W179

B660.   ____. "New Music." Musical America 76 (April 1956):
20.

Review of the score of Sicilienne. "Watered-down
Ravel in idiom, this music nonetheless has delicacy
and charm, and is far more difficult to play well than
it looks."
See: W192

B661.   ____. "New Songs and Cycles by American Composers."
Musical America 72 (December 15, 1952): 26.

Review of the score of Flight for Heaven. "The essence of Herrick's poetry is verbal felicity, the
chiseled phrase and the faultless verbal rhythm. But
Rorem's music is rhythmically weak, harmonically commonplace, and emotionally tepid."
See: W24

B662.   ____. "New Vocal Compositions by American Contemporaries." Musical America 71 (January 15, 1951): 29.

Review of the score of <u>The Silver Swan</u>. "...a setting
for high voice of Ben Jonson's lyric that combines the
harmonic palette of Ravel with an English folk-song
pattern of development and line...While neither very
original or distinguished in substance, it is a very
effective song for a skilled vocalist."
<u>See</u>: W74

B663. _____. "Some Younger American Composers." <u>Tempo</u> 64
(Spring 1963): 25-28.

Ned Rorem is included among the composers discussed.
About Rorem, "...a prolific and profoundly gifted
writer of arts songs. He has written two short operas
which reveal a plentiful invention although they lack
dramatic concentration.   We can expect an exciting
work in his forthcoming full-length opera commissioned
by the Ford Foundation. Although Rorem is best known
as a song composer, his chamber and orchestral music
is equally interesting.   His 'Eleven Studies for
Eleven Players,' for example, is an exquisitely fan-
ciful and witty work."
<u>See</u>: W206

B664. _____. "Songs by Rorem, Flanagan." <u>Musical America</u> 79
(March 1959): 79.

Review of the February 24, 1959 concert of Rorem and
Flanagan compositions. Patricia Neway, soprano, with
Ned Rorem, piano, premiered <u>What Sparks and Wiry
Cries</u>; <u>Lullaby of the Woman of the Mountain</u>; <u>Bedlam
(Visits to St. Elizabeths)</u>; and <u>Love</u>. Other Rorem
songs included were <u>Mourning Scene</u>; <u>Cycle of Holy
Songs</u>; <u>Look Down, Fair Moon</u>; <u>To You</u>; <u>Spring</u>; and
<u>Alleluia</u>.
<u>See</u>: W2, W15, W23, W44, W46, W83, W91, W96, W100,
W109

B665. _____. "Works for Flute by American Composers." <u>Musi-
cal America</u> 71 (June 1951): 30.

Review of the score of <u>Mountain Song</u>, for flute and
piano. The work "...combines a wistful melody with an
accompaniment that is transparent in texture, if a bit
lush harmonically."
<u>See</u>: W209

B666. Salisbury, Wilma.   "'Missionaries' Win Converts."
<u>Cleveland Plain Dealer</u>, November 5, 1986, sec. F,
p. 9.

Review of the November 3, 1986 performance of <u>End of
Summer</u>. "Strung together in contrasting sections, the
backward-looking work played off sweet melodies and
nostalgic harmonies against fast figurations and showy
cadenzas."
<u>See</u>: W207

B667. Salzman, Eric. "Day Music." <u>Stereo Review</u> 31 (September 1973): 122.

Review of Desto DC 7151 recording of Day Music. "They form an attractive, rather loose group of inventions full of character and charm." The recording also includes Leon Kirchner's Sonata Concertante.
See: D21

B668. _____. "Folk Play Listed As Opera Project." New York Times, October 25, 1961, p. 33.

Announcement that Ned Rorem was commissioned by the New York City Opera through the Ford Foundation's opera program to write an opera based on Du Bose and Dorothy Heyward's Mamba's Daughters.

B669. _____. "The Nantucket Songs." Stereo Review 48 (November 1983): 86.

Review of CRI SD 485 recording of The Nantucket Songs and Women's Voices. The recording of The Nantucket Songs is the premiere at the Library of Congress in 1979. "These two song cycles have a great deal in common: both are miscellaneous collections of texts dealing with vastly different subjects and states of mind; neither has a dramatic or lyric thread except for the composer's own sensibility in arranging the texts and putting music to them." Women's Voices are settings of poems by women. They "...are more personal and inward in feeling than The Nantucket Songs."
See: D11

B670. _____. "ROREM: Serenade on Five English Poems for Mezzo-Soprano, Violin, Viola, and Piano." Stereo Review 46 (February 1981): 108.

Review of Grenadilla GS-1031 recording of Serenade on Five English Poems. "...Serenade (1975) is a charming lyric setting of poems by Fletcher, Shakespeare, Tennyson, Hopkins, and Campion, and it is effectively sung here by Elaine Bonazzi. The texts are framed by instrumental solos beautifully played by excellent musicians...and the recording is well made." It is paired with Starer's Quartet for Piano and Strings.
See: D27

B671. Sanders, Linda. "Musical Lives." Review of The Later Diaries of Ned Rorem, by Ned Rorem. The Nation 238 (February 25, 1984): 231-233.

Review of The Later Diaries of Ned Rorem, which was originally published as The Final Diary. "The writing, most of which is superbly stylish, sometimes lapses into preciousness; and some thoughts are more trouble to unravel than they are worth..." However, the author concludes, "...the Diaries are the work of a 'real' writer, not a composer/dilettante."
See: W287

B672. Sandow, Gregory.   "Present Tensions."   Village Voice
      (New York, N.Y.), October 8, 1985, p. 84.

      Three short essays in which the author presents some
      contradictions of modern music. In "New Romanticism,"
      some differences in what he calls the "modernist"
      composers (Schoenberg and Druckman) and the "non-
      modernist" (Rorem) are explored.

B673. "Santa Fe Festival Will Feature Distinguished Composer."
      Albuquerque Journal, February 15, 1980, sec. C, p. 7.

      Written in anticipation of the Santa Fe Chamber Music
      Festival with Ned Rorem as composer-in-residence. In-
      formation is given about the performers as well as a
      schedule of the Santa Fe, Seattle and New York City
      concerts.

B674. "The Santa Fe Music Festival."   Film for Television,
      1982.   Filmed July-August 1982 by KNME-TV, Albuquer-
      que, NM.   Fort Worth, TX: Fort Worth Productions,
      1982.

      Combines interviews with Aaron Copland, Ned Rorem and
      William Schuman along with performances of their cham-
      ber music. Selections from Rorem's Winter Pages are
      included. Presented on PBS, November 23, 1983.
      See: W223

B675. Sargent, Winthrop.   "Musical Events."   New Yorker 47
      (June 12, 1971): 88-89.

      Review of the June 1971 performance of Symphony No. 1.
      "Rorem's symphony is, by present-day standards, a fine
      composition. It may not be a symphony in the tradi-
      tional sense. But it is a coherent work in five move-
      ments, containing a minimum of noise and a fair amount
      of melodic invention."
      See: W243

B676. Satz, Arthur. "Ned Rorem: Musician of the Month." High
      Fidelity/Musical America 26 no. 8 (August 1976): MA
      4-5.

      Interview with Ned Rorem shortly after he was awarded
      the Pulitzer Prize for Air Music. In addition to Air
      Music, he discusses his approach to song composition
      and poets; his means of supporting himself through
      commissions, performances and publication; and his
      attitude toward teaching. About the latter: "The
      money is tempting, but your creativity dies."
      See: W224

B677. Schaefer, Theodore.   "Music Reviews." Notes (Music Li-
      brary Association) 8 (March 1951): 405-406.

      Review of the score of The Silver Swan. "The vocal
      line in this song betrays an entirely instrumental
      design with no appreciation for the capacities of the
      voice in high tessitura on vowel sounds...Even the

technical prowess of a Tourel or Berger is not likely
to make for advantageous performance."
See: W74

B678. Scheider, John.   "The Guitar Works of Ned Rorem."
Soundboard 11 no. 1 (1984): 28-32.

Detailed analyses of Rorem's compositions for guitar:
Romeo and Juliet and Suite For Guitar.
See: W213, W220

B679. Schneider, John. "Atlanta Symphony: Rorem 'String Symphony.'"   High Fidelity/Musical America 36 no. 3
(March 1986): MA 14.

Review of the October 31, 1985 premiere of String Symphony, "...a stunning work that deserves to have the
major orchestras standing in line to perform it."
See: W241

B680. Schonberg, Harold C. "Opera: 'Miss Julie' at City Center." New York Times, November 5, 1965, p. 32.

Review of the November 4, 1965 premiere of Miss Julie.
The reviewer calls it "...a brilliant production of a
not very successful operatic version of 'Miss Julie.'"
See: W178

B681. Schwartz, Elliott. "The American Bicentenary."   Sound-
ings 5 (1977): 88-93.

Description of American music which was premiered during the bicentennial year (1976). Included was the
Pulitzer Prize winning Air Music "...a ten-movement
work in which the orchestra is subdivided into a variety of unorthodox chamber groupings."
See: W224

B682. Schwarz, K. Robert. "The King's Singers: Rorem 'Pilgrim
Strangers.'"   High Fidelity/Musical America 35 no. 3
March 1985): MA 25-26.

Review of the November 16, 1984 premiere of Pilgrim
Strangers.   "Ned Rorem's Pilgrim Strangers was the
focus of the evening's program...one of the finest of
Rorem's recent scores."
See: W150

B683. "7 Paeans for St. Luke's."   New York Times, March 15,
1973, p. 55.

Announcement that Ned Rorem was one of seven composers
commissioned to write works celebrating the 150th
Anniversary of St. Luke's Chapel of Trinity Parish.

B684. Shawe-Taylor, Desmond.   "Musical Events." New Yorker 49
(December 10, 1973): 181-185.

Review of the November 25-26, 1973 concerts of Rorem

compositions including Trio; Day Music; Night Music;
Last Poems of Wallace Stevens; War Scenes; Gloria;
Ariel; and Bertha. "In some of these performances,
the composer played the difficult piano parts in a
style as clean and professional as his composition.
But the hollowness of the ideas, for all the clarity
of their handling, was increasingly exposed in the
course of the two concerts."
See: W32, W98, W106, W108, W172, W205, W210, W222

B685. Sherman, Robert. "Ax Gives Premiere of Rorem's Eight
Etudes." New York Times, May 9, 1976, p. 46.

Review of the May 6, 1976 premiere of Eight Etudes for
Piano. "Sometimes reflective, the pieces are more
frequently charged with a propulsive, brilliant
clangor as they challenge the pianist to make artistic
unity out of the constant contrasts of speed, tension,
dynamics or linear motion."
See: W185

B686. _____. "Recital: Joyce Mathis in Premiere of Rorem
Work." New York Times, November 6, 1976, p. 9.

Review of the November 4, 1976 premiere of Women's
Voices. Described as "spellbinding," the work "...is
consistently compelling and the evocative performance
by Miss Mathis superbly accentuated its shifting dramatic moods."
See: W103

B687. Shulgasser, Barbara. "Setting the Tone." Review of
Setting the Tone: Essays and a Diary, by Ned Rorem.
New York Times, July 17, 1983, sec. 7, p. 17.

"In the essays reprinted from various publications,
Mr. Rorem's imagery is fresh and arresting. When he
looks beyond himself to such subjects as Cosima Wagner
as well as Auden and Coward, he is capable of providing canny insights, and he offers a particularly
luminous essay on the music teacher extraordinaire
Nadia Boulanger."
See: W296

B688. Shulgold, Marc. "Sidlin Leads Long Beach Symphony."
Los Angeles Times, March 28, 1987, sec. 6, p. 3.

Review of the March 26, 1987 performance of Lions.
"...they did a poised and polished reading of Ned
Rorem's heavily dramatic 'Lions'...Though nearly a
quarter-century old, the work retains its freshness
and spontaneity, deftly mixing dreamy four-square
tonality with subtly shifting dissonances."
See: W233

B689. Shupp, Enos E., Jr. "Organ." The New Records 48 no. 1
(March 1980): 15.

Review of Gothic D-87904 recording which includes six

selections from Ned Rorem's A Quaker Reader. Concerning A Quaker Reader: "Rorem's suite, of which we
hear six of eleven pieces, is played beautifully; it
too sounds good most of the time, although the hard-
driven climaxes rankle." The record includes works by
Bach, Distler, Hindemith, and Sokola.
See: D26

B690. Simmons, David.   "London Music."   Musical Opinion 96
(August 1973): 552-554.

Review of a July 15, 1973 London recital by Shirley
Verrett, soprano, with Warren Wilson, piano. "I am
yet to know and understand what the fluent musical
asset-stripping inspiration provided by Ned Rocem
[sic], entitled The Resurrection, was trying to un-
fold. Admittedly it is a pretty tough task to set any
of the Bible these days, and the subject tends to be a
little on the transcendental side. So a series of
chords, which sounded like a contradiction in terms,
shall we say Conservatoire-Gershwin, did not gain any
prizes from this distracted critic."
See: W68

B691. Singer, Samuel L.   "Composers and Works Get a Hearing or
Two."   Philadelphia Inquirer, February 23, 1981, sec.
A, p. 17.

Review of the Philadelphia Art Alliance's "Meet the
Composer--Second Hearing" concert of February 22, 1981
which featured Rorem's After Reading Shakespeare. The
work "...employs practically every technical trick in
the string player's arsenal..."
See: W200

B692. Sjoerdsma, Richard Dale.   "Music Review."   Notes (Music
Library Association) 28 no. 4 (1972): 783.

Review of the score of King Midas. "The songs of King
Midas exemplify his typical concern for linear con-
struction, his interest in a variety of contrapuntal
techniques, his fondness of syncopation, and his
predilection for ostinato figures...King Midas is
obviously not intended for amateur performers. The
musical demands of the songs require technically
secure singers and an accomplished pianist. Neverthe-
less, these songs will reward serious study, and the
cantata should prove to be a valuable addition to the
modern concert repertoire."
See: W40

B693. Skei, Allen B.   "Music."   Review of Setting the Tone:
Essays and a Diary, by Ned Rorem.   Library Journal 108
no. 6 (March 15, 1983): 587.

"The present collection--previously published essays
and reviews together with the latest installment in
his ongoing diary--often shows him at his best, as
when writing about books and music and their creators,

and sometimes at his self-indulgent worst, as in the case of the diary."
See: W296

B694. Skenazy, Paul. "Paris Sizzles in Diaries from Literary Set." Review of The Later Diaries of Ned Rorem: 1971-1972, by Ned Rorem. San Jose Mercury (California), August 12, 1984, Arts & Books, p. 26.

"Ned Rorem, a noted composer, managed to scandalize the musical world...when he published the first two volumes of his diaries in 1966 and 1967...The present book follows these earlier selections in format and significance. It mixes anecdote, character, portrait, gossip, name-dropping, travelogue and confessional into a continuously entertaining pastiche."
See: W287

B695. "Sketches of the Winners of the 60th Pulitzer Prizes in Journalism and the Arts." New York Times, May 4, 1976, p. 48.

Brief biographical sketches of the 1976 Pulitzer Prize winners, among them, Ned Rorem for Air Music.
See: W224

B696. Smith, Liz. "John Malkovich 'Burning' to Move on." New York Daily News, February 26, 1988.

Mention of Ned Rorem's recently published The Nantucket Diary of Ned Rorem. "This Pulitzer Prize-winning American composer has created another compelling reading experience. I think it's the best, most mordant and most thoughtfully rueful of his four diaries. I loved every word of it, even the complicated parts about music, which I hardly understood. What a treasure--Ned Rorem's head!"
See: W290

B697. Smith, Patrick J. "North Carolina Sym. (Gosling)" High Fidelity/Musical America 27 no. 7 (July 1977): MA 36.

Review of the March 9, 1977 New York premiere of Assembly and Fall.
See: W225

B698. Snook, Paul. "Classical Hall of Fame." Fanfare (September-October 1979): 126-128.

Review of Grenadilla GS-1031 recording of Serenade on Five English Poems. "...Rorem has given us a completely integrated concert work which in some respects almost constitutes a chamber concerto for four solo musicians."
See: D27

B699. Sobolewska, Ingrid. "Tully Hall." Music Journal 32 no. 1 (January 1974): 42.

Review of the November 26, 1973 all-Rorem concert during which Day Music, The Last Poems of Wallace Stevens, War Scenes and Gloria were performed. "In a good grasp of the mood of the times, the composer's music is bright, expressive and just impersonal enough to maintain a brittle shell about it."
See: W32, W98, W108, W205

B700. Sokolov, Raymond. "Community Concert: Wake for a Local Hero." Wall Street Journal, March 2, 1984, p. 24.

A review of a concert honoring Paul Jacobs. "Ned Rorem accompanied two singers in works by Debussy."

B701. "Solo for Cello, with a Shakespearean Twist." New York Times, March 14, 1981, p. 28.

Written in anticipation of the March 15, 1981 premiere of After Reading Shakespeare. Sharon Robinson tells of her reasons for requesting the commission of a solo cello work.
See: W200

B702. Songs of Love and Affection. New York: Boosey & Hawkes, Inc., 1985.

Contains Little Elegy.
See: W41

B703. Srodoski, Joseph. "Records." Music Journal 33 no. 7 (September 1975): 50-51.

Brief review of Louisville LS 733 recording of Rorem's Piano Concerto in Six Movements. "Rorem's handling of the piano and orchestra is brilliant."
See: D34

B704. Steinberg, Michael. "The Final Diary." Review of The Final Diary, 1961-1972, by Ned Rorem. New York Times, November 17, 1974, sec. 7, p. 6.

The reviewer compares this volume with previous diaries saying, "...it seems duller." However, he concludes, "The lasting pleasures are those one takes in Rorem's intelligence, in the good ear behind the prose, in his essential, unfearing straightness: theatrical he is, and narcissistic to a fault, but he doesn't pretend and he doesn't apologize. No one that opinionated can help providing good (and startling) company, at least intermittently."
See: W286

B705. _____. "Words and Music." Review of An Absolute Gift; A New Diary; by Ned Rorem. New York Times, May 21, 1978, sec. 7, p. 12.

"It's a tired, dispirited book, one which suggests that Mr. Rorem is writing a diary because he's known

for writing diaries, because it's somehow expected...
Sometimes--and this is where an absolute gift is most
likely to awaken interest--one meets Ned Rorem the
composer, a professional commenting on the professional scene and, like many of his colleagues, angry
at the way music is swallowed up in show biz and
hype."
See: W284

B706. "Sterling Staff International Competition (SSIC); Composers Offer Works For Auditions." The Triangle of Mu
Phi Epsilon 66 no. 2 (1972): 13-14.

Brief announcement that Ned Rorem would be one of four
composers contributing works to the Sterling Staff
International Competition.

B707. Stoneman, E. Donnell. "Books." Review of The Final
Diary, by Ned Rorem. The Advocate (February 28,
1975): 16.

"Rorem has apparently lived his life with one eye on
the printed account eventually to be published...one
is faced with the inexcapable conclusion that the
image Rorem has spent over four decades and three
volumes to create has not been worth the effort."
See: W286

B708. Stoop, Norma McLain. "The Many Masks of Ned Rorem."
After Dark (January 1971): 18-22.

A discussion of Ned Rorem as "...a many-faceted
personality still sifting through his talents and
experiences for individual identity."

B709. Straus, Noel. "Gershwin Concert Offers New Work." New
York Times, May 9, 1949, p. 20.

Review of the May 7, 1949 premiere of Overture in C.
Winner of the 1949 Gershwin Award, the work "...was
imaginatively scored, with novel and striking percussion effects, and possessed emotional intensity, as
well as strength and vitality."
See: W236

B710. Strongin, Theodore. "Julia [sic] Marlowe on Harpsichord
Scans Music of 20th Century." New York Times, December 16, 1964, p. 51.

Review of the December 15, 1964 premiere of Lovers.
"Mr. Rorem's 10 brief scenes do not build into a
whole...They are varied in speed, closely related in
material and at times have moments of interesting
eccentricity in the scoring..."
See: W208

B711. _____. "'New' Old Music Performed Here." New York
Times, April 3, 1968, p. 37.

Review of April 2, 1968 performance of <u>Water Music</u>. "For Mr. Rorem, 'Water Music' is a relatively violent work, with outbursts of combined percussion and wood-wind sonorities spurring the soloists along...The piece lasts about 15 minutes and has all the external earmarks of a major effort."
<u>See</u>: W247

B712. _____. "3 Stellar Singers, at Town Hall, Present a Ned Rorem Program." <u>New York Times</u>, December 13, 1968, p. 57.

Review of an all-Rorem concert at Town Hall, December 12, 1968. Specifically mentioned were: <u>Poems of Love and the Rain</u>; <u>I Am Rose</u>; and the premiere of <u>Some Trees</u>.
<u>See</u>: W34, W64, W76

B713. "Suit Yourself." Review of <u>Setting the Tone: Essays and a Diary</u>, by Ned Rorem. <u>Washington Post</u>, September 23, 1984, sec. W, p. 8.

"Ned Rorem is...one of the few music critics who can be mentioned in the same breath with Virgil Thomson ...No matter what the subject, Rorem responds to it in an intensely personal way, writes with precision and wit, and reveals a remarkable mix of sympathy, learn-ing, and discrimination."
<u>See</u>: W296

B714. Summers, Mary Lois. "The Songs of Ned Rorem on Reli-gious Texts and Themes." D.M.A. diss., Southwestern Baptist Theological Seminary, 1982.

B715. Susa, Conrad S. "Alice Esty." <u>Musical America</u> 84 (February 1964): 34.

Review of the January 13, 1964 concert in honor of Francis Poulenc. Ned Rorem's <u>For Poulenc</u> received its premiere. "Rorem's 'Poulenc'...was a beautiful exam-ple of this composer's ingenuous blending of music and text. He composes tunes worth remembering."
<u>See</u>: W25

B716. _____. "Ned Rorem Musical Settings." <u>High Fidelity/ Musical America</u> 19 no. 3 (March 1969): MA 30-31.

Review of the December 12, 1968 recital of Rorem songs during which <u>Some Trees</u> was premiered. "His music is frankly tonal, harmonically elegant, lyrically supple, and rhythmically pert, deriving largely from the mod-ern French cuisine of Ravel and Poulenc with certain characteristic injections of Americanisms here and there."
<u>See</u>: W76

B717. Tangeman, Robert. "Music Reviews." <u>Notes</u> (Music Library Association) 11 (June 1954): 438.

Review of the score of From An Unknown Past. "Rorem's style indicates sensitivity to his texts and a gift for lyrical melody..."
See: W130

B718. Tartak, Marvin. "Music Reviews." Notes (Music Library Association) 32 no. 4 (1976): 885-886.

Review of the scores of Fables and Three Sisters Who Are Not Sisters. Concerning Fables: "All in all, a misfire; one detects a facile hand and a disinterested heart." Concerning Three Sisters Who Are Not Sisters: "Rorem's music is ideally suited to Stein's works; they turned him on to some of his most delightful thoughts. Though not much happens theatrically, the musical structure shines through; recurring musical motives follow the repetitive interior rhymes of Stein's text in intense fascination."
See: W175, W180

B719. Taubman, Howard. "Katchen, Pianist, Heard in Recital." New York Times, March 1, 1951, p. 32.

Review of the February 28, 1951 New York premiere of Sonata No. 2 for piano.
See: W191

B720. _____. "Theater: A Play Returns." New York Times, January 2, 1964, p. 33.

Review of the January 1, 1964 performance of Tennessee Williams's play The Milk Train Doesn't Stop Here Anymore for which Ned Rorem wrote the incidental music. The music is described as "...Oriental in intent with its gongs and bells but also lush in an Occidental way..."
See: W273

B721. Teachout, Terry. "Tailored Impulses." Review of Setting the Tone: Essays and a Diary; The Paris and New York Diaries; The Later Diaries, by Ned Rorem. National Review 36 no. 13 (July 13, 1984): 48-49.

Review of a new publication by Ned Rorem and reissues of previously published books. "If Ned Rorem's music is, in the best sense, 'conservative,' his prose--or at least part of it--is often another matter altogether." The Paris and New York Diaries "...may be sampled anew in an elegant reissue...combined into a single volume of manageable length..." The Final Diary reissue has been "...(sensibly) renamed The Later Diaries of Ned Rorem...Setting the Tone merits close reading by anyone seriously interested in classical music today..."
See: W286, W292, W296

B722. Terry, Walter. "Dance: Balletic Ramrod from Missoula." Saturday Review 4 (September 17, 1977): 50-51.

Review of the 1977 Summer Festival at Forest Meadows Center of the Arts, Dominican College, San Rafael, California. Ned Rorem, composer-in-residence and Stuart Sebastian, choreographer-in-residence collaborated "...in a ballet that highlighted the festival: Competitions." Danced by the Marin Civic Ballet and based on Rorem's Eleven Studies for Eleven Players, Stuart choreographed vignettes about the human competitive responses. "The result is brilliant."
See: W206, W250

B723. Tetley-Kardos, Richard. "The Journal Reviews." Review of Music and People, by Ned Rorem. Music Journal 26 no. 10 (December 1968): 104.

Brief review of Music and People. "...his constantly interesting mind and opinions on practically everything, ranging from the wittily superficial to the deeply perceptive, make enjoyable and worthwhile reading."
See: W288

B724. _____. "The Journal Reviews." Review of Music from Inside Out, by Ned Rorem. Music Journal 25 no. 5 (May 1967): 61.

Brief review of Music from Inside Out. "Here, he makes evident an acutely perceptive awareness of the subtleties of the creative mind, and proves himself to be a highly articulate and often brilliant writer."
See: W289

B725. _____. "The Journal Reviews." Review of The New York Diary, by Ned Rorem. Music Journal 25 no. 10 (December 1967): 70.

Brief review of The New York Diary. "There is the brilliant, pungent, colorful writing, the indiscriminate banalities, the famous, fascinating people floating through its pages--and last, but certainly not least, there is the revealing and usual shocking self-expose."
See: W291

B726. "35mm Music Man." Utah Alumnus 43 (Winter 1967): 20-22.

Ned Rorem discusses his role as composer-in-residence at the University of Utah. "This is the kind of assignment that should not last more than two years ...A teacher begins to believe what he says after that long a time and becomes sterile." He also discusses the contemporary composer's role in the Arts.

B727. Thoresby, Christina. "Music in France." Musical America 74 (August 1954): 11.

Review of the premiere performance of Ned Rorem's Second Piano Concerto. "This extremely attractive and

lively work, which has a distinctly American character at times, should prove a winner in the concert hall, for it gives the soloist plenty of scope in both lyrical and virtuoso piano playing, and is effectively scored for an orchestra with a large percussion section."
See: W228

B728. Tircuit, Heuwell. "A Brahms Collection Among the New Albums." San Francisco Chronicle, March 11, 1973, p 30.

Review of Turnabout TV-S 34447 recording of Symphony No. 3 by Ned Rorem and William Schuman's Symphony No. 7. "Rorem's Third Symphony is...an 'easy' piece to take, but a mite tedious in its Hindemith-like insistence on single motives repeated beyond cause of merit...Still, everything considered, this is an important pair of American works, well recorded."
See: D47

B729. _____. "Classical Albums." San Francisco Chronicle, January 20, 1974, p. 26-27.

Review of Desto DC-1751 recording of Day Music. "For once, he sounds like he belongs to the 20th Century, and has almost managed to set aside his passion for pseudo-Faure pleasantries." Record includes Kirchner's Sonata Concertante.
See: D21

B730. _____. "Mostly Moderns..Among the New LPs." San Francisco Chronicle, March 18, 1973, p. 32.

Review of Orion ORS 7268 recording of Lions, by Ned Rorem and works by Hovhaness, Colgrass and Floyd. "The Rorem is a dream piece, again with popular music elements creeping in..."
See: D42

B731. "TNB Interviews Ned Rorem." NATS Bulletin 39 no. 2 (1982): 5-7+.

A lengthy interview with Ned Rorem discussing his work as a song composer. In answer to a question concerning his choice of texts: "...I choose whatever, as the Quakers say, speaks to my condition. I might love a great poem but feel that music would be superfluous ...Another poem, less great might be more appropriate. I don't need to understand a poem...so much as to react kinetically to it..." On interpretation of song: "There is no one right way to perform any piece; there are as many right ways as there are true performers." On diction, "...good diction does interfere with vocal sonority, but the interference is corrective, not negative. A singer should assume his voice is gorgeous beyond compare, then forget about it; thus he can concentrate wholly on text." On critics:

"Critics are mere pilot fish nibbling around the edge of what really matters (even when it matters not)..."

B732. "To Perform 'Holy Songs' By Rorem." _Utah Chronicle_ (Salt Lake City, Utah), February 3, 1967.

The announcement of the program for the 19th Annual Chamber Music Festival includes _A Cycle of Holy Songs_. There is brief mention of the premiere of _Lions_ at the recent Festival of Contemporary Music and the announcement of Rorem's resignation as the University of Utah's composer-in-residence.
See: W15, W233

B733. Todd, Arthur. "The National Ballet." _Dance Observer_ 30 no. 3 (March 1963): 37-40.

Review of the February 16, 1963 performance of _Early Voyagers_, choreographed by Valerie Bettis "...to an exciting and highly theatrical score by Ned Rorem..."
See: W254

B734. Toms, John. "Maverick Composer Honored." _The Sunday Oklahoman_ (Oklahoma City, OK), May 5, 1985, p. 3.

Report of Rorem's lecture, informal talks with faculty and students, and the concert of his music during a visit to the campus at Northeastern State University at Tahlequah, OK, April 21-23, 1985.

B735. Trimble, Lester. "Third Symphony." _Stereo Review_ 28 (June 1972): 89.

Review of Turnabout TV S34447 recording of Rorem's _Third Symphony_ and William Schuman's _Symphony No. 7_. "Ned Rorem's Third Symphony...is a work that makes the orchestra sound gorgeous. Its moods are those of a younger man, and one whose many years of living in France...led him to adopt certain French attitudes toward musical organization...It is harmonically and melodically as handsome as it is in orchestration, and if its main endeavor seems to be to sing beautiful songs and to please the listener...that is a perfectly respectable aim."
See: D47

B736. Turner, J. Rigbie. "Books." Review of _Pure Contraption_, by Ned Rorem. _Music Journal_ 32 no. 3 (March 1974): 6.

"...Mr. Rorem is a clear, stylish writer, often aphoristic, and shows himself to a trenchant and frequently witty critic."
See: W295

B737. _____. "N.Y. University." _Music Journal_ 30 no. 10 (December 1972): 78.

Brief review of the October 4, 1972 performance of Ned

Rorem's Three Sisters Who Are Not Sisters.
See: W180

B738.   _____. "Tully Hall." Music Journal 32 no. 1 (January
1974): 42.

Review of the November 26, 1973 all-Rorem concert
which included the New York premieres of Night Music
and Ariel; and the world premiere of Bertha, which was
described as "...witty and often touching."
See: W106, W172, W210

B739. Turok, Paul. "Records." Music Journal 31 no. 8 (October 1973): 9.

Brief review of Desto DC 7151 recording of Rorem's Day
Music. "Splendid performances and recording."
See: D21

B740. 20th Century Composers Intermediate Piano Book: Easy to
Moderately Difficult Contemporary Piano Pieces.   New
York: C. F. Peters Corporation, 1981.

Contains the first movement of Barcarolles.
See: W182

B741. "U. of U. Concert Features Works by Ned Rorem."   Salt
Lake Tribune (Utah), February 5, 1967, p. W9.

Brief announcement that the University of Utah's cham-
ber Music Festival would include a performance of
Cycle of Holy Songs.
See: W15

B742. "UNCC Opera." The Charlotte Observer, January 30, 1986,
sec. A, p. 17.

Brief announcement of the February 4 & 6 1986 performance of Three Sisters Who Are Not Sisters.
See: W180

B743. Underwood, T. Jervis.   "Flute Review." Woodwind World-
Brass & Percussion 20 (January-February 1981): 32-33.

A review of the newly published Romeo and Juliet for
flute and guitar with a description of the piece and
degree of difficulty.   "...Rorem knows how to write
effectively for both instruments."
See: W213

B744. Veilleux, C. Thomas.   "Rorem: Book of Hours." The New
Records 45 no. 8 (October 1977): 6.

Review of CRI SD-362 recording of Rorem's Book of
Hours. "The best...is Ingrid Dingfelder's performance
of works by Ned Rorem...Dingfelder is a charming flut-
ist, the music is refreshing..."   Recording includes

Bohuslav Martinu's _Trio_.
    See: D8

B745. Von Rhein, John. "Cuyahoga Valley Arts Ensemble: Rorem
    Premiere." _High Fidelity/Musical America_ 26 no. 9
    (September 1976): MA 15.

    Review of the May 23, 1976 premiere of _Serenade on_
    Five English Poems. "Rorem's gifts as a sensuous
    melodist are less apparent here than in earlier works,
    yet there is no mistaking the graceful curve and nat-
    uralness of his lyricism for the work of any other
    composer."
    See: W112

B746. _____ . "Diaries and Profiles: Naughty Notes about
    Today's Musical Life." Review of _Setting the Tone_, by
    Ned Rorem. _Chicago Tribune_, October 16, 1983, sec.
    12, p. 14-15.

    "Rorem writes about music and musicians, performers
    and teachers, poets and critics...in content the book
    is rich. Even its flippest idiosyncrasies provoke
    thought, just as its prejudices and passions compel
    the reader to examine his own."
    See: W296

B747. _____ . "Ferris Chorale's Superb Concert a Fitting
    Birthday Gift for Rorem." _Chicago Tribune_, March 26,
    1984, sec. 5, p. 7.

    Review of the March 23, 1984 concert which included
    Gloria; From an Unknown Past; Three Motets on Poems of
    Gerard Manley Hopkins and _Letters from Paris_. _Letters_
    from Paris was the "...most atmospheric piece on the
    program...sweet with nostalgia, full of delicate but
    telling strokes of tone-painting..."
    See: W32, W130, W138, W163

B748. _____ . "Ned Rorem, Both of Him, Returns Home to Chicago
    in Search of Boundless Love." _Chicago Tribune_, April
    20, 1986, sec. 13, p. 18.

    Written in anticipation of the Chicago premiere of _An_
    American Oratorio. Rorem recalls his boyhood in
    Chicago and his friendship with Margaret Hillis who
    conducts the work.
    See: W118

B749. _____ . "Ned Rorem's Akron Diary." _Akron Beacon Jour-_
    nal, September 12, 1976, magazine sec., p. 20-16+.

    Ned Rorem is interviewed during a four day period
    spent in Akron for the premiere of _Serenade on Five_
    English Poems, and a series of lectures, master
    classes and readings at the University of Akron and
    Kent State University.

See: W112

B750. _____ . "'Oratorio' Celebration Doesn't Leave Out Dark
Side." Chicago Tribune, April 26, 1986, sec. 2, p. 9.

Review of the April 24, 1986 performance of American
Oratorio.   "The music is nostalgic, bittersweet,
conservative in the composer's typically lucid, main-
stream, neo-Romantic style."
See: W118

B751. _____ . "Rorem AAI Premiere a Coup." Akron Beacon Journal, May 24, 1976, sec. B, p. 14.

Review of the May 23, 1976 premiere of Serenade on
Five English Poems. "Rorem's 1975 song cycle is a
strong, sensitive, deeply felt and elegantly wrought
piece of vocal chamber music. One can pay it no
higher tribute than to say it does not belie Rorem's
reputation as one of our most gifted composers for the
human voice."
See: W112

B752. _____ . "Rorem Song Cycles: Between Emotions and Sounds
Felt." Chicago Tribune, November 24, 1980, sec. 2,
p. 6.

Review of the November 21, 1980 concert of Ned Rorem
song cycles. Nantucket Songs "...demonstrates Rorem's
sensitivity in choosing texts which are not only good
poetry, but which invite musical elaboration." Wom-
en's Voices "...seems rather joyless, even if some of
the poetry...is not."
See: W52, W103

B753. _____ . "Sound Survivors: 14 Master Composers Score a
Place in History." Chicago Tribune, May 17, 1987,
Arts sec., p. 18.

Ned Rorem is included among a group of American composers whose works are likely to secure them a place
in history. "Sometimes it appears as if Ned Rorem is
keeping the art of American vocal music alive single-
handedly...Rorem through his music has merged an
American sensibility with French refinement, to lovely
and persuasive effect."

B754. _____ . "Two New books Speak Volumes About Music."
Review of An Absolute Gift, by Ned Rorem. Chicago
Tribune, February 12, 1978, sec. 6, p. 10.

"...the book is full of the man's genius for observa-
tion—at once candid, witty, poignant, urbane, clear-
eyed—and his flair for the aphorism steeped in wry."
See: W284

B755. Wadia, Roy. "Finest Chamber Concert from Verdehr Trio."
The Daily (Bombay, India), April 9, 1986.

Review of the March 31, 1986, world premiere of Ned Rorem's End of Summer. "The music truly speaks for itself...the interplay of themes and the sense of continuity and musical pulse make this composition most effective. This is contemporary programme music at its most accessible and tuneful."
See: W207

B756. Walsh, Michael. "Where the New Action Is." Time 125 (February 4, 1985): 82.

Review of the January 4, 1985 premiere of An American Oratorio. "Rorem's new oratorio, based on texts by Poe, Longfellow, Twain, Crane, Melville, Whitman, Emma Lazarus and Sidney Lanier, is one of four premieres this season for the prolific composer, and it too treads familiar ground. Best known for his art songs and his candid, elegantly written diaries recounting his life and loves in Paris, New York and elsewhere, the composer, 61, has long been a conservative voice in American music. He speaks in a basically breezy 1940s tonality which is leavened by a few more recent technical advances. In An American Oratorio, Rorem's style works effectively with gentle poems like Poe's To Helen, but it missed the force and majesty of Crane's bitter War Is Kind or Lazarus' noble ode to the Statue of Liberty, The New Colossus. The reach of the texts generally exceeds the composer's grasp."
See: W118

B757. Ward, Charles. "Rorem's Works Stem from Literary Interest." Houston Chronicle, October 31, 1986, p. 9.

Interview in anticipation of Ned Rorem's participation in the Southwest Native Arts Festival at the University of Houston, November 1, 1986. In a program entitled Conversations With Ned Rorem, he will talk about the song cycle, War Scenes before it is performed by William Parker, baritone.
See: W98

B758. _____. "Symphony Program Mix of Light, Serious Tones." Houston Chronicle, April 14, 1986, Houston sec., p. 6.

Review of the April 12, 1986 concert which featured the premiere of Ned Rorem's Frolic. "Rorem's jaunty short piece...was a tongue-in-the-cheek look at the fanfare that drew much from the 20th-century Parisian with an insouciance."
See: W231

B759. Warren, Linda. "Ned Rorem's Book of Hours: Analysis and Study Guide." American Harp Journal 7 no. 2 (1979): 27-29.

Detailed analysis of Book of Hours. Includes information about the premiere.
See: W201

B760. Webster, Daniel. "He'll Hear His Songs of 1951 Sung--
for the Second Time." <u>Philadelphia Inquirer</u>, December
9, 1984, sec. I, p. 14.

Written in anticipation of the December 9, 1984 performance of <u>Six Irish Poems</u>. Rorem discusses the
history of the composition; his philosophy concerning
revision of early works; his work at Curtis Institute;
popular and contemporary music.
<u>See</u>: W113

B761. _____. "Music: Camerata Specially Tailors Songs from
Four Centuries." <u>Philadelphia Inquirer</u>, March 20,
1986, sec. D, p. 9.

Brief review of the March 19, 1986 concert which included two songs from <u>Last Poems of Wallace Stevens</u>.
"The layered emotion within each song was uncovered
partially by the singer who appeared to find her bear-
ings by the music rather than in the variegated images
of the text."
<u>See</u>: W108

B762. _____. "Music: Soprano, Cellist Share Curtis Spotlight." <u>Philadelphia Inquirer</u>, April 20, 1984, sec.
C, p. 3.

Review of the April 19, 1984 concert celebrating
Curtis Institute's 60th anniversary. "Ned Rorem's
shard of a song, 'I Am Rose,' about 15 seconds of
music, was an instant of skill and wit."
<u>See</u>: W34

B763. _____. "New Albums Feature American Art Songs." <u>Phila-
delphia Inquirer</u>, January 5, 1986, sec. I, p. 9.

Review of recordings GSS 104 and Leonarda LPI 116.
Concerning GSS 104, a collection of Rorem songs: "Ned
Rorem has written songs from his earliest days as a
composer..." The songs are "...instrumentally clear,
subtly shaped to express each word's resonance...
eminently singable." Concerning Leonarda LPI 116,
<u>Last Poems of Wallace Stevens</u>: "The added instrument
makes this cycle symphonic, and the vivid language of
the nine poems prompts music of extraordinary emotional range."
<u>See</u>: D29, D30

B764. _____. "Reuniting Composer and Performer." <u>Philadel-
phia Inquirer</u>, January 30, 1979, sec. C, p. 6.

Review of the January 29, 1979 all-Rorem concert which
included <u>Rain in Spring</u>; <u>My Papa's Waltz</u>; <u>Visits to
St. Elizabeths</u>; <u>War Scenes</u>; and <u>Eleven Studies for
Eleven Players</u>.
<u>See</u>: W51, W66, W96, W98, W206

B765. _____. "Spoleto Opens with an Explosive 'Butterfly.'"
<u>Philadelphia Inquirer</u>, May 29, 1983, sec. H, p. 1.

Review of Winter Pages performed May 29, 1983 at the Spoleto Festival in Charleston, S.C. "Listeners could see the Rorem music evolving. Written for violin, cello, bassoon, clarinet and piano, the work is auto-biographical in its references to piano exercises and kinds of music, but an explosive and lyrical explora-tion of sonorities and form."
See: W223

B766. _____. "20th-Century American by 1807 & Friends." Philadelphia Inquirer, November 18, 1986, sec. D, p. 3.

Review of the November 17, 1986 performance of Trio for Flute, Violoncello and Piano. "The piece is theater with three musical players, each given a star turn full of humor, serious lyricism and sentimen-tality."
See: W222

B767. Wechsler, Bert. "New York." Music Journal 38 no. 10 (November–December 1980): 42–43.

Review of the August 1980 Santa Fe Chamber Music Fes-tival concert at Tully Hall during which The Santa Fe Songs and Day Music were performed.
See: W110, W205

B768. _____. "Now, Just Which Century Is This?" New York Daily News, January 30, 1988, p. 16.

Review of the January 28, 1988 premiere of Ned Rorem's Death of Moses. It was "...a six minute straight-forward re-telling, with organ, of four paragraphs from Deuteronomy with some decoration and then a more worked out final paragraph. A more poetic translation of the Bible passage might have added literary splen-dor to the undoubted interest of the music."
See: W125

B769. _____. "Opera." Music Journal 37 no. 4 (May–June 1979): 51.

Review of the performance of the revised version of Miss Julie in April 1977. "This is a strong opera both in music and drama."
See: W178

B770. Weissmann, John S. "Reviews of Music." The Music Review 10 (February 1949): 75–76.

Review of the score of Four Madrigals. These "...four madrigals on texts by Sappho were inspired by the more sensuous Italian madrigalists. It seems that the har-monic possibilities attracted Roren [sic] more than the contrapuntal aspect of the form; yet his harmonies tend to be too rich, too cloying in effect, and one often feels aimlessness in their progressions."
See: W129

B771. _____ . "Reviews of Music." The Music Review 15 (May 1954): 152-153.

Review of the score of Flight for Heaven. "The music shows sincerity of feeling and there is considerable solicitude for easily singable melodic line. The last song is preceded by a piano interlude which recapitulates the first song's thematic material and so a certain formal unity is achieved."
See: W24

B772. Werle, Frederick. "Publishers' Mart." Musical Courier 153 no. 6 (April 1956): 45.

Review of the scores of Lullaby of the Woman of the Mountain and Rain In Spring. "...lyrical melody, a refined style...sincere expression...with the simplest means...two of the most outstanding songs by a contemporary composer."
See: W46, W66

B773. "Whacking About." Utah Chronicle (Salt Lake City, UT), November 17, 1965.

Announcement of Ned Rorem's appointment to teach at the University of Utah and mention of his plan to "create an opera for the cinema." Also quoted was Time (November 12, 1965) in which Rorem is said to have stated, "'Utah is such a boring state...I know it will be good for my work.'"

B774. Wierzbicki, James. "CSO Has Premiere of Pulitzer Winner." Cincinnati Post, May 4, 1976, p. 13.

First hand account by the journalist who informed Ned Rorem that he had received the Pulitzer Prize for Air Music.
See: W224

B775. Willis, Thomas. "Symphony Season Ends With a Whimper." Chicago Tribune, June 16, 1972, sec. 2, p. 11.

Review of the June 15, 1972 concert which included Ned Rorem's Concerto in Six Movements. "The descriptively titled six movements...ramble about in a conglomerate style suggestive of late Ravel, punctuated at odd moments with ear-splitting chords."
See: W227

B776. _____ . "Symphony's 'Air Music' Thrills Composer." Chicago Tribune, January 8, 1977, sec. 1, p. 15.

Review of the January 6, 1977 performance of Air Music. "...there is no gainsaying the music's elegance and basic quality. His major strengths are expressive and formal...he can spin a supple arching melody whose effect lingers in the memory even as the

pitches recede."
        See: W224

B777. Wilson, J. Kenneth.   "Publishers' Mart."   Musical
        Courier 153 no. 4 (March 1, 1956): 50.

        Brief review of the scores of Ned Rorem's Alleluia;
        What If Some Little Pain; Philomel; Little Elegy; and
        On a Singing Girl."   Concerning Alleluia: "Performed
        as directed...the effect will be biting, cynical, and
        powerful."   Concerning What If Some Little Pain:
        "...an expressive use of counter-melody in the accom-
        paniment against a slowly moving, sustained vocal
        part."   Concerning Philomel: "In this...the composer
        appears as a master of lyrical expression who under-
        stands...the force and emotional power inherent in the
        subtle use of deceptively simple modulations and chro-
        matic changes."   Concerning Little Elegy and On a
        Singing Girl: "They are both examples of a sensitive
        artist's craft."
        See: W2, W41, W58, W60, W99

B778. "Words and Music."   Horizon 23 no. 8 (August 1980): 12.

        News item concerning the premiere of a new work based
        on poems by Witter Bynner and the schedule for the
        Santa Fe Chamber Festival performances in Santa Fe,
        Seattle and New York.
        See: W110

B779. "Works by Ned Rorem Premiered."   Music Clubs Magazine 45
        no. 3 (February 1966): 23.

        Brief announcement of the October 28, 1965 premiere of
        Lions; the November 4, 1965 premiere of Miss Julie;
        and CRI Records release of Poems of Love and the Rain.
        See: D6; W178, W233

B780. "The Works of Ned Rorem."   New York: Boosey & Hawkes,
        Inc., n.d.

        "...contains full details of all works of Ned Rorem
        published by Boosey & Hawkes."   Includes works through
        1977 with information about premieres.
        See: W27, W32, W33, W40, W63, W64, W76, W98, W106,
        W108, W112, W115, W138, W141, W151, W157, W172,
        W175, W176, W180, W185, W189, W201, W205, W206,
        W208, W210, W213, W215, W224, W225, W227, W229,
        W230, W232, W233, W237, W242, W244, W245, W247

B781. Zakariasen, Bill.   "'I Write What I Mean and Shut Up!'"
        New York Daily News, February 2, 1982, Manhattan sec.,
        p. 1+.

        Review of the New York premiere of Remembering Tommy,
        and an interview in anticipation of the premiere of
        Winter Pages.   Concerning the latter Rorem says, "It
        reflects...my two hometowns...I don't know what I'll

put in the program notes, but I know the audience as usual will hear what it is told to hear."
See: W223, W239

B782. ____. "New Rorem Finds Favor." New York Daily News, February 7, 1981. (Located in Newsbank, Review of the Arts [Microfiche], Review of Performing Arts, July 1980-June 1981, 104:D8, fiche).

Review of February 5, 1981 premiere of Ned Rorem's Sunday Morning. "'Sunday Morning' was inspired by the poem of the same name by Wallace Stevens, and is in eight sections. Rorem's writing is colorful, communicative and on occasion powerful...All in all, a successful work, though overall, it sounds like an incomplete sketch for something bigger."
See: W242

B783. Zarr, Wayne. "Music Reviews." Notes (Music Library Association) 28 no. 4 (1972): 780-781.

Review of the scores of Some Trees and Poemes pour la paix. Concerning Some Trees: "These pieces are in all ways extraordinary. The texture is a rare one in song composition, and the three voices are used with imagination and skill." Concerning Poemes pour la paix: "Patriotic, statuesque, restrained, these songs are illuminated by Rorem's mastery of expressive writing and love of all things French."
See: W63, W76

B784. Zimmerman, Paul D. "Candid Composer." Newsweek 72 (December 23, 1968): 79-80.

Written on the occasion of the all-Rorem concert in December 1969. "The Town Hall concert, which featured superbly dramatic performances by Phyllis Curtin, Beverly Wolff and Donald Gramm, to Rorem's piano accompaniment, only confirmed the 45-year-old composer's place as the custodian of the lieder tradition in America."

Appendix I
Alphabetical List of Compositions

This appendix is an alphabetical list of Ned Rorem's compositions. It includes individual songs in song cycles; works
which may have been published under collective titles; distinctive subtitles; and working titles by which compositions
may have been known for a time. The "W" numbers which follow
each title refer to corresponding numbers in the "Works and
Performances" section of this volume.

Abel, W88
Absalom, W1, W77
An Absent Friend, W129
Address by Dionysus, W40
Adieu, Farewell Earth's Bliss, W136
After Great Pain, W105
After Long Silence, W105
After Reading Shakespeare, W200
The Air Is the Only, W64
Air Music, W224
The Airport, W27
All Glorious God, W116
All Hail the Power of Jesus Name, W117
Alleluia, W2
An American Oratorio, W118
Anacreontiche, W3
An Angel Speaks to the Shepherds, W4
The Animals Sick of the Plague, W175
The Anniversary, W171
Another Epitaph, W24
Another Sleep, W5
Antics for Acrobats, W248
Any Other Time, W110
The Apartment, W27
The Apparition, W64
Ariel, W106
Arise, Shine (Surge, illuminare), W119
Armenian Love Songs, W120
As Adam Early in the Morning, W6, W30
The Ascension, W139

The Sun and the Frogs, W175
Sun of the Sleepless, W115
Sunday Morning, W242
Sundown Lights, W115
Surge, illuminare, W119
Suspiria, W130
Symphony No. 1, W243
Symphony No. 2, W244
Symphony No. 3, W245

Te Deum, W162
Tears, W130
That We May Live (incidental music), W279
Thee God, W163
Thoughts of a Young Girl, W52
Three Calamus Poems, W86
Three Incantations from a Marionette Tale, W87
Three Motets on Poems of Gerard Manley Hopkins, W163
Three Poems of Baudelaire, W164
Three Poems of Demetrios Capetanakis, W88
Three Poems of Paul Goodman, W12, W26, W100
Three Prayers, W165
Three Scenes from "The Iliad," W134
Three Sisters Who Are Not Sisters, W180
Three Slow Pieces, W221
The Ticklish Acrobat, W181
To a Common Prostitute, W86
To a Young Girl, W77, W89
To Anthea, Who May Command Him Anything, W24
To Daisies, Not to Shut So Soon, W24
To Jane, W90
To Music, to Becalm His Fever, W24
To My Dear and Loving Husband, W103
To the Ladies, W103
To the Sun, W115
To the Willow-Tree, W24
To You, W91
Toccata, W194, W198
Trio for Flute, Violoncello and Piano, W222
Truth in the Night Season, W166
The Tulip Tree, W29, W92
The Holy Songs, W15, W167
Two Poems of Edith Sitwell, W93
Two Poems of Plato, W94
Two Poems of Theodore Roethke, W95
Two Psalms and a Proverb, W168

Up-Hill, W52
Upon Julia's Clothes, W24

Views from the Oldest House, W199
Violin Concerto, W246
Virelai, W169
The Virgin's Cradle-Hymn, W127
Visits to St. Elizabeths (Bedlam), W96
Vita summa brevis, W105

The Waking, W30, W97
War Scenes, W98

Appendix II
Chronological List of Compositions

The "W" number which follows each title refers to the corresponding number in the "Works and Performances" section of
this volume.

1943   Four-Hand Piano Sonata, W187
           The Seventieth Psalm, W159

1944   Doll's Boy, W17
           Overture for G.I.'s, W235
           Song of Chaucer, W80

1945   Dawn Angel, W16
           Lost in Fear, W257
           A Psalm of Praise, W65
           A Song of David, W81

1946   Absalom, W1
           Alleluia, W2
           Cain and Abel, W173
           Concertino da Camera, W203
           The Long Home, W142
           On a Singing Girl, W58
           Reconciliation (from Five Poems of Walt Whitman), W23
           Spring and Fall, W84
           That We May Live (pageant), W279

1947   At Noon upon Two (incidental music), W262
           Bawling blues, W7
           Catullus: On the Burial of His Brother, W10
           Fantasy and Toccata, W186
           Fire boy (puppet show), W269
           Four Madrigals, W129
           Jail-Bait Blues, W38
           The Lordly Hudson, W42
           Mongolian Idiot, W50
           Mourning Scene from Samuel, W109
           Near Closing Time, W53
           A Sermon on Miracles, W157

Spring (Hopkins), W83
String Quartet No. 1, W218

1948 Concerto for Piano, No. 1, W226
Death of the Black Knight, W252
Dusk (incidental music), W267
Echo's Song, W19
Hippolytus (incidental music), W270
Mountain Song, W209
A Quiet Afternoon, W190
Requiem, W67
Sonata I, for Piano, W194
Three Incantations from a Marionette Tale, W87
Toccata, W198
Two Poems of Edith Sitwell, W93

1949 Barcarolles, W182
Cock-A-Doodle-Doo (incidental music), W265
Little Elegy, W41
Overture in C, W236
Pastorale, W188
Penny Arcade, W59
Rain in Spring, W66
Seconde sonate pour piano, W191
The Silver Swan, W74
The Sleeping Palace (from Four Poems of Tennyson), W28
Sonata for Violin and Piano, W217
What If Some Little Pain..., W99

1950 Concerto for Piano, No. 2, W228
Flight for Heaven, W24
I will Always Love You, W35
Il n'y a plus rien a vivre (incidental music), W271
Lullaby of the Woman of the Mountain, W46
Philomel, W60
Sicilienne, W192
Six Irish Poems, W113
String Quartet No. 2, W219
Symphony No. 1, W243
Three Slow Pieces (1950, 1959, 1970), W221

1951 Another Sleep, W5
Ballet for Jerry, W249
The Call, W9
Cycle of Holy Songs, W15
From an Unknown Past, W31, W130
Love in a Life, W45
Mélos, W259
The Nightingale, W55
O Do Not Love Too Long, W56
To a Young Girl, W89
Whisky, Drink Divine, W102

1952 An Angel Speaks to the Shepherds, W4
A Childhood Miracle, W174
A Christmas Carol, W11
Dorian Gray (ballet), W253
The Mild Mother, W49
The Resurrection, W68

1953   Boy with a Baseball Glove, W8
        Clouds, W12
        The Corinthians, W124
        Cradle Song, W14
        Design, W229
        Eclogues, W20
        Epitaph, W24
        A Far Island, W126
        Five Prayers for the Young, W127
        For Susan, W26
        Gentle Visitations, W131
        I Feel Death, W135
        In A Gondola, W36
        Jack L'Eventreur, W37
        Love, W44
        The Midnight Sun, W48
        Pippa's Song, W61
        Poèmes pour la paix, W63
        Rondelay, W69
        Sally's Smile, W71
        Six Songs for High Voice, W114
        Song for a Girl, W79
        Song to a Fair Young Lady, Going Out of Town in the
            Spring, W82
        The Tulip Tree, W92

1954   Anacreontiche, W3
        Four Dialogues, W27
        Sonata III, for Piano, W195
        Three Poems of Demetrios Capetanakis, W88
        Youth, Day, Old Age, and Night, W104

1955   All Glorious God, W116
        Burlesque, W184
        Christ the Lord Is Ris'n Today, W123
        Early in the Morning, W18
        I Am Rose, W34
        Poem for F, W62
        The Poets' Requiem, W151
        Sing My Soul, His Wondrous Love, W161
        The Young Disciple (incidental music), W280

1956   The Robbers, W179
        See How They Love Me, W72
        Symphony No. 2, W244
        What Sparks and Wiry Cries, W100

1957   As Adam Early in the Morning, W6
        Conversation, W13
        Five Poems of Walt Whitman, W23
        The Lord's Prayer, W43
        O You Whom I Often and Silently Come, W57
        Settings for Whitman (spoken voice), W277
        Sinfonia, W240
        Such Beauty as Hurts to Behold, W85
        Suddenly Last Summer (incidental music), W278
        To You, W91
        Visits to St. Elizabeths (Bedlam), W96

1958   Eagles, W230
        Pilgrims, W237
        Slow Waltz, W193
        Symphony No. 3, W245
        The Ticklish Acrobat, W181

1959   The Cave at Machpelah (incidental music), W264
        Early Voyagers (ballet), W254
        Last Day, W177
        Memory, W47
        Miracles of Christmas, W146
        My Papa's Waltz, W51
        Night Crow, W54
        Root Cellar, W70
        Snake, W75
        Three Slow Pieces (1950, 1959, 1970), W221
        Two Poems of Theodore Roethke, W95
        The Waking, W97

1960   Eleven Studies for Eleven Players, W206
        Motel (incidental music), W274
        Polish Songs, op. 74, by Chopin (orchestral arrange-
            ment), W281
        Prayers and Responses, W155
        Trio for Flute, Violoncello and Piano, W222

1961   The Anniversary, W171
        Ideas for Easy Orchestra, W232
        King Midas, W40
        Virelai, W169

1962   Caligula (incidental music), W263
        Two Psalms and a Proverb, W168

1963   Color of Darkness (incidental music), W266
        Eleven by Eleven (ballet), W255
        The Emperor (incidental music), W268
        For Poulenc, W25
        Four Poems of Tennyson: (1-3), W28
        Lady of the Camellias (incidental music), W272
        Lift Up Your Heads (The Ascension), W139
        Lions, W233
        Poems of Love and the Rain, W64

1964   Antics for Acrobats (ballet), W248
        Excursions (ballet), W256
        Laudemus tempus actum, W137
        Lovers, W208
        The Milk Train Doesn't Stop Here Anymore (incidental
            music), W273
        Two Poems of Plato, W94

1965   Miss Julie, W178

1966   Feed My Sheep, W22
        Hearing (song cycle), W33
        Letters from Paris, W138
        Love Divine, All Loves Excelling, W143

Lovers (ballet), W258
Proper for the Votive Mass of the Holy Spirit, W156
Sun, W115
Truth in the Night Season, W166
Water Music, W247

1967   A Birthday Suite, W183
Dancing Ground (ballet), W251
He Shall Rule from Sea to Sea, W133
Progressions, W260
Sculptures, (ballet), W261

1968   Bertha, W172
Some Trees, W76
Spiders, W197
Three Sisters Who Are Not Sisters, W180

1969   Concerto in Six Movements, W227
Two Holy Songs (choral arr. from Cycle of Holy Songs,
     1951), W167
War Scenes, W98

1970   Fables, W175
Gloria, W32
The Pastry Shop (incidental music), W282
Praises for the Nativity, W153
Three Slow Pieces (1950, 1959, 1970), W221
The Young Among Themselves (incidental music), W283

1971   Ariel, W106
Canticle of the Lamb, W121
Day Music, W205
The Nephew (incidental music), W275
Panic in Needle Park (incidental music for film), W276

1972   Canticles, W122
Last Poems of Wallace Stevens, W108
Night Music, W210
The Serpent, W73

1973   All Hail the Power of Jesus Name, W117
Four Hymns, W128
In Time of Pestilence, W136
Little Prayers, W141
Missa brevis, W147
Solemn Prelude, W216
Three Motets on Poems of Gerard Manley Hopkins, W163
Three Prayers, W165

1974   Air Music, W244
Prayer to Jesus, W154
To Jane, W90
Where We Came, W101

1975   Assembly and Fall, W225
Book of Hours, W201
Eight Etudes, W185
Serenade on Five English Poems, W112

1976   Hearing (opera), W176
         A Journey, W39
         A Quaker Reader, W189
         Sky Music, W215
         Women's Voices, W103

1977   Arise, Shine (Surge illuminare), W119
         Competitions (ballet), W250
         Romeo and Juliet, W213
         Sunday Morning, W242

1978   O magnum mysterium, W148
         The Oxen, W149
         Shout the Glad Tidings, W160

1979   After Reading Shakespeare, W200
         Miss Julie (revised), W178
         The Nantucket Songs, W52
         Remembering Tommy, W239

1980   Back to Life, W107
         The Santa Fe Songs, W110
         Suite for Guitar, W220

1981   Give All to Love, W132
         Views from the Oldest House, W199
         Winter Pages, W223

1982   After Long Silence, W105
         Little Lamb, Who Made Thee? W140
         Mercy and Truth Are Met, W144
         Praise the Lord, O My Soul, W152
         Three Calamus Poems, W86

1983   An American Oratorio, W118
         Dances for Cello and Piano, W204
         Picnic on the Marne, W211
         Whitman Cantata, W170

1984   Organ Concerto, W234
         Pilgrim Strangers, W150
         Violin Concerto, W246

1985   End of Summer, W207
         Septet: Scenes from Childhood, W214
         String Symphony, W241

1986   Frolic, W231
         Homer, W134
         Seven Motets for the Church Year, W158
         Song & Dance, W196
         Three Poems of Baudelaire, W164

1987   Armenian Love Songs, W120
         Death of Moses, W125
         Schuyler Songs, W111
         Te Deum, W162

1988   Bright Music, W202

Praising Charles (Fanfare and Flourish), W212
Quaker Reader (orchestral version), W238

In Preparation:

1988   Choral Work, untitled, W298
        Goodbye My Fancy, W299
        Society of Friends, W300

Appendix III
Alphabetical List of Literary Sources

The "W" numbers which follow each name refer to the corresponding numbers in the "Works and Performances" section of this volume.

Anonymous, Liturgical and Traditional, W2, W9, W11, W14, W21, W32, W43, W49, W55, W102, W116, W122, W128, W130, W147, W148, W153, W155, W156, W158, W160, W161, W162
Ashbery, John, W52, W76
Auden, Wystan Hugh, W64

Baif, Jean-Antoine de, W63
Barnfield, Richard, W60
Baudelaire, Charles, W164
Beaumont, John, W139
Bible. New Testament, W4, W68, W124
Bible. Old Testament, W15, W65, W81, W109, W119, W122, W125, W133, W144, W152, W159, W166, W167, W168
Bishop, Elizabeth, W13, W96
Blake, William, W105, W115, W140
Boleyn, Anne, consort of Henry VIII, King of England, W103
Boultenhouse, Charles, W87, W269
Bradstreet, Anne, W103
Browning, Robert, W36, W45, W61
Burns, Robert, W105
Bynner, Witter, W110
Byron, George Gordon, Baron (Lord Byron), W115

Campion, Thomas, W112
Capetanakis, Demetrios, W88
Carew, Thomas, W105
Carroll, Lewis, W127
Catullus, Gaius Valerius, W10
Chaucer, Geoffrey, W80, W169
Cocteau, Jean, W151
Coleridge, Mary Elizabeth, W103
Crane, Stephen, W118
cummings, e.e., W17, W64

Index

Page numbers, e.g., p.4, refer to pages in the "Biography," numbers preceded by a "W" to the "Works and Performances" section, numbers preceded by a "D" to the "Discography," and numbers preceded by a "B" to the "Bibliography."

About the Author

ARLYS L. MCDONALD is Head of the Music Library at Arizona State University, Tempe, AZ. She is author of "Phoenix" in *New Groves Dictionary of American Music* (1986).

**Recent Titles in
Bio-Bibliographies in Music**

Daniel Pinkham: A Bio-Bibliography
Kee DeBoer and John B. Ahouse

Arthur Bliss: A Bio-Bibliography
Stewart R. Craggs

Charles Ives: A Bio-Bibliography
Geoffrey Block

Cécile Chaminade: A Bio-Bibliography
Marcia J. Citron

Vincent Persichetti: A Bio-Bibliography
Donald L. Patterson and Janet L. Patterson

Robert Ward: A Bio-Bibliography
Kenneth Kreitner

William Walton: A Bio-Bibliography
Carolyn J. Smith

Albert Roussel: A Bio-Bibliography
Robert Follet

Anthony Milner: A Bio-Bibliography
James Siddons

Edward Burlingame Hill: A Bio-Bibliography
Linda L. Tyler

Alexander Tcherepnin
Enrique Alberto Arias

Ernst Krenek: A Bio-Bibliography
Garrett H. Bowles, compiler